THE BUSINESS
OF BUILDING A
BETTER
W●RLD

THE BUSINESS
OF BUILDING A
BETTER
W●RLD

The Leadership Revolution That Is Changing Everything

Edited by

DAVID COOPERRIDER
and AUDREY SELIAN

BK

Berrett–Koehler Publishers, Inc.

Berrett-Koehler Publishers, Inc.
1333 Broadway, Suite 1000
Oakland, CA 94612-1921
Tel: (510) 817-2277
Fax: (510) 817-2278
www.bkconnection.com

ORDERING INFORMATION

Quantity sales. Special discounts are available on quantity purchases by corporations, associations, and others. For details, contact the "Special Sales Department" at the Berrett-Koehler address above.
Individual sales. Berrett-Koehler publications are available through most bookstores. They can also be ordered directly from Berrett-Koehler: Tel: (800) 929-2929; Fax: (802) 864-7626; www.bkconnection.com.
Orders for college textbook / course adoption use. Please contact Berrett-Koehler: Tel: (800) 929-2929; Fax: (802) 864-7626.

Distributed to the U.S. trade and internationally by Penguin Random House Publisher Services.

Berrett-Koehler and the BK logo are registered trademarks of Berrett-Koehler Publishers, Inc.

Printed in the United States of America

Berrett-Koehler books are printed on long-lasting acid-free paper. When it is available, we choose paper that has been manufactured by environmentally responsible processes. These may include using trees grown in sustainable forests, incorporating recycled paper, minimizing chlorine in bleaching, or recycling the energy produced at the paper mill.

Library of Congress Cataloging-in-Publication Data

Names: Cooperrider, David L., editor. | Selian, Audrey, editor.
Title: The business of building a better world : the leadership revolution that is changing everything / edited by David Cooperrider and Audrey Selian.
Description: First edition. | Oakland, CA : Berrett-Koehler Publishers, Inc., [2020] | Includes bibliographical references and index.
Identifiers: LCCN 2021033457 (print) | LCCN 2021033458 (ebook) | ISBN 9781523093649 (hardcover) | ISBN 9781523093656 (adobe pdf) | ISBN 9781523093663 (epub)
Subjects: LCSH: Leadership. | Social responsibility of business. | Social change.
Classification: LCC HD57.7 .B877 2020 (print) | LCC HD57.7 (ebook) | DDC 658.4/092—dc23
LC record available at https://lccn.loc.gov/2021033457
LC ebook record available at https://lccn.loc.gov/2021033458

First Edition
26 25 24 23 22 21   10 9 8 7 6 5 4 3 2 1

Book producer: Westchester Publishing Services
Text designer: Pamela Rude
Cover designer: Nita Ybarra

CONTENTS

FOREWORD

Jesper Brodin (CEO, Ikea) and Halla Tómasdóttir (CEO, the B Team)

FOR ALL THAT HUMANITY HAS lost and endured in the recent past, climate change remains the biggest challenge of our time. It threatens our way of life, our resilience, and our safety. And while words can inspire, it is action that sparks change and creates hope for the future. Seeing as this book is already in your hands, you just might feel the same.

We are in a critical decade, maybe the most important one for humankind. History will remember us for the actions we take or fail to take.

The question to ask yourself: How will I choose to lead during this decade?

We choose to lead with purpose and values. Our values animate our core humanity. They compel us to take a stand for people, to take responsibility for a more green and just world, to protect and sustain the planet—a home we all share, the only home we have—for our families, communities, and generations to come. Our values guide us as individuals and as business leaders, for there is no business beyond our planetary boundaries and only fading opportunity in a world with a broken social contract.

Values-based leadership is needed now more than ever as climate change has accelerated and converged with multiple global crises: a once-in-a-century pandemic, widespread economic turmoil, a reckoning on race, democratic backsliding, mass migration, the crisis of social media, and rising inequality alongside diminishing trust in public institutions.

But a crisis of conformity still plagues boardrooms and leadership ranks around the world. Nearly 90 percent of *Fortune* 500 CEOs are white men. Only two are Black women. Globally, women occupy a mere one in five seats in the boardroom. With rare exception, senior leadership in business and government falls far short of fairly reflecting the diversity of our workforces and customers, of our communities and constituencies. The COVID-19 pandemic has made matters worse, disproportionately imperiling the economic security of people of color and setting back gender equality 25 years. The crisis of conformity also extends to leaders, irrespective of their gender, race, ethnicity, orientation, or ability, who continue values-deficient incentive structures, often through inaction. When we change who is in leadership, we change how we do business.

To be sure, well-intentioned leaders in business, government, and civil society are creating opportunities and impacting positive change every day. We are humbled to know and work with so many of them. But when we take a big step back and focus our gaze at the systems level, we see an economic model that is truly broken. Ours is a system ill-prepared to mitigate—and surely not built to solve—today's interdependent crises. Indeed, the view is commonly held that our economic model bears meaningful responsibility for the inequality and despair tearing at our social contract.

Along with staggering hardship and human loss, the COVID-19 pandemic brought us a narrow window of opportunity to reimagine and redesign the systems in which we live, prosper, and pursue our purpose. This moment demands an ambitious reset of our economy. It calls for bold leadership and radical collaboration across industries and sectors. Let's create a new economic paradigm, with humanity as its beating heart. Let's "right the rules" in time to achieve the 2030 Agenda for Sustainable Development and deliver on our promise to the Paris Climate Agreement.

With much on our minds, forgive us for burying our introduction. In 2013, Richard Branson and Jochen Zeitz cofounded the B Team to work across business and government and help solve some of the world's most intractable challenges. Today, as a global collective of CEOs and civil society leaders, we have a clearer sense of what future generations need from us. We are advocates for a better way of doing business, with a focus on bringing the global economy in line with Earth's boundaries, cultivating equitable representation in leadership and achieving transparency in corporate governance. Our agenda ladders up to one overarching goal: to build, by 2030, an inclusive economy that works for all people and communities while safeguarding our natural environment.

In our pursuits, we convene leaders across business, labor, civil society, and government. We collaborate deeply with partners and across our networks. We amplify the stories of mission-aligned leaders around the world, and we reflect with candor on our struggles and setbacks. We are transparent in our ambition: engaging in public and corporate policy-making processes and driving adoption of new norms and incentives that can orient business toward a broader bottom line. Mindful of our privilege while embracing the benefits of our platform, we strive to uplift tomorrow's leaders as vigorously as we catalyze change today.

Our bold vision is of a world where global inequality gaps are closed. Where gender balance and equitable representation at all levels of leadership are the norm. Where businesses thrive with accountability and integrity at their core. Where our economy is regenerative, and we've delivered a just transition for the world's workforce.

Thankfully we are not short on guides to light our path. In this volume, *The Business of Building a Better World: The Leadership Revolution That Is Changing Everything*, David Cooperrider and Audrey Selian bring together a treasure trove of thought leaders and some of the most path-breaking CEOs of our time. The book is imaginative, empirically researched, and actionable. What is more, this book is not just about the future. In prompting leaders to aspire to something greater, it can help shape the future. As Paul Polman, B Team leader and former CEO of Unilever (as well as a chapter coauthor in this volume), writes in the book's early pages:

> What we are witnessing is a shift that is all-embracing, rapid, irreversible, extending to the far corners of the planet and involving practically every aspect of business life. What we are witnessing is a world increasingly divided by companies that are known as part of the problem and those that are leading the solution revolution.

Taken together, this international group of authors affirms that the journey toward an inclusive economy is possible only with bold leadership from business—and that those who take the lead will benefit enormously. Whether you are a titan of industry or a budding entrepreneur, you'll find wisdom and inspiration in the chapters ahead.

We hope, too, that you see this volume for what it truly is: a call to action of historic urgency. The world's crises are interdependent. The socioeconomic challenges we face are intergenerational. Our economic model is broken, but we can build a better world if leaders everywhere commit to brave, collaborative action today. A new leadership playbook can deliver change in this decade—provided we summon the courage and elevate our leadership to meet this moment.

Twenty-first-century leaders accelerate innovation while reducing risk. They follow the science. They see diversity in leadership for the competitive advantage it is and the bottom-line benefit it brings. They understand that the clock is ticking, future generations are counting on us, and that "history has its eyes on us."

How will you choose to lead? How will history remember you?

PREFACE

THIS BOOK WAS PREPARED as a gift for the tens of thousands of participants—executives, students of management and young future leaders, societal entrepreneurs, change agents, sustainable design thinkers, management educators, and thought leaders—who will attend the fifth Global Forum for Business as an Agent of World Benefit in the fall of 2021.

The Global Forum series was launched and hosted on October 14, 2006, at Case Western Reserve University's Weatherhead School of Management and was founded in partnership with the United Nations Global Compact, now the largest corporate sustainability network in the world with 12,000 corporations, together with the Academy of Management, the preeminent professional association for management and organization scholars with a community of over 20,000 management scholars spanning 130 countries. Designed to unite the creative power of good theory with leading-edge practice, bringing executives and leaders together with the finest business researchers—the Global Forum was described by its first keynote speaker, one of the century's great strategy thinkers Dr. C. K. Prahalad, as "a leadership institute for tomorrow." The series mission: the realization of a generative economy in the service of life, whose ultimate aim is a world of "full spectrum flourishing," defined as:

> a world where businesses can excel, all persons can thrive, and nature can flourish, now and across the generations.

This book, *The Business of Building a Better World: The Leadership Revolution That Is Changing Everything*, was made possible by three sources.

First, this book has its roots and home in a center at Case Western Reserve University's Weatherhead School of Management. It is a center that was catalyzed when we were invited by then-secretary general of the United Nations,

Kofi Annan, to facilitate the largest meeting in history between the UN and business leaders. The summit catalyzed the greatest growth years of the UN Global Compact. This work and its vast potential also inspired Chuck Fowler, the cofounder and former CEO of Fairmount Minerals and later chairman of the board of Case Western Reserve University. Chuck is one of the finest human beings and CEOs we have ever had the privilege to know. Chuck and his family foundation stepped forward. The Char and Chuck Fowler Family Foundation are dedicated to improving people's lives, and it was their transformational gift to the university that built the Fowler Center for Business as an Agent of World Benefit. This book, as well as our global forum series, would not have been possible without this foundation, which today is splendidly led in part by Chann Fowler-Spellman and Holley Fowler Martens. We owe a huge debt of gratitude to Chuck Fowler. Moreover, we can only hope to do our small bit to extend his living legacy as a humanitarian and hopeful believer in our young leaders. "There is so much power in great education," said Chuck, "especially the kind of education that empowers our students and future leaders *to lead with values,* to lead purpose-driven lives, and to *do good, do well* for all of humankind and our earth."

Second, we want to celebrate the "better business and better world" vision of Harry Halloran and the catalytic gift of Halloran Philanthropies for this book and what has become perhaps the largest data bank in the world for studying innovations at the intersection of business and society. It contains student-led interviews of pathbreaking leaders from all parts of the world, housing nearly 4,000 "business for good" interviews and over 3,000 published cases (see www.aim2flourish.com). Harry has been and is a courageous and values-led leader in the business for good movement. In addition, one of the inspirations behind this project is the former president of Halloran Philanthropies. His name is Tony Carr, and he is truly a visionary and our tireless thought partner. Tony has handed off his president role to Brian Halloran, who is a futurist and who resonates with this volume, helping to advance corporations that are future fit and future forming. We also would like to recognize the research funding making this *New Theory of Business* Project a reality; it came in the form of a grant, generously given, by the University of St. Thomas, a long-standing leader in corporate responsibility, ethics and leadership studies.

Third, we want to thank our partners. Our publishing partner and Fifth Global Forum cohost and coproducer is Berrett-Koehler Publishers. Their mission—connecting people and ideas to create a world that works for all— aligns perfectly with this book. They believe that the solutions to the world's greatest challenges will come from all of us, and that when we are motivated by love, caring, and a desire to contribute, we can accomplish more than people who are scrambling to win. Here we wish to thank the founder of Berrett-Koehler Publishers, Steve Piersanti, for his encouragement to dream big and better. The people at Berrett-Koehler have been truly awesome to work with; they are real pros, including the president and CEO David Marshall, our dedicated editor Anna Leinberger, and the core BK digital summit team with Kylie Johnston and Zoe Mackey. We especially recognize the work of the exceptional team at Fowler Center; everyone on our advisory board, all of our faculty colleagues—and specifically Megan Buchter, the director of the Fowler Center and Joseph Bianchini, the center's coordinator. Moreover, the dean of the Weatherhead School, Manoj Maholtra, has always been an advocate of the idea of business of building a better world and his support for our work, as always, is appreciated. But perhaps most important, sometimes we feel we were born under a lucky star to work amid such people and organizations. The authors of this book are some of the greatest thought leaders of our time and they form a treasure trove of insight, inspiration, and grounded hope for *The Business of Building a Better World*.

Finally, we wish to dedicate this book. Few have "walked the talk" the way Harry Halloran has through his lifetime of building and investing in businesses that serve community. This volume is dedicated to Harry Halloran and Joseph "Tony" Carr, whose deep commitment to positive values in business through practice and altruism has inspired so many, including ourselves.

Harry is the earliest, most positive source of inspiration for this project, which originated from his vision and heart as a respected business leader, philanthropist, and impact investor. In preparation for this project, Harry helped set the stage by funding a world-class empirical research effort documenting the history of human well-being. In many ways, this project is a sequel that now specifically focuses on realizing the potentials of good business as a force for well-being. Harry's belief in the dignity of work, in human community and solidarity, in moral and stakeholder capitalism, and in the positive goodness that can be propelled through purpose-driven innovation and entrepreneurship—constitutes the cornerstone callings that fuel the research questions, inspiration, and values of this volume. He has been and is a courageous and values-led leader in the "business for good" movement.

—∞—

This extraordinary compilation is also dedicated to our families, and notably our children and our grandchildren. For Audrey Selian, this is dedicated to her husband Mardit Matian; her children, Raphael Masis and Maya Alessandra Gayané; as well as to her parents, Alexander and Ani. It is also dedicated to the Singh Family, and notably Tom Singh, thanks to whom so much opportunity and learning about the practical power of positive business has been inspired. For David Cooperrider, this is dedicated to David and Nancy Cooperrider's first two grandchildren, Hugo David Lyons and Reverie Burkey Cooperrider—both were born reminding us of the miracle of life on this planet during the writing of this book.

David Cooperrider and Audrey Selian
Case Western Reserve University, 2021

1

Introduction

A Moonshot Moment for Business and the Great Economic Opportunities of Our Time

DAVID COOPERRIDER AND AUDREY SELIAN

ONE OF HUMANITY'S GREATEST GIFTS is that in times of profound shock and disruption, new perspectives are forged. Such moments tend to be historical ones—moments when new possibilities for humanity can be established and new eras born. Could it be that we are standing at the threshold of the next episode in business history?

The quest in this book is ultimately to explore the profound new enterprise logic propelling the "business of building a better world"—ways that the field of business is increasingly becoming an *agent of change* and a *partnership power* for building a better world—together with all of this serving as a catalyst for the "betterment of your business." Moreover, this includes all the new ways that *The Business of Building a Better World* can lead inside the enterprise to bold new waves of innovation, business outperformance, and what we call full-spectrum flourishing. Flourishing enterprise is something every industry leader increasingly wants. Flourishing enterprise, as we shall discover, is about people being inspired every day and bringing their whole and best selves into their businesses; it's about innovation arising from everywhere; and most important, it is about realizing sustainable value with all stakeholders. These include customers, communities, shareholders, and societies, all coexisting ultimately within a thriving, not dying, biosphere.

SOMETHING REMARKABLE IS UNDERWAY

The relationship of business and society—and the unprecedented search for mutual advances between industry and the world's profound upheavals—has become one of the decisive quests of the twenty-first century. As we stand now in what scientists are calling the "decade of determination," the stakes could not be higher for humanity and planet Earth. Like dials on a seismograph, we have stood stunned as the decade of the 2020s has arrived with *unprecedented* disruptive preludes: megafires in January; a global pandemic in March; an economic crash in April with bankruptcies putting millions out of work; and protests across the planet for racial justice and inclusive systemic change in June and beyond. Only just a few months earlier, we listened to the rising voices of millions of millennials and Gen-Z young leaders, including *Time* magazine's Person of the Year Greta Thunberg and over 7 million strikers from six continents. For them, the entire era of climate gradualism "is over." As our youth stepped onto podiums in a series of high-level venues with world leaders—from the Assembly Hall of the United Nations to Davos in Switzerland, where thousands of business leaders gathered at the World Economic Forum—young people cried out for a war-time mobilization commensurate with the state of "climate emergency," urging everyone to embrace the empirical evidence, pointing to articles such as the one in *Bioscience* signed by tens of thousands of scientists stating: "We're asking for a transformative change for humanity" (Ripple et al. 2020).

To be sure, these voices are scarcely alone. Many executives too are seeing a world where society is being irreversibly mobilized. BlackRock's CEO Larry Fink, for example, declared in front of Wall Street that climate action has now put us "on the edge of a fundamental reshaping of finance" (Fink 2021). These are not the words of a scientist or activist but the conclusions of the head of the largest investment company in the world, managing over $7 trillion in assets. Perhaps most important, however, is that trajectories like this are advancing significantly beyond words on a piece of paper. The past decade saw, for example, sustainably directed assets under management triple to more than $40 trillion globally so that they now represent $1 of every $4 invested (Lang 2020).

Indeed, positive disruptions across the business landscape are booming, and in many cases, they are propelling companies to outperform—not incrementally but significantly. Companies such as Toyota are, right now, building net-positive cities that give back more clean energy to the world than they use while leveraging artificial intelligence and biotechnologies to reinvent and individualize medicine, turn waste into wealth, propel zero-emissions mobility, and even purify the air that people breathe. Corporations such as Unilever, Danone, Westpac, Grameen Bank, Nedbank, and Greystone Bakeries have turned theory into reality with base-of-the pyramid innovation and social business strategies demonstrating how the enterprising spirit can eradicate human poverty and inequality through inclusive prosperity, profit, and dignified work. Thousands of entrepreneurial initiatives have been launched, as smaller companies like Frontier Markets in Rajasthan, Aakar Innovations in Mumbai, or Springhealth in Orissa emerge against the odds to serve the underserved and to tackle the proverbial "last mile" with a passion that many giants have struggled to emulate. Growing companies like Mela Artisans work to generate sustainable livelihoods for artisanal communities under a purposeful brand, while hundreds of for-profit health-tech innovators, like those found under the Baraka Impact umbrella, drive at top speed toward a world in which affordable access and health systems strengthening are a unifying mission. Companies such as Terra Cycle, Nothing New, Nike, and Interface are designing the future of circular economy modalities that leave behind zero waste—only "foods or nutrients" that create truer wealth through symbiotic *economies of cycle* while leveraging digital technologies that serve to dematerialize and decouple growth from harm. Likewise, revolutionary enterprises such as Solar Foods signal the potential of Schumpeter's great "gale of creative destruction." Their remarkable and, as yet, largely unknown, story of industry reinvention, has been sighted as one of the "biggest economic transformations of any kind" heralding the possibility of making food 20,000 times more land-efficient than it is today while propelling a future where everyone on earth can be handsomely fed, using only a tiny fraction of its surface (Monbiot 2020).

The biggest new management story of our time thus is not only about the individual business responses alone but about the rapid rise in collective impact. It's about what scholars and leaders are calling business "megacommunities." Consider the Global Investors for Sustainable Development. Taken together, they manage over $16 trillion in assets—and they are strategically prioritizing SDG investments across every sector and region of the world (GISD n.d.). Likewise, 2021 heralded the accelerated mobilization of over 200 companies such as Apple, Orsted, Woolworths South Africa, Salesforce, Patagonia, Tesla, Unilever, Schneider, Tata, Google, Levi Strauss, Microsoft, and Ikea, each one galvanizing their enterprises to be 100 percent renewable-energy leaders. In addition, this year also grew another worldwide partnership called Business Ambition 1.5°C, where hundreds more companies are rallying their 5.8 million employees, with headquarters in 36 countries, to reach net-zero emissions by 2050 via what's called the "ambition loop" (United Nations Global Compact n.d.). In the last few months, we've seen the number of net-zero commitments rise to more than 1,500 corporations worldwide (Lubber 2021). And we all know that somewhere in the world, it's already tomorrow. Microsoft, Interface, Unilever, and Natura—all and more are aiming higher, far beyond the sustainability agendas of "less bad."

These are examples of trends and megatrends, almost overnight turning into transformative trajectories. Indeed, while researching this book, we were privileged to sit down with many of the vanguard CEOs leading the revolution. The 6,000 interviews now in the Fowler Center's large and growing database involve not just the stuff of dreamers. They are the case studies of the bold, brave, and successful *savvy of doers*. Paul Polman, the former CEO of Unilever and chair of the International Chamber of Commerce, for example, spoke during a personal interview (Paul Polman and David Cooperrider, pers. comm., March 7, 2019) with penetrating purpose and urgent optimism, drawing on years of delivering industry-leading outperformance. He referred to the "shifting of the tectonic plates"—not a small step but a giant leap from our industrial age paradigm of business to its successor. He asserted:

> What we are witnessing is a shift that is all-embracing, rapid, irreversible, extending to the far corners of the planet and involving practically every aspect of business life. What we are witnessing is a world increasingly divided by companies that are known as part of the problem and those that are leading the solution revolution in this, the era of massive mobilization. What we are witnessing is the birth of a comprehensive new enterprise logic, one that can not only create better value and truer wealth but can also be a platform for building the twenty-first-century company, the kind of enterprise that will be loved by its customers and stakeholder communities, emulated by its peers, and prized by all those who care about the next *decisive decades* of our planet.

The future, whether we are ready for it or not, is imminent. Some call what we are witnessing the worldwide solution revolution. Others call it the rise of a new mission economy. Whatever our age comes to be called, there will be winners and losers. Deep enterprise transformation will arrive, of course, in sputtering fits and starts. It will be sparked here and there by seemingly minor innovations. But then, as in every revolution, it will be set ablaze by adjacent embers, until the flames become something of a new Olympic standard, altering conceptions of business and society *excellence* forever.

We invite you into our journey, the call of our times, and the exciting, bold, and innovation-inspiring chapters written by the foremost thought leaders and successful CEOs in the field of management—*and the business of betterment.*

OUR JOURNEY

This book has been written to help leaders, entrepreneurs, change agents, executives, practical scholars, and young future managers join with and lead what Paul Polman referred to as the "solution revolution." In this book, we serve as a guide to the emerging new enterprise logic—future-fit, future-ready, and future-forming—while helping to uncover the potentials for higher peaks of *better* prosperity, built on shared and regenerative value, with intergenerational concern and world-changing actualization. As we speak to each of the three parts of this volume and each chapter, we refer to figure 1.1 as the synthesis of our concept, as it relates to its meaning—and how—to elicit business *outperformance* together with business *outbehavior.*

Taken altogether, the chapters in this book form a natural union in their combined conviction that the fundamental purpose of business *is* building a better world and that there are multiplier opportunities before us—to *outperform* in *competitive excellence* terms and to *outbehave* the field *in collaborative advantage* terms. Moreover, the perspective offered here is new in its conception of how being *a platform for world change* "out there" is rapidly and paradoxically becoming one of the most inspiring *and* repeatable ways for bringing the "in here" of the enterprise powerfully alive.

As seen on the right side in figure 1.1, there is a largely underrecognized, underanalyzed, and underdeveloped new continent of leadership, a wide new axis of management potential, to be appreciated.

Of course, there are many facets to the framework. Each chapter will illuminate one or more of them in detail through major examples, data sets and trends, and the surfacing of deeper enterprise logics combined. In the spirit of foreshadowing the more precise threads woven through this book, there are three big lenses or ideas that make the positive loops between all the elements reverberate together even more powerfully. These cornerstones include: (1) the exciting new research on *mission economy* dynamism; (2) the idea of organizations as *positive institutions or strengths-attracting platforms* for "outbehavior"; and (3) the advanced leadership frontier of *outside-of-the-building* systems thinking that may be the most powerful way to bring "the inside of enterprise" to life. Let's start with the idea of mission economics.

The Betterment of Business +
The Business of Betterment

Creating Shared Value
Purpose-Driven Shareholder and Stakeholder Business Outperformance+

Thick Value: multi-Capital Wealth Management
Stakeholder relationship value; brand admiration management innovation, culture, natural capital renewal etc. All the tangible and 'intangible assets."

Entrepreneurial Humanocracy: from bureaucracy to fully human organizational designs.

Positive Revolution in Products and Markets: every world problem potential net-positive product in disguise—reconceiving needs, products, and customer endearment and empowerment.

Disruptive Circularity: from efficiencies of scale to efficiencies of circularity, technology dematerialization, and regenerative design.

Radical Transparency Advantage: embracing extreme transparency as markets become truer and freer of externalities.

SOURCES OF COMPETITIVE EXCELLENCE FOR LEADING IN THE GENERATIVE ECONOMY

Mirror Flourishing

Platform for World Betterment
Human Outbehavior in the Mission Economy

Anticipatory Global Learning: scaling up excellence through 10X learning, sharing, open innovation, and ambitious X-Prizes.

New Impact Tri-sector Innovation: Win-win-win partnerships unlocking new sources of value and moonshot dynamism.

Mission Economy Business Megacommunities: Creating B2B magnification of strengths and systems change.

Strategic Convening and C-Connectivity: Accelerating community betterment and regenerative inclusive growth.

Enhancing & Elevating Human Lives: Inviting customers and stakeholders to platforms for flourishing and conscious leadership.

SOURCES OF COLLABORATIVE ADVANTAGE THROUGH BUSINESS AS AN AGENT OF WORLD BENEFIT

FIGURE 1.1 The mirror flourishing two-axis model of *The Business of Building a Better World*

6

1. *Mission economics: Why so dynamic?*

We know from economic history that epochal shifts in the logic of business have typically begun in response to underlying changes like what we call "the envelope of enterprise." This includes tectonic shifts in society's expectations, ecosystem and economic disruptions, and world system dynamics. The record of the last century shows that business organizations do not change easily from within, whereby changes outside the organization are most likely to be a trigger of fundamental transformations in the purpose, organizational designs, and leadership priorities of the firm (see Zuboff and Maxim 2004; Hamel and Breen 2007). We tend to think of these fundamental shifts in negative terms, for example, as devastating pandemics, world wars, and so on. These are of course powerful, often black swan events, and they are well-known change catalysts. But what's also true and not as commonly appreciated is that fundamental shifts also come not only when society changes its mind but also when there is an enormous *elevation* of aspiration. This is where the research on mission economics becomes telling. Mission economies, just as negative macroevents often do, can propel mighty shifts.

Moreover, and according to the data of one of the economic theory's rising stars (Mazzucato 2021; Mazzucato and Penna 2015), economic systems are most dynamically alive, technologically innovative, adaptive, prosperous, more fully human, and apt to *propel betterment* for all when they unleash an economy's entrepreneurial spirit in a trisector way *in the service of* mission. How do we know? Mazzucato and her colleagues have studied over 100 examples across countries, cultures, and virtually every continent. The Kennedy-era moonshot is a notable example in the work of Mazzucato (2020; 2021). We still thrill to John F. Kennedy's mission economy when he said, "We choose to go to the Moon in this decade and do the other things, not because they are easy, but because they are hard, because that goal will serve to organize and measure the best of our energies and skills, because that challenge is one that we are willing to accept, one we are unwilling to postpone." The word *moonshot* originally meant a "long shot" and is increasingly used to describe a monumental effort and lofty goal; in other words, "a giant leap" for humankind. What then, for example, have the studies of moonshot or mission economics discovered?

For one thing, missions create alignment of a society's economic engine, entrepreneurial spirit, and symbiotic coalitions and partnerships, while becoming organizationally and technologically transformative. Landing a person on the moon propelled and produced unprecedented payoffs and large numbers of unpredictable spinoffs, creating entirely new markets and industries. It lifted a nation's sense of hope and fueled inspiration, success, purpose, signifi-cance, and a desire to cooperate. And the record abounds of the economic pro-ductivity and vast benefits for all of humankind. In *Apollo's* success, we experienced the birth and growth of the internet; small computers, nanotech-nology; clean energy; X-rays; and the lists go on. Just the internet itself, as a public good and business catalyst, has enabled humanity to create thousands upon thousands of new businesses and millions of new jobs.

It is in this spirit that many of the chapters in this book see too, that to an extent unimaginable a decade ago, a macroworld project with a shared agenda calling upon all of humankind and unprecedented in scope and scale, *is* taking on form and substance. The original moonshot model offers insights and in-spiration for pursuing global goals and "earthshots" today. To avoid some of the worst outcomes of climate change, the world must cut carbon emissions by 45 percent by 2030 and achieve net-zero by 2050. An achievement like that will, among other things, call upon investments and innovation in areas as dif-ferent as building smart cities, transforming vast mobility industries, propelling the renewable energy economy, creating circular and regenerative approaches to manufacturing, turning waste into wealth, and building out regenerative agri-culture and new food systems. That is the signature marker of what mission economies do.

Today's earthshot, propose the authors, includes the example of the 17 Sus-tainable Development Goals (SDGs) that is fast emerging and accelerating as the largest macroproject in recorded history. The scope and need dwarf the collaborations to heal the ozone layer or the global eradication of smallpox and the COVID-19 pandemic. It has dwarfed initiatives like the Marshall Plan, and it is ultimately even dwarfing humankind's leap to the moon.

As one looks at figure 1.1, the idea of an emerging mission economy is both a megatrend and a valuable lens for making sense of advanced leadership (right axis) of the new theory of business, as well as a megatrend propelling and help-ing to explain the surge in the left "Creating Shared Value" side, depicting the rise in sustainable enterprise and regenerative business. Many things in this volume will make better sense as we appreciate mission economy dynamism.

2. *Why is the* Shared Value *business paradigm—itself a relatively new enterprise logic—suddenly bursting out together with this largely undefined new emerging axis of management, where institutions show up as powerful platforms not just for* outperformance, *but for* outbehavior?

For us, the concept of outbehavior is a good place to start and has several significant meanings. First, we draw attention to the work of Dov Seidman

(2007) who wrote what he called a "how" book, not a "how-to" book *recogniz-ing that in our hyperconnected world of extreme transparency, there is no longer such a thing as private organizational behavior.* In this internetworked economy, it is becoming increasingly difficult for organizations to succeed just based on what they make or do. It's not long before someone else is making the product or service, better. It's not long before others are doing it cheaper. People instantly compare price, features, and services effectively making the *what* into a commodity, where differentiation becomes blurred or blotted out, and distinctiveness itself is not long-lasting. How long is it before Costco has matched the price of a Walmart? Certainly not long.

Yet there is one area where tremendous variation exists, and it is not so much in outperformance as in *outbehavior.* In a world that's yearning for trust and hope, it's increasingly about the "how"—the outbehavior of bringing character strengths into the world, like honesty and integrity, hope and inspiration, or more humanity, fairness, courage, and wisdom into our communities. It doesn't hurt that everything organizations do today can live online forever. Wherever organizations show up, their reputations arrive before they get there.

So while it's true that the term *outbehave* is not to be found in dictionaries as are words like *outperform, outfox,* and *outproduce,* we posit that this kind of language truly matters. The idea that organizations can excel in the *how* of outbehavior needs such a word. Indeed, words make worlds. Seidman (2007, 17–18) is clear: "We know how to outspend and outsmart our rivals, but we know relatively little about how to outbehave them.... Show me a venture capitalist that asks entrepreneurs, 'How do you plan to scale your values?' and I'll be interested in investing in their fund." Could it be that in the twenty-first century, outbehavior is the strongest and higher-quality path to success and significance?

The second meaning of *outbehavior* is even more important. Harvard's Rosabeth Moss Kanter's newest leadership book *Think Outside the Building: How Advanced Leaders Can Change the World One Smart Innovation at a Time* (2020) indeed takes leadership to a new place. The days of viewing the corporation as a fortress or castle are gone, and what we are seeing emerge is "outside of the building thinking to improve the world." For Kanter (who also has a chapter in this book) the next frontier for business leaders is to innovate *outside of the building,* at the interface of business and society, as an agent of world betterment. Still underanalyzed and underappreciated as a form of economic and human value, this kind of *out*behavior is also a new kind of *out*performance. For, according to Kanter, good companies can promote diversity in their ranks while making little difference in systemic racism outside of their walls.

The opportunity truly is to deploy a new leadership force for the world. The creativity of outside-the-building skills and sensibilities—activating allies; linking business communities; finding trisectoral assets in unexpected places; working to align complex and competing interests; opening minds; starting movements; harnessing tools for awakening enthusiasm for change; spanning professions of many disciplines; harnessing the renewable power of a positive purpose; creating big enough tents to unite and multiply siloed strengths—all of these are part of what Kanter calls "societal entrepreneurship" and what we refer to as the platform model of business as an agent of world benefit. Platforms are not programs for change; they are bigger than that.

Platform business models—for example Wikipedia, or Patagonia's new activation platform that connects thousands of customers to one another and to hundreds of causes they can join—serve to harness and create large, scalable networks of users, human strength combinations, and resources that become ecosystems of cocreation. These produce scaled-up action and turn action into an effective antidote to despair while augmenting impact and driving human well-being. Platforms create communities and markets with network effects that allow users to interact, learn, enliven—and collaborate. Instead of being the means of production, platforms are the means to connection.

More academically, Cooperrider and Godwin (2011) in the *Oxford University Handbook of Positive Organizational Scholarship* talk about change making, with its usual focus on change management on the inside of the building, where *the enterprise* is the object of organization development and change. But then they pose a question, a thought experiment. What if we conceived of institutions not as the clients of change but as *the* change agents for attracting resources, partners, persons, communities, customers, coalitions, investors, and mission-aligned change makers of every kind? The larger concept involves the discovery and design of positive institutions:

> *Positive institutions* are organizations and structured practices in culture or society that serve to elevate and develop our highest human strengths, combine and magnify those strengths, and *refract our highest strengths outward in world-benefiting* ways leading, ultimately, to a world of full-spectrum flourishing. (Cooperrider and Godwin 2011, 737)

The world is the ultimate context for *the business of business is betterment.* And because of this, every organization's future will be of larger scope and greater purpose than it has been in the past. Every part of the field of management will indeed speak more fully to the destiny of humanity and nature.

So why—beyond being a force for good—will such platforms for world-changing as a new axis of advanced leadership matter in high-performance business terms? The answer, illustrated from the chapters and other recent research, revolves around what unites the right and left sides of figure 1.1. It's called the "mirror flourishing" effect, and it proposes one radical message: *building a better world is the most potent force on the planet—for generating on the inside of the firm the most engaged, empowered, and innovation-inspired enterprise every leader wants.*

3. What if every business aspired to become a positive institution and platform for building a better world?

This is the question we want every reader to consider in the rich tapestry of chapters to follow. Could it be that as we as human beings doing good flourish and come more alive on the "in-here," inside ourselves? Beyond the sustainability literature, there are now more than 500 scientific studies on this "doing good and doing well" dynamic. Steven Post and J. Neimark (2008) summarize many of them in a book titled *Why Good Things Happen to Good People,* whereupon they argue that this reverse flourishing, or mirror flourishing effect, is the most potent force on the planet. The possibilities are vast. For one thing, the reversal of so much of the active disengagement in the workplace, as well as the depression and heartsickness in our culture at large, might well be reversed and easier to accomplish than we think. There are more than 200 million businesses, literally countless numbers, operating across and around our blue planet. Imagine the positive mirror flourishing effect of millions of enterprise initiatives reverberating, scaling up, amplifying, and engaging—us.

OUR THREE-PART VOLUME

Our exploration begins in part 1, entitled "The Business of Business Is Betterment," with a set of chapters that offer a new theoretical perspective for understanding how and why the business of building a better world is not only taking a quantum leap through the multistakeholder logic of "shared value creation" (see Porter and Kramer's 2011 HBR classic and Kramer's chapter in this book) but how this towering and expanding conceptual breakthrough of shared value is only the beginning.

Part 1 opens with a contribution by Marga Hoek in chapter 2, ranked by Thinkers50 as one of the top new management thinkers in the world. For Hoek, there is, as we previewed the concept, a powerful *mission economy* dynamic at work—a driving force and unstoppable force; "a new era in which there is every reason for businesses to want to save the world."

Chapter 3, by Harvard's courageous leadership theorist Rosabeth Moss Kanter, speaks to the new axis or next frontier of what she calls advanced leadership "outside of the building." She writes: "It's not enough to be good within their own operations and capabilities." Advanced leadership changes the underlying institutions that shape systems. Moreover, "the gaps, the cracks between institutional walls, are the places that produce innovation opportunities."

Mark R. Kramer follows, in chapter 4, with a short contemporary commentary on the classic article that he wrote with Michael Porter called "Creating Shared Value: How to Reinvent Capitalism—and Unleash a Wave of Innovation and Growth" (2011). Kramer expands the idea that competitive advantage can be found in providing market-driven solutions to the world's greatest social, ecological, and human challenges. The research, he concludes, is clear: "There is no reversing the fundamental recognition that managing business as a force for good is a winning strategy."

In the next chapter (5) the originator of the concept of "triple bottom line" John Elkington and his colleagues Roberts and Kjellerup Roper write a fascinating contribution called "Green Swans: The Coming Boom in Regenerative Capitalism." The title tells it all. "A Green Swan," the authors write, "delivers exponential progress in the form of economic, social, and environmental wealth creation." If we are indeed entering the dynamism of perhaps the world's most unprecedented mission economy—for which the authors provide evidence from all over the world—then we could be heading toward some sort of positive breakthrough future. Is it a certainty? Absolutely not. Is it a choice? Absolutely yes.

Finally, in the closing chapter (chapter 6) of part 1, CEO Naveen Jain, one of the world's most imaginative entrepreneurs and exponential technology visionaries who helped found Singularity University and the X-Prize, articulates the power of the moonshot mindset with his coauthor John Schroeter. For them, the essence of moonshot thinking is *thinking big*. It's what every business today needs to do. The authors share business examples, one after another, and conclude: "Now, in thinking big, what is the best way to create a $100 billion company? Answer: help a billion people live better lives."

Part 2 of this book raises the stakes involved. It's called "Net Positive = Innovation's New Frontier," and is composed of a set of chapters that together embrace the "best of the best," vitally raising the bar with a great sense of urgency, impatience, and brutal honesty regarding the stakes involved. It begins with one of the world's most respected CEOs, Paul Polman, former head of

Unilever as well the International Chamber of Commerce, together with Andrew Winston, a strategic advisor to many leading companies including 3M, Marriott, DuPont, and others. The title of chapter 7 sets the stage: "Net-Positive Business and the Elephants in the Room." The new horizon is a north star, not a short-term plan; there is no company today that can claim to be net positive. "Business has no choice but to play an active role," say the authors and, "when we face the systemic hurdles head on, we can create net-positive businesses that serve the world."

Next, in chapter 8, Bart Houlahan and Andrew Kassoy, cofounders of the B-Corporation movement, trace the historic shift happening in business toward true markets, extreme transparency, real accountability, and the toppling of the statue of Milton Friedman; that is, the view that the only business is business. By the start of 2021, there were 3,800+ certified B Corporations in more than 70 countries.

Raj Sisodia, the cofounder of the conscious capitalism movement, follows next in chapter 9 and speaks to the kind of mirror flourishing that can happen when we achieve a Copernican revolution, where the business of betterment is at the center of the business universe: "We need to put the life-affirming essentials—human and planetary flourishing—at the center. Everything else, including profits, must revolve around and serve those transcendent goals."

Chapter 10 by R. Edward Freeman, often called the academic father of the stakeholder theory of the firm, along with coauthors Joey Burton and Ben Freeman, presents the data sets and the proposal that stakeholder capitalism is here to stay, and that we are on the cusp of the new story of business. And unlike others that say it's purely being driven by the younger generations (which is true), the larger reality is that what we are witnessing is "three generations, one voice." Thus: "We must be the generations that create a better world for those to follow us."

In chapter 11, Gillian M. Marcelle and Jed Emerson—two of the great thinkers in the arena of blended capital and multidimensional capital—ask us to be inspired by and to "incorporate the alternative understandings of value and stewardship" that emanate from ancient African, Asian, indigenous, and feminine traditions. One aspect is a return to the reality and quality of relational being, where we see and acknowledge the deepest qualities that make us human.

Finally in chapter 12, Roger Martin, a prolific researcher and business school dean, provides a remarkable history lesson—the story of how business models stripped humanity out of management theory. He argues that any business guided by these models "will be doomed to failure" as the humans involved will come to understand the missing humanity and feel its counterproductive impacts. They will fail "because humanity will eventually undermine systems devoid of humanity." High on the agenda of the business of building a better world is a fully human design, not as an afterthought but a centrally embedded reality.

In part 3 (called "The Ultimate Advantage: A Leadership Revolution That Is Changing Everything"), the authors agree that the human dimension and shift from sustainability-as-less-harm to the quest for full-spectrum flourishing *is a driving force* for all the hope and promise of this moment of leadership reset. In management, Peter Drucker spoke to us (David Cooperrider and Peter Drucker, pers. comm., 2003) in common sense terms when he said: "Just as a vital organ such as one's heart cannot thrive in a body overcome by cancer, a business resides in, our societies, the biosphere, and the earth." Indeed, worldviews of bifurcation or separation no longer serve us. There is no long-term business case at all for destroying the envelope of enterprise. Can we acknowledge the interdependence of business and society, that one cannot flourish without the other, the concomitant systems logic of mirror flourishing?

To do this, argue the authors, we must essentially elevate our view of what it means to be human. They turn to the crossroads of state-of-the-art human science, the biology of enlivenment, and the field of neuroscience (some of it made possible by technology advances like MRI) that all show that altruism is real and that impulses to goodness and caring (for newborns, for example) reside in our genes. We see increasing validation of the fact that emotions of love and kindness are precious and vital to every one of us in life; that rich meaning and activation of moral purpose raises our happiness and our immune systems; that extreme isolation and loneliness kills; that when a friend living less than a mile away becomes happy, it will increase the probability that you are happy by 25 percent (Fowler and Christakis 2008), whereby our states of well-being, even dimensions of our physical health flow through networks, and more.

In chapter 13, Kim Cameron, one of the founders of the field of positive organizational scholarship (POS), shares his insights on the back of the study of hundreds of organizations that have faced major crises. In an overwhelming number of these, unprecedented levels of crisis were followed by deteriorations in productivity, quality, trust and ethics, and customer and stakeholder loyalty. Yet a select few organizations flourished and bounced back higher. What was the difference that made all the difference? In every exceptional case, it had to do with outbehavior where leaders were described in virtuous terms or descriptors: compassion, dignity, forgiveness, kindness, trustworthiness, and higher sense of purpose in their cultures. Cameron concludes: "In considering how business can be a better contributor to world benefit, prioritizing virtuousness, may be among the very best strategies to pursue."

If that sounds radical, then chapter 14 by Michele Hunt, former EVP of Herman Miller and now researcher and writer, may push the envelope. Can a company be powered by love? How can a great leader *not* be in love with their bold dreams, with authentic and mighty purpose, with unleashing the human excellence that people are endowed with, and indeed with serving? She argues that love is the most powerful, transcendent, and energetic force in the lives of real leaders. Under Hunt's leadership at Herman Miller, the company became *Fortune's* "Most Admired Company," the best company for women and working mothers, the most environmentally responsible in the United States, and named the "Best Managed Company in the World." This was love in action.

In chapter 15 Chris Laszlo (lead author of an emerging Stanford University business classic, *Flourishing Enterprise: The New Spirit of Business*) and Ignacio Pavez from Chile share that we are in the midst of a consciousness revolution and one that's changing everything. Based on their studies of "positive-impact corporations" committed to going beyond the Hippocratic oath, where doing less harm is no longer an industry-leading leadership ideal, they define success by positive impact value. Their aim is "to increase economic prosperity, contribute to a regenerative natural environment, and improve human well-being." This chapter brought us to reflect on many wisdom traditions and great adages, for example, the words of Thomas Aquinas when he said: "To live well is to work well"—where good living and good working are inseparable.

Chapter 16, by Udayan Dhar and Ronald Fry, is based on a grounded theory study drawn from perhaps the largest innovation bank in the world on the topic of the business of world betterment. Housed at the Fowler Center for Business as an agent of world benefit at Case Western Reserve University, the AIM2Flourish database holds more than 3,000 interviews with businesses from over 130 countries whose mission is to advance both the UN SDGs and create economic value for investors. Dhar and Fry rigorously draw a randomized subset of 36 business and society innovations from this dataset and uncover a series of clear success factors of nearly every element of our dual-axis model. Their analysis uncovers "recognizing the enterprise [itself] as a change agent," the platform model of positive institutions, as well as the success factors of social and ecological embeddedness; long-term orientations to value creation; incorporation of circular value chains; and the convening power of collaborative boundary spanning.

The final chapter in this volume is about the thrill of putting all of this—notably the elements from figure 1.1—together and in practice. Chapter 17 is written by Nadya Zhexembayeva, known for creating a new discipline beyond change management called reinvention, and David Cooperrider, thought leader and originator of the theory of appreciative inquiry. Together they share the skills and sensibilities of the reinvention mindset and how it counters the *Titanic* syndrome, where patchwork never succeeds. They distill key lessons with their own experiences of reinvention, through helping companies bring hundreds and sometimes thousands of internal and external stakeholders "into the room" as collaborating partners. Nadya, David, and their colleagues have helped lead Appreciative Inquiry Reinvention summits with companies such as Apple, Interface, Clarke Industries, Walmart, Whole Foods, and with business megacommunities such as the UN Global Compact, which now involves some 10,000 corporations and regional networks of companies in every region of the world.

Their number-one conclusion after years of reinvention design on a vast array of management topics? The business of betterment is the most potent force on the planet for generating—both on the inside and outside of the firm—the most engaged, empowered, and innovation-inspired enterprise every leader wants. And what the world needs.

REFERENCES

Cooperrider, David L., and Lindsey Godwin. 2011. "Positive Organization Development: Innovation-Inspired Change in an Economy and Ecology of Strengths." In *The Oxford Handbook of Positive Organizational Scholarship*, edited by Gretchen M. Spreitzer and Kim S. Cameron, 737–50. New York: Oxford University Press.

Fink, Larry. 2021. "Larry Fink CEO Letter." BlackRock. https://www.blackrock.com/corporate/investor-relations/larry-fink-ceo-letter.

Fowler, James H., and Nicholas A. Christakis. 2008. "Dynamic Spread of Happiness in a Large Social Network: Longitudinal Analysis over 20 Years in the Framingham Heart Study." *BMJ* 337, a2338. https://doi.org/10.1136/bmj.a2338.

Freedman, Andrew. 2019. "More Than 11,000 Scientists from around the World Declare a 'Climate Emergency.'" *Washington Post*, November 5. https://www.washingtonpost.com/science/2019/11/05/more-than-scientists-around-world-declare-climate-emergency/.

Gladwell, Malcolm. 2002. *The Tipping Point: How Little Things Can Make a Big Difference*. New York: Back Bay Books.

Global Investors for Sustainable Development Alliance (GISD). N.d. "The GISDAlliance." Accessed May 12, 2021. https://www.gisdalliance.org/.

Hamel, Gary, and Bill Breen. 2007. *The Future of Management*. Boston: Harvard Business School Press.

Kanter, Rosabeth M. 2020. *Think Outside the Building: How Advanced Leaders Can Change the World One Smart Innovation at a Time*. New York: PublicAffairs.

Lang, Kristen. 2020. "Building a More Equitable, Just and Sustainable Economy Is No Longer an Ideal. It's Imperative." Reuters Events—Sustainable Business, October 8. https://www.reutersevents.com/sustainability/building-more-equitable-just-and-sustainable-economy-no-longer-ideal-its-imperative.

Lubber, Mindy. 2021. "Net Zero Gaining Momentum like Never before among Investor and Business Community." *Forbes*, January 6. https://www.forbes.com/sites/mindylubber/2021/01/05/net-zero-gaining-momentum-like-never-before-among-investor-and-business-community/?sh=3b9186af8bf0.

Mazzucato, Mariana. 2020. *The Value of Everything*. New York: Public Affairs.

Mazzucato, Mariana. 2021. *Mission Economy: A Moonshot Guide to Changing Capitalism*. New York: Harper Business Books.

Mazzucato, Mariana, and Caetano C. Penna, eds. 2015. *Mission-Oriented Finance for Innovation: New Ideas for Investment-Led Growth*. London: Pickering & Chatto.

Monbiot, George. 2020. "Lab-Grown Food Will Soon Destroy Farming—and Save the Planet." *Guardian*, January 8. https://www.theguardian.com/commentisfree/2020/jan/08/lab-grown-food-destroy-farming-save-planet.

Porter, Michael E., and Michael R. Kramer. 2011. "Creating Shared Value: How to Reinvent Capitalism—and Unleash a Wave of Innovation and Growth." *Harvard Business Review*, January. https://hbr.org/2011/01/the-big-idea-creating-shared-value.

Post, Steven, and Jill Neimark. 2008. *Why Good Things Happen to Good People: How to Live a Longer, Healthier, Happier Life by the Simple Act of Giving*. New York: Broadway Books.

Ripple, William J., Christopher Wolf, Thomas M. Newsome, Phoebe Barnard, and William R Moomaw. 2020. "World Scientists' Warning of a Climate Emergency." *BioScience* 70, no. 1: 8–12.

Seidman, D. 2007. *How: Why How We Do Anything Means Everything . . . in Business (and in Life)*. Hoboken, NJ: John Wiley.

United Nations Global Compact. N.d. "Business Ambition for 1.5°C." Accessed May 11, 2021. https://www.unglobalcompact.org/take-action/events/climate-action-summit-2019/business-ambition.

Zuboff, S., and J. Maxim. 2004. *The Support Economy: Why Corporations Are Failing*. New York: Penguin Books.

PART
ONE

THE BUSINESS OF BUSINESS IS BETTERMENT

2

The Trillion-Dollar Shift

Business for Good Is Good Business

MARGA HOEK

THIS IS THE ERA when business for good is good business. A new era in which there is every reason for businesses to want to save the world. Responsible business models and capital investment can be pivotal drivers for good and can open many exciting markets as well. Rather than seeing sustainable practices as problems or growth limiters, companies should embrace sustainability as a domain of huge growth potential. We are currently experiencing a trillion-dollar shift in business and capital opportunities—a $12 trillion opportunity to be precise—just in this decade alone.[1] Sustainable brands are outperforming nonsustainable brands both in revenue as well as growth, as consumers increasingly vote with their feet. Shareholders have been putting pressure on investors to integrate environmental, social, and governance (ESG) in a materialized way; some investors are going further to adopt full-fledged impact and mission into their private equity transactions. Yet, it is not only a $12 trillion opportunity, it is also a $12 trillion need as the world requires a radical turn of the tide. In that sense, business and the world's challenges are mutually dependent.

THE SDGS: THE MORAL AND BUSINESS COMPASS FOR THE WORLD

Recognizing the many challenges faced throughout the world, the UN Sustainable Development Goals (SDGs), adopted by 193 countries in September 2015, can be used as a compass to direct sustainable business and investment. The SDGs (shown in figure 2.1) are the blueprint for the world we want to have, and they provide one language and one set of goals, targets, and

FIGURE 2.1 The UN Sustainable Development Goals (https://sdgs.un.org)

indicators to guide us to eradicate broad challenges including hunger, poverty, inequality, and injustice and climate change by 2030. From the initiation of the SDGs in 2015, we have been fortified in focus and more unified in approach. This has contributed to a precise specification and the materialization of solutions needed to restore and sustain the world.

Investors predominantly use ESG as a tool to monitor both risks and opportunities in business. Both the 17 SDGs as well as ESG methods refer broadly to the same challenges, albeit that the SDGs are more specific. ESG performance on investments is becoming increasingly important, as sustainable investments outperform nonsustainable ones. Throughout the COVID-19 crisis, it has become abundantly clear: investment for good is a good investment, as sustainable investments have proven to be more resilient. The pandemic has been a wake-up call for decision makers and a positive catalyst for ESG. J. P. Morgan found the broadly defined ESG investor market doubled in 2020 to $80 billion. The high engagement private equity approach taken by impact investors has flourished even more; the Global Impact Investing Network indicated in June 2020 an updated estimated market size of $715 billion.[2]

Business, investment, and society's challenges are all mutually dependent. As societal challenges create clear needs for solutions, there are huge growth markets to be unlocked. Imagine in this warming world, the need for cold is no longer a luxury. Nearly 2.8 billion people now live in hot areas and this number is rising rapidly. It is predicted that 90 percent of the world's population will be living in hotter climates by 2100. Access to air conditioning will therefore become a crucial need and will become a major industry. It is also an industry that is currently being disrupted since its negative footprint must be eliminated. So new ways of cooling our cities, our rural communities, and our transportation need to be invented. Already, 470 million people are living in rural communities in hot areas where they have no access to electricity. As we must diminish and ultimately prevent the use of fossil energy, new technology at scale is needed to face these challenges and those companies bringing innovative, truly sustainable solutions will experience tremendous growth.[3]

The Challenge for Business: Minimize Negative Impact on All SDGs, Focus on Creating Positive Impact on the Most Relevant SDGs

The SDGs come with a huge prize, and prioritizing SDGs for this purpose is crucial. Companies should expect to minimize their negative impact on all SDGs. At the same time, they should focus on creating a positive impact on a select few of the SDGs, to ensure significant influence. For example, many companies like the global retailer Gap, Inc. concentrate their efforts on

SDG 5: gender equality. The McKinsey Global Institute estimates that the market impact of products and services that focus on gender equality could add up to $28 trillion, or 26 percent of annual global GDP by 2025.[4]

By focusing on the SDGs, companies are directing their business behavior toward creating sustainable workforces and sustainable markets. Business and capital, when assuming the responsibility as a force for good, create many exciting prospects and opportunities for growth and endurance.

SHARED VALUE AND THE NEW MEANING OF GROWTH

Minimizing negative societal impact and focusing on creating positive impact indicate a new business imperative. It means business is becoming part of the solution rather than the problem. If companies can create a net-positive impact across the totality of their operating footprints, it means we can restore the world and its assets. It also means, for instance, that we can move from carbon neutrality toward carbon positivity by removing the overload of carbon in our atmosphere. The wheels are beginning to turn here. It has been the case for many years that carbon neutrality and mission zeros were considered the ultimate goals, but by now carbon is considered a resource for new materials. Carbon removal and sequestration are now considered to be a $5.9 trillion global opportunity. This includes building materials, fuels, agricultural materials, and consumer goods.

This way of thinking and action is representative of the shared value business model. The concept of shared value, often referred to as CSV (creating shared value) was first introduced by the trailblazing researchers and business strategists Michael Porter and Mark R. Kramer. This business model asserts that value for society and financial value are positively (rather than negatively) related. It cannot be overstated that financial success does not need to come at the expense of society or the environment; creating a positive impact on society and the environment does not need to come at the expense of profit. The same applies to the connection among markets, growth, competitiveness, and sustainability. This way of thinking is about recognizing positive synergies and is, by essence, opportunity-driven.

We Must Disconnect Growth from Negative Impact and Reconnect Growth to Positive Impact on Our World. Then We Can Speak of Growth as a Force for Good.

Building on the ambition to move from reducing negative impact to creating a positive one, the CSV model will become the business-driven model pervading sustainable global business and capital. The shared value model is characterized by the principle of "doing well by doing good." CSV shows that financial, societal, and environmental benefits can be achieved simultaneously. In fact, at the core of the model are societal and environmental issues that serve as the drivers in propelling profitable shared-value business cases across a wide spectrum of companies and industries. In this regard, CSV is the ideal business model to support the realization of the SDGs. It is the new sustainable economic model.

Companies can contribute in meaningful ways, and shared-value business cases often touch many SDGs at the same time. Carpet manufacturer Interface changed course years ago to create a positive impact with its growth. Unilever, Nike, Nestlé, DSM, and others are also well on their way to changing course. All are working to eliminate their negative impact and create positive impact as they strive to put more back into society and the environment than they take out. They aim to become CO_2 positive by developing more renewable energy than they need themselves and therefore to be in a position to supply energy to others in their surroundings. In these cases, growth is good. Examples like these show that growth in this respect makes a positive impact on the world, and we can look at growth as something that contributes to the world rather than takes from it.

In the coming decades, growth must at the very least be disconnected from negative impact associations and connected instead to positive impact. The value of growth is the creation of value for society and the environment, and certainly not the exploitation of the world's assets. Exploitive growth with insular financial gain can no longer be tolerated and will, in fact, eventually lead to its demise as it is simply not sustainable. Growth as a force for good, positive impact, and scaling up sustainable activities is the new meaning of growth.

MARKET OPPORTUNITIES: SDG SWEET SPOTS

According to a landmark report launched by the Business and Sustainable Development Commission (BSDC) entitled *Better Business, Better World*, achieving the SDGs opens up $12 trillion in market opportunities.[5] While other reports mention different numbers, the essence of the matter here is that there are huge growth markets related to solving societal challenges.

For companies' considerations, it is crucial to know where those opportunities are and thus we can identify the major growth markets, namely food and agriculture, cities, energy and materials, and health and well-being. They represent around 60 percent of the real economy and are critical to delivering the

SDGs at the same time. We can refer to these growth markets as sustainable "sweet spots." These sweet spots have the potential to grow two to three times faster than the average GDP over the next 10 to 15 years. The same report notes there is a $4 trillion annual investment opportunity existing in these sectors, which could unlock opportunities worth more than $12 trillion by 2030, conservatively calculated.

Companies can consider making new products and market decisions as a consequence. This means companies in industries such as construction can, for instance, move away from low-margin competitive offerings to high-value, less competitive environments. This, of course, assumes quite radical, innovative approaches, but it can be done. Take, for example, the amazing project that started at Mexico's hospital Torre de la Especialidades. An innovative façade tiling was introduced that neutralizes smog in a city that is considered one of the most polluted. The Berlin-based firm Elegant Embellishments designed the building's face, which is now capable of neutralizing chemicals produced by 8,750 cars a day. And it looks truly beautiful at the same time, creating ecological as well as aesthetic value. Being a designer or producer of such solutions lifts your company out of the spectrum of current competitors since you create a whole new league of value that will be in high demand.

Preventing food loss and waste is a significant part of the food and agriculture sweet spot. While the loss is predominantly happening at the beginning of the food cycle, most food waste is caused at the end of the supply chain by consumer and retail behavior in developed countries. This should be easier to solve than the issues farmers in developing countries face with food loss, but it still demands concerted effort, focus, innovation, and scale.

In the United States alone, nearly half of all food is thrown away, with consumers accounting for 40 percent of that. In France, consumers also generate the most waste, causing 67 percent of the 7.1 billion tons of waste in the country. Retail and other food vendors also generate their fair share of the total waste in developed countries. For instance, in the United Kingdom, the food and hospitality industry wastes 920,000 tons of food, costing £2.5 billion each year.[6]

Recognizing the amount of economic loss should propel every business to find solutions. This does not only apply to businesses directly related to food, like supermarkets or restaurants, but every company. Think of company cafeterias or business meetings with lunch provided. Solutions for companies are available. Startup businesses like Copia collect leftover food from a meeting, for example, and deliver it to charities in their area, offering companies a tax benefit for their charitable contributions and helping society by redirecting perfectly good food to those in need. For restaurants and catering companies contending with the fine line of having enough fresh food on hand while not creating unnecessary overexpenditure, technological solutions are providing an economical remedy. Q-point, for example, is a Dutch consultancy that has developed a data collection and estimation solution to food purchasing and planning for restaurants and catering companies to avoid oversurplus resulting in waste. They are currently expanding their scope to develop applications tailored to hospitals, theme parks, and company restaurants.

THE ECONOMIC PRIZE

Achievement of the SDGs brings with it economic gains for the economy at large, which substantially adds to the total prize shared by the private sector. This is an important factor since GDP impact is still generally ignored. It is important to note, however, that achieving the SDGs brings with it a huge GDP prize—much higher than any company can account for.

Global disasters exacerbated by climate change (SDG 13) caused $210 billion in losses in 2020 as several countries, including the United States and China, battled hurricanes, floods, and wildfires, according to a report by insurance company Munich Re. The worldwide monetary losses in 2020 were up 26.5 percent compared to 2019 costs of $166 billion, and $82 billion worth of damage was insured last year, up from $57 billion in 2019.[7]

Health and well-being (SDG 3) confront us with the fact that currently, more people die from obesity than from lack of food. The impact of an overweight population on public health translates to an incredible increase in health expenditure. About USD PPP 311 billion will be spent every year by OECD countries to treat diseases caused by the overweight. In total, this issue alone will cost 52 countries 8.4 percent of their total health spending whereas the United States will spend nearly 14 percent of its health budget on obesity and the overweight. Issues relating to overweight also affect the labor market, since obesity reduces the employment rate and increases early retirement, absenteeism, and presenteeism. As a result, the workforce in the abovementioned 52 countries will be reduced by the equivalent of 54 million full-time workers. Through the combined effects of overweight on life expectancy, health expenditure, and the labor market, GDP will be 3.3 percent lower on average in OECD countries.[8]

The other side of the same coin is the upside. Solving these challenges prevents costs and will free us up from the enormous economic burdens that come along with ever-growing societal challenges. Research from the McKinsey Global Institute, for instance, indicates that achieving gender equality alone (SDG 5) would add at least $12 trillion to global growth by 2025.[9]

New markets are emerging and, at the same time, some current markets are starting to fade. The market demand for nonsustainable energy sources and sugary refreshments are examples of shifts in consumer awareness and behavior. The business cases for these and other detrimental products will also become negative as soon as inclusive pricing is made a reality. Currently, it is still cheaper in most cases to create products using virgin materials rather than recycling, since we do not put a fair price on resources and externalities like pollution. Nonsustainable products nowadays often have a double advantage: they barely pay the price for their negative footprint and, in the case of fossil energy, benefit from subsidies. As soon as tax systems include the CO_2 price and ecological costs, now still called externalities, nonsustainable business cases will be deemed loss-making. This would already happen if the world would just stop subsidizing fossil energy since according to the International Monetary Fund, the fossil fuel industry is still subsidized worldwide to the tune of $5.2 trillion.[10] The Business Commission calculated that the impact on the value of the sweet spots referred to above would rise by around 50 percent if ecological costs were to be integrated. Incorporating the SDGs in business initiatives and strategies helps companies shape their business endeavors for enduring success.

SCALE HAS IMPACT

Corporations are some of the largest economic entities in the world, ranking higher than many countries. Now imagine if those giants create positive societal and environmental value, the tide may be turned. While large companies often transition slowly to a sustainable business model, small companies can move faster. A tanker simply doesn't shift course as easily as a speedboat. There are currently many highly innovative startups with high growth potential arising around the globe. These startups are born from the orientation toward these new markets and the solutions to the problems facing our world. Several innovative startups and scale-ups are incorporating this new meaning of growth from the floor of their foundation. Their business models are often based on creating a positive impact on the world.

Good things happen when small meets big. Large companies can benefit from the innovation and purpose-driven culture of the startup, and the startup can benefit from the network and funds of the large company to scale up faster. There are different ways that large companies and small are coming together.

One way involves the large companies using the ambidextrous business model to nurture breakthrough innovation. An "ambidextrous organization" keeps its regular business endeavors going at the same time while creating or incorporating business units that have their unique processes, structures, and cultures. These business units either identify new opportunities, develop new products or services, or protect a new venture within the umbrella of the large company.

Corporate venture capital (CVC) is a great form of "small meets big" that, when done right, is mutually beneficial for both corporations and investees. The strength of the CVC model is twofold. First, innovative ideas are effectively linked to economies of scale and financial power. Second, this model helps large companies to accelerate the achievement of their long-term sustainable objectives. The growth in CVC is fueled by numerous disruptive, transformative trends, which are greatly increasing the pace of innovation and business endeavors. Large companies are therefore looking for faster "shortcuts" to enter new markets and accelerate growth. They are not only looking to innovate with manageable risk and an assurance of a financial return, but they are also increasingly using corporate venture capital to realize their long-term goals. If done well, CVC offers large companies a shortcut to future offerings and offers small companies an accelerated growth path.

TECH FOR GOOD

It is said that data is the new gold. Data serves many purposes, one of which is that it is an excellent way to have an honest dialogue on how businesses can commit to the SDGs. The intersection of business and societal needs can be navigated by data analysis, which enables all parties to see concrete results and shift course as necessary. Data providers are in a unique position to accelerate and strengthen the mobilization of sustainable capital investment. Through regional, interregional, and global forums for knowledge-sharing, technical assistance, and data-sharing, data analyses and projections can serve as powerful motivators to decision making.

Examples of how the combination of AI and data analytics are being used for good can be seen in many industries. One primary area where the market is expanding is in smart city design. Academics and business leaders are currently exploring areas where AI can improve city design, the quality of life of inhabitants, and optimize city operations. Using this technology, city planners can produce design solutions that transform urban spaces, track resident well-being and behavior, and analyze data for new insights. Because of the data generated by smart cities, planners can better design them to address resident needs. Sensors placed on buildings can track how people move around and interact with a property. This can provide valuable information about how to save both money and energy.

Technology is the biggest accelerator for sustainability in the 2020s, or at least it should be. In the next decade, every company, regardless of the sector, needs to go tech. Small and big data, robotics, AI, drones, and other innovative technologies offer new pathways to sustainability as well as business opportunities.

NEW GENERATIONS IN DEMAND

Sustainability will become much more important to big and small companies throughout this decade, as new generations become the largest portion of both consumer and workforce markets. Millennials are already a large proportion of these markets, and they have noticeably started to be a driver for sustainable change. As employees, they demand purpose-driven companies, and as consumers, they are willing to pay more for sustainable products and supply-chain practices. Generation Z, entering the workplace and consumer market right after them will continue to demand action and take action themselves. Greta Thunberg has amazed the world with her straightforward confrontations which she has delivered on every world stage by now. Boyan Slat has won the prestigious Champion of the Earth UN prize by making clear that less plastic won't suffice and that we "must get rid of the mess," since otherwise, we will have more plastic in the sea than fish by 2050. Many, if not most, startups are purpose-driven companies with the mission to improve the world. A McKinsey study showed that 90 percent of Gen Z expects brands to take a responsible approach to societal issues.[11] Companies will have to get a move on if they want to become, and stay, relevant since they will need to respond rapidly and at scale to the major changes ahead in workforce and consumer demands.

Millennials and Generation Z are not only interested in ethical businesses but in ethical work relationships as well. Millennials are the stewards of change, and they will champion the shift to business for good becoming the norm rather than the exception.

LEADERSHIP FOR GOOD

People have power, even more so today than ever before. A Cone Communications study in the United States shows that 87 percent of people will purchase a product because a company advocated for an issue they cared about, and 76 percent will refuse to purchase a company's products or services upon learning it supported an issue contrary to their beliefs.[12] The study also revealed that 90 percent of U.S. people surveyed would boycott a company if they discovered that the company was using dishonest or irresponsible business practices. We can each be a leader for good and inspire and support each other to build a sustainable life for ourselves and the generations to come.

The world needs our business solutions, and they are needed sooner rather than later. The solutions not only need to come quickly, but they also need to be scaled up as rapidly as we can. The scale of our business and capital solutions simply must meet the scale of our global challenges. We have entered a new decade. The decade of sustainability.

NOTES

1. Business and Sustainable Development Commission, *Better Business, Better World*, 2017.

2. "Why Covid-19 Could Prove to Be a Major Turning Point for ESG Investing," J. P. Morgan Equity Research, July 1, 2020, https://www.jpmorgan.com /insights/research/covid-19-esg-investing.

3. Richard Mahapatra, "Heatwave Effect: 2.5 Billion People to Have Air Conditioners by 2050," Down to Earth, August 1, 2019, https://www .downtoearth.org.in/news/climate-change/heatwave-effect-2-5-billion-people -to-have-air-conditioners-by-2050-65948.

4. Jonathan Woetzel, Anu Madgavkar, Kweilin Ellingrud, Eric Labaye, Sandrine Devillard, Eric Kutcher, James Manyika, Richard Dobbs, and Mekala Krishnan, "How Advancing Women's Equality Can Add $12 Trillion to Global Growth," McKinsey & Company, September 16, 2020, https://www.mckinsey .com/featured-insights/employment-and-growth/how-advancing-womens -equality-can-add-12-trillion-to-global-growth.

5. Business and Sustainable Development Commission, *Better Business, Better World*.

6. Oakdene Hollins, *WRAP-Overview of Waste in the UK Hospitality and Food Service* (Banbury, UK: Wrap, 2020), https://wrap.org.uk/sites/default/files/2020 -10/WRAP-Overview%20of%20Waste%20in%20the%20UK%20Hospitality%20 and%20Food%20Service%20Sector%20FINAL.pdf.

7. "Record Hurricane Season and Major Wildfires—The Natural Disaster Figures for 2020," Munich RE, January 7, 2021, https://www.munichre.com/en

/company/media-relations/media-information-and-corporate-news/media
-information/2021/2020-natural-disasters-balance.html.

8. Michele Cecchini, *Heavy Burden of Obesity: The Economics of Prevention* (Paris: OECD, 2019), https://www.oecd.org/health/health-systems/Heavy -burden-of-obesity-Policy-Brief-2019.pdf.

9. Woetzel et al., "How Advancing Women's Equality."

10. "Climate Change: Fossil Fuel Subsidies," International Monetary Fund, accessed May 17, 2021, https://www.imf.org/en/Topics/climate-change/energy -subsidies.

11. Tracy Francis and Fernanda Hoefel, "'True Gen': Generation Z and Its Implications for Companies," McKinsey & Company, November 2018, https:// www.mckinsey.com/industries/consumer-packaged-goods/our-insights/true -gen-generation-z-and-its-implications-for-companies.

12. "2017 Cone Communications CSR Study," Cone, 2017, https://www .conecomm.com/research-blog/2017-csr-study.

3

Taking Leadership to a New Place

*Outside-the-Building Thinking
to Improve the World*

ROSABETH MOSS KANTER

BUSINESS LEADERS INCREASINGLY acknowledge their responsibilities to create benefits for multiple stakeholders, beyond just financial benefits for owners and shareholders, and they are increasingly reporting on environmental, social, and governance performance to ensure accountability for their actions. However, change within a company doesn't necessarily change the system that created and perpetuates problems that threaten and diminish well-being. Instead, business leaders must "think outside the building"—beyond their silos and sectors—to exercise leadership to solve complex problems plaguing the world—including literal "plagues" such as COVID-19. In addition to pandemics, the problem set includes climate change, racial justice, gender equity, health disparities, education shortfalls, and extreme poverty.

THE NEED FOR ADVANCED LEADERSHIP

Great leadership within the boundaries of an organization is a start, but systemic or institutional change requires additional actions and sensibilities that are part of what I call "advanced" leadership. Advanced leadership attempts to change the underlying institutions that shape systems. It requires challenging sometimes opaque assumptions about the world, and it rarely can be accomplished by one organization acting alone, regardless of how "good" that entity is. Advanced leadership is inherently entrepreneurial, as it seeks problem-solving innovations, but it reflects "systems entrepreneurship," attempting change in an entire system of activity across many players.

Here's an example of the difference: good companies can promote diversity in their ranks yet make little difference in systemic racism outside of their walls. Black professionals might find highly paid work with equal opportunity in a good "supercorp" company (one that combines profits with social good) but face systemic discrimination in the rest of their lives outside of the workplace, such as redlining or residential bias practices that attempt to exclude them from attractive housing in wealthy neighborhoods, even though they could well afford it. U.S. Senator Cory Booker has often told the story about how his Black parents achieved successful executive careers at a major global tech giant—a company known for great leadership on workforce diversity. But they still faced systemic barriers when they tried to buy a house in suburban New Jersey. They were prevented from seeing and bidding on houses in neighborhoods real estate agents considered white-only until they used a white friend as a front to trick realtors into accepting their bid on a house in what they considered a "restricted, white-only" neighborhood. This story ended well for the Booker family, and local ordinances were changed as a result, but numerous Black American families still suffered from de facto housing segregation.

In short, the next frontier for business leaders is systemic or institutional change. How to accomplish this is underanalyzed, and the leadership tools that are needed are underrecognized and underdeveloped. This means that business executives can be underprepared. A newly promoted general manager of a remote country subsidiary of a multinational company was bewildered about his new role because it brought him in contact with the world beyond company and customers. He had studied to be a good engineer and then rose as a respected manager of engineering and product teams. Now, he complained, he was expected to be a diplomat and work with national and local government officials, community activist organizations, and the media, all of which he knew little about, let alone their agendas and associations. Welcome to life outside the building.

The relationship between business and society is complicated and multifaceted, especially as circumstances, norms, and technologies change; systems that worked well or at least were unchallenged in one era become problematic in others. Pharmaceutical companies bring great benefits on some dimensions— major scientific breakthroughs that save lives, reduce suffering, and end pandemics with new vaccines—but are pilloried on others—with pricing in the United States that perpetuates health disparities and marketing that generates overprescribing and the opiate epidemic. Sometimes businesses offer solutions, but sometimes they are part of the problem.

To be an agent of world benefit, companies must move from having reduced their negative externalities, such as air pollution, to positive actions that solve a problem, such as slowing global warming. That is a higher standard than simply "do no harm." It's not enough to be good within their operations and capabilities. The question is how to lead wider problem-solving efforts that produce systemic change.

INSTITUTIONS AND THE CHALLENGE
OF SYSTEMIC CHANGE

Institutions are the set of established structures, norms, assumptions, and pathways that guide societal action and have the legitimacy to carry out certain societal functions, such as education, health care, or the provision of goods and services. They constitute part of what we commonly refer to as "the system." Sometimes institutions become associated with physical structures that house them, such as "the Church" for religion, hospitals for health, or schools and campuses for education. Buildings are just metaphors for structures that tend to set boundaries for activities and assumptions, as manifestations of institutions that represent pathways for action and give shape to a system that becomes more fixed and fortress-like over time. Occupants—incumbents—act as though they alone own the issue and set up barriers to other approaches. That's how problems get stuck in structural silos and thinking gets stuck inside already-established assumptions about action pathways. It's hard for most people to veer off well-trod trails. That's why advanced leaders must be trailblazers.

Systemic problems share five overlapping characteristics. Understanding these systemic issues makes clear how business—itself an institution—can play a role and what skills business leaders can exercise.

System Gaps: A Mismatch between Resources and Needs

Systems are locked into place with boundaries that exclude, whether deliberately or unintentionally. Institutional problems occur when systems advantage some over others; some groups find access to resources readily available, and so they have an interest in defending the system, while others fall into the cracks and might not be able to press for change because of their resource limitations. Even though resources exist that would benefit them, they have no way to get them. That is in part because of assumptions about system design—about the "right way" to do things—which blind leaders to other possibilities.

In some cases, assets or resources that exist are misapplied, unapplied, or unable to reach the target. Gaps in access to healthcare have been exposed not only in the COVID-19 pandemic but also in earlier disasters, reflecting assumptions about the best ways and best places to deliver care. After Hurricane Katrina devastated low-lying areas of New Orleans, largely inhabited by a poor Black population, the inadequacy of a large central hospital for care delivery became clear; the people most in need had no way to get there. Following the disaster, civic leaders began to reimagine the system to get care to where the people are, including mobile clinics and clinics in public schools, which themselves were being reinvented to bring the innovation of charter schools. A later program in Baton Rouge brought health services to barber shops, where Black men congregated and in which they had high trust. Retail pharmacies developed primary care clinics in their stores; fashion retailer Nordstrom began to offer mammograms in theirs.

In other instances of mismatch and gaps, food or medicine sent to disaster areas can decay at entry ports because of inadequate logistics to move them to places where people are hungry or ill. Wasted but safe and edible foods might be available in affluent suburbs but nowhere near the people who need them. Imagine if there were a distribution system and retail outlets to bring nutrition to food deserts. That's an institutional gap to be filled—which former Trader Joe's president Doug Rauch did when he founded Daily Table, which converted food about to go to waste into nutritious affordable groceries, thereby addressing climate change (methane from food waste) and health (nutrition for low-income people).

Underutilized assets present opportunities for system change. Gaps represent opportunities. To solve urban transportation problems, entrepreneurs saw a gap and chance for matching unutilized private cars and their owners with discretionary time with potential passengers who needed a ride. Uber and Lyft grew quickly in the United States and in other parts of the world. Ride-sharing alleviated community space problems (limited parking) and created freelance work (which itself has migrated from "gigs" as independent contractors to claims of "employees" seeking benefits).

One of the first tenets of advanced leadership is that thinking outside the building—that is, beyond current assumptions and the usual suspects to identify other possible partners—involves challenging assumptions about how things must work. It's often not resources that are in short supply; what's missing are human imagination and leadership to find new pathways that make better matches. The gaps, the cracks between institutional walls, are the places that produce innovation opportunities.

Big Scope and Complexity, with Many Facets and Layers

Big problems are not easily contained by institutional boundaries. Seemingly unrelated activities in different industries turn out to bear on the problem. There are ripples beyond core issues. Whatever the issue is, it is of great importance to many parties, some of who are invisible to institutional champions. Sometimes the role of business is not central, but business practices affect the problem and can help solve it.

As long as the system appears healthy on the surface, it's hard to get attention to the underlying system's dysfunctions; institutions are often taken for granted as long as everything is working. Extreme weather events have brought attention to climate change and moved it higher on the agenda. The COVID-19 pandemic brought attention to infrastructure inequities affecting remote work or remote education, such as lack of broadband for good internet connections. Parsing a problem enlarges its scope. To reduce U.S. educational inequities involves a range of other factors—family situations, hunger and malnutrition, health challenges, transportation problems, and more—requiring action well beyond the classroom. Peeling the onion reveals more layers of connected problems. There is not just one problem but many.

Sometimes the significance of a major systems problem is unrecognized until problems mount—traffic, for example, is merely a daily annoyance of a rush-hour commute for people without awareness of the larger system context surrounding transportation availability and policy choices. Attempts to put the issue into an existing container or to isolate it in a silo are doomed to fail. Even fast-growth companies like ride-sharing startup Uber neglected to see all facets of the system—ignoring and behaving antagonistically toward the government got them thrown out of some countries. A few years into their venture they stopped saying they were "only a technology company" and claimed to be a greener cities solution. And then it turned out that ride-sharing did not reduce traffic congestion. How much turmoil could the company be saved, and how many benefits for the world could have been created if they had looked more broadly at all layers of the system? Ignoring the full scope of the systems issues they are affecting hurts businesses.

Advanced leaders must peel off the layers, understand the complexities, and look broadly at areas beyond the immediate. Rather than staying within their comfort zones, leaders must be guided by their sense of purpose, their mission to bring beneficial change by "dreaming big," looking for the widest manifestations possible, and including them in problem statements.

Ambiguity—Vague or Unspecific Goals and Pathways

This is a corollary of big scope. What exactly does it mean to tackle climate change or racial justice? The problem is defined at a high level of abstraction. That can be a good thing because it means the wider context is included, but it also obscures the path to problem-solving and makes consensus difficult. Unlike the routine problems of daily life, big problems are hard to pin down. Saving dolphins is easier to comprehend than saving oceans. But even this simpler goal has a great deal of uncertainty associated with it, and there is no clear path to action.

Intractable institutional problems are inherently ambiguous as well as complex. There is no single clear goal to be pursued, let alone a consensus about its meaning. Statements on the problem can't easily be translated into action implications. Stating the problem is not enough, as the issue connotes many different things, pointing in different directions for solutions. This means that the route to change is not well mapped. And the routes that are mapped are exactly what is reinforcing the current state of the system. Using established pathways doesn't open the way to solving the problem.

Staying literally or figuratively inside the building will not help clarify goals or find productive new lines of action. Too many companies engage with society through charitable contributions, giving what I've called "spare change" instead of seeking "real change." The pathway is already there to direct funds, established nonprofit organizations need funds, and the rest is easy. But whether that produces world benefits or maintains the existing system is questionable. Moreover, sometimes the cause that leaders seek to address is defined too generally and ambiguously to support innovation. Trader Joe's Doug Rauch, mentioned earlier, thought he was dealing with just a local mismatch problem, so perhaps he could set up a distribution mechanism for getting day-old bread to food banks. But had he settled on that somewhat stale idea (humor was part of his leadership style), he would not have hit upon his well-publicized successful new retail idea addressed to three issues, rather than one: food insecurity, health (affordable nutrition), and climate change (saving food from being wasted and producing greenhouse gases).

When goals aren't clear, it is much easier to settle on paths that exist rather than wandering far afield to explore and gather abundant information and experiences from a very wide range of people and places, including unexpected ones not at first assumed to have anything to do with the problem. For Rauch and other advanced leaders, participating in a culture of constant learning and opening the mind to new ideas produces new angles on problems that can stimulate new action opportunities. Businesses can break through closed minds and closed systems by sending people out into the world for open-ended exploration. Inside an organization, leaders can listen to voices from below—which is especially important as employee activism grows.

Limited Mandates and Lack of Authority

Clearly, no one is in charge of the big problems plaguing the world, including business. Who has the sole charter to cure cancer, end racial or gender discrimination, or clean up the oceans? The big scope of system problems means that no single entity or person, however powerful—monarch, president, prime minister, CEO, or designated executive—can wave his or her executive order, and bingo, it's fixed—assuming that elites would want to fix the matter anyway. In fact, rather than one entity, there are often many with pieces of expertise if not authority. For intractable systems problems, no one entity has a monopoly on legitimate control or governance rights over all aspects of the problem. That's certainly true of environmental challenges such as the oceans, over which no nation has sovereignty. This is also true of practically every other major societal predicament, which can face multiple jurisdictions and multiple claimants to "owning" the problem, standing at different points and coming from multiple sectors and industries.

Multiple potential sources of authority mean that current approaches and structures can't handle the problem alone. Each chips away at just their slice of it, while the problem seems even more intractable. The continuing existence of the problem undermines the authority of existing entities because it exposes their inability to create effective change and thus threatens their power. Other concerned parties who attempt to act might lack legitimate authority or even a formal organizational position.

That lack of clear mandates and authority is a good thing, for several reasons. First, it means that persuasion instead of a position power must be the mode of action, and the quality of ideas should improve in the process. In addition, because responsibility for changing institutions to solve the problem is spread over many entities, benefits are enlarged because many entities benefit. A food company helping farmers with sustainable agriculture generates many benefits. The company has a steady supply, the farmers have customers, and the planet benefits from more environmentally friendly practices.

But it requires advanced leadership sensibilities to navigate these complex systems. The COVID-19 pandemic has illuminated the tangle of NGOs, UN agencies, and governments dealing with the public health emergency, rather than a single responsible party or a clear chain of command. Sometimes this is the result of a longstanding system design—such as the American federal system, with "shared" responsibility for such major public concerns like education and health care, lending confusion to who can do what when, as was seen in the early days of America's COVID-19 response; these were marked by lack of consistency across states and with the federal government, arguably resulting in unnecessary deaths. Where did business fit?

When there is no king, coalitions reign. MITRE Corporation and the Mayo Clinic allied with over 1,000 companies and healthcare systems to coordinate the private sector response to COVID and contribute to the public sector response. The COVID-19 Healthcare Coalition took as its mission to help save lives by providing real-time insights to aid healthcare delivery and help protect U.S. populations. Each coalition member brought its unique assets, sharing resources and plans, and working together with infectious disease experts and researchers to support those on the front lines in responding to COVID-19. Business members included tech giants Amazon Web Services, Microsoft, Salesforce, and numerous healthcare systems and research centers. Coalition subgroups helped get competitors to work together on mission-critical activities such as diverting production to make protective equipment or applying data analytics for decision makers to help save lives.

Forming coalitions and leading within them are hallmarks of advanced leadership. Advanced leaders take the initiative to ally with other organizations to create a de facto mandate with shared responsibility, using persuasion rather than authority to act on a problem. They volunteer and solicit other volunteers with a sense of purpose, with a combination of hubris and humility. They don't wait to be asked, but they don't try to dominate either.

Multiple Conflicting Stakeholders

As I've said, the complexity of big systems problems also makes them contentious. With many dimensions to the problem and many groups involved, conflicting interests and perspectives are likely. Each group might view it differently. (Who is aggrieved? Who deserves help?) Stakeholders might bring a different disciplinary lens to it. (Law? Medicine? Education? Finance?) Some might want to see the problem addressed their way to bring benefits to their specific group—or perhaps they don't want to see it solved at all because they benefit from the status quo. Each group has its priorities and would benefit differentially from particular solutions. Degrees of concern vary; those who care a lot are likely to get very active or very agitated and make a disproportionate amount of noise. Moreover, as stakeholders work to advance their interests, they might advocate without regard to the welfare of the whole, sometimes intentionally and sometimes because they can't see the whole.

Because no one discipline or approach can solve the problem alone, stakeholders often compete for action rights. Claims by one set of professionals (e.g., physicians over patient health care) are contested by other groups (e.g., insurance companies making health decisions for the same patients). It can be hard to find a common cause, let alone unite people behind it. Intractable institutional problems remain that way because there is no agreement about what should be done. Squabbling among stakeholders deflects time and energy from problem-solving action. Stakeholder conflict is more debilitating when there is a status gap among groups that means that elite voices, for example, might receive more attention than those of people at the grassroots. And incumbents—those who have power today—can dominate the narrative at the expense of others.

Having an impact on significant societal problems involves aligning stakeholders, or at least a subset of them, behind a common goal. The goal must be capacious enough to transcend separate interests and enabling compromise— that everyone gets at least some of what they want while directing their actions toward the common goal. Forging such coalitions or joining them as contributors is the ultimate exercise of advanced leadership. Leaders must be able to suspend single-minded pursuit of merely their interests (e.g., traditional U.S. business associations pursuing tax cuts or less-stringent regulations) to advocate for attention to the interests of all stakeholders (e.g., declarations by the Keidanren business federation in Japan and the Business Roundtable in the United States). Thus, leaders must listen to the needs and arguments of stakeholders who are very different from them, whether in sector, industry, or worldview, and then determine how to work together to benefit a larger goal without losing their separate identities.

TOWARD A BETTER PLACE

Solving big problems means shifting from adversarial to collaborative approaches. For example, a Dutch bank known as a good corporate citizen was targeted by climate activists who staged protests outside its headquarters over development projects it financed that had deleterious effects on the environment—precisely, some said, because the bank was supposedly such a good corporate citizen. Leaders could have found many ways to quash the protests and undermine the activist organizations. They could have shut their doors and stayed inside the building. But instead, they chose a collaborative approach. They invited the activists into the bank to educate them. They became leaders in defining a set of environmental principles other banks could follow, which eventually included most of the world's largest banks. A Brazilian subsidiary became the first commercial bank to trade carbon credits, in partnership with the World Bank.

To be effective champions of world benefit, advanced leaders learn to speak many languages—their own and those of the myriad groups in the communities around them. Unlike their lives inside corporate bubbles, they must know how to learn from others more than telling them what to do. They must be able to listen to others who disagree with them. They must ally with competitors and empathize with former opponents.

To improve the world takes a cross-sector, multistakeholder coalition. This is a new organizational form that is not well understood and for which leaders are often not prepared. It is the ultimate of outside-the-building systemic thinking. And it just might be the best vehicle for moving the needle on significant problems with the characteristics I've described. One path-breaking example is West Side United in Chicago, a collaboration of six major hospital systems, numerous community organizations with equal seats at the table, banks and other financial investors, small businesses, and Chicago city government, with the mission of closing the racial longevity gap for over a half million people in that area through projects aimed at health and economic viability.

Business has many roles to play in the quest for a better world. Sometimes business is the main instigator of action and convener of coalitions; sometimes it is a bit player in a supporting role. Sometimes there are direct business opportunities, for example, for new ventures or enhanced products and services. Sometimes business is the visionary innovator that develops the models for change; sometimes it is the culprit behind the problems or the recalcitrant laggard preventing change.

In recent years, there has been a great deal of progress in reframing the role of business so that it serves society. The agenda ahead is to orient businesses to work more boldly and imaginatively in partnership with government and communities to tackle major world problems calling out for systemic, institutional change. Will business leaders rise to the challenge and add advanced leadership skills to their portfolios?

Adapted from R. M. Kanter, *Think Outside the Building: How Advanced Leaders Can Change the World One Smart Innovation at a Time* (New York: Public Affairs/ Hachette, 2020).

4

A Decade That Transformed the Role of Business in Society—A Snapshot

MARK R. KRAMER

IN 2011, WHEN MICHAEL PORTER and I published the "Creating Shared Value: How to Reinvent Capitalism—and Unleash a Wave of Innovation and Growth" in the *Harvard Business Review*, we suggested that too much attention was focused on the conflict between business and society rather than on synergy and interdependence. The COVID pandemic we are currently living through has powerfully demonstrated that the private sector cannot survive without a healthy society and that societies encounter massive hardship when companies cannot succeed. Indeed, without all three sectors working together— government subsidizing the economy, business maintaining employment and developing vaccines, and nonprofits providing immediate assistance to those in need—we could never survive the pandemic. Such a trisector approach, I believe, is at the core of solutions to all the world's major problems.

In our article, however, we focused solely on the role of business in improving society. We believed then—like today—that many of the greatest opportunities for new sources of profit and competitive advantage can be found in providing market-driven solutions to the world's problems. We did not claim that conflicts between profit and social well-being never exist; of course, they happen all the time, especially between the pressures for short-term profit maximization and the reality of long-term social and environmental challenges. Neither did we suggest that corporate philanthropy is moot or that corporate social responsibility should be replaced. Both remain essential corporate obligations.

Instead, we realized that most companies in the world today operate on business models developed decades ago, before we understood the perils of climate change, the social and dietary determinants of health, or acknowledged the deep racial inequities in our society. These companies designed their operations, products, and services without considering the associated societal costs, reinforced by classical economic theory that taught such factors were mere externalities to be addressed by the government.

Today, however, we understand that the salt, fat, and sugar in our diets, the carbon emissions from our cars, and the structural racism that pervades our country, all affect the value and profitability of our companies. Many companies still try to ignore these facts and preserve their old business models for another few quarters, while others have struggled to adjust their operations without confronting the magnitude of change required. Shared value companies, however, find new opportunities for growth and differentiation by designing new business models that embrace these facts and affirmatively improve society.

The decade since our article was published has seen ever-growing momentum, from many sources and under many different banners,[1] all promoting the idea that businesses can benefit from creating positive social impact. Our theory has found numerous practical examples, several of which are now used as teaching cases at Harvard Business School.[2] Some of the world's largest companies, such as Walmart, have explicitly embraced shared value as central to their strategy and operations.[3] Other companies have profoundly changed their industries. Discovery Ltd., a global health and life insurer based in South Africa has reinvented its industry by developing a rewards system that incentivizes healthy behaviors, resulting in a decade-longer life expectancy and 15 percent lower medical costs for its members. Tesla has become one of the world's most valuable companies by proving the viability of emission-free electric cars. PayPal has invented a new form of small business financing that disproportionately helps businesses owned by women and people of color that have difficulty obtaining bank financing, generating over $15 billion in profitable loans. Cisco has trained more than 4 million people around the world in network administration, many of who never finished high school, enabling them to earn a comfortable living while eliminating one of the biggest constraints on the company's growth.

The evidence of changing attitudes toward the role of business continues to build. For the last seven years, *Fortune* magazine has published an annual list of companies that profit from changing the world for the better, now counting hundreds of examples.[4] The Business Roundtable has endorsed the idea that companies must consider the welfare of all stakeholders.[5] BlackRock CEO Larry Fink has cautioned companies that climate change is leading to a fundamental reshaping of finance and that companies must embrace a social purpose beyond profit.[6] The few investment funds that go beyond ESG metrics to apply a shared value lens have consistently outperformed the market,[7] while impact investing, characterized by the twin objectives of financial returns and social impact, has grown exponentially.[8] In short, the world has been moving steadily toward what we called creating shared value.

And yet, old paradigms die hard. The skepticism and pressure for short-term shareholder profits remain deeply entrenched. Many MBA students still graduate believing that maximizing shareholder value is their only objective and that "nonfinancial" factors are irrelevant to securities valuation. ESG investing continues to rely on unverified checklists of voluntary disclosures, most of which are neither material to the company nor the world. Companies claim commitment to the UN's Sustainable Development Goals, yet analyses of their actual behavior and business plans show that they will never reach their stated ambitions.[9] Activist investors threaten to disrupt long-term corporate plans with quick tricks to pump up stock prices. For all the progress being made, the sad truth is that most businesses still do not intentionally create positive social impact as part of their core strategy and operations.

Despite these laggards, the trend is clear that social issues are inescapable business issues and that neither CSR nor philanthropy are adequate responses. Instead, companies must reinvent their products to deliver social value, restructuring their value and supply chains to align with social and environmental realities. They must strengthen the industries and regions where they operate in ways that expand markets, support stakeholders, and improve their competitive context. As governments have become increasingly dysfunctional around the world, the role of corporations in solving the world's problems has become irrefutable.

The evidence is increasingly clear that the companies that do embrace the concepts of shared value, by whatever name they choose, are succeeding, while those that try to handle social and environmental issues only through traditional "light touch" CSR and philanthropy are rapidly losing value.[10] Academic theories may come and go, the language of "creating shared value" may gain or lose popularity, but there is no reversing the fundamental recognition that managing business as a force for good is a winning strategy.

NOTES

1. Similar approaches include work by Jed Emerson (Blended Value), Stuart Hart (Mutual Benefit), Wayne Visser (Integrated Value), and Robert Phillips (Stakeholder Value).

2. Harvard Business Publishing Education, 2021, https://hbsp.harvard.edu /search?N=4294930434&Nrpp=25&Ntt=creating+shared+value&action=refined.

3. "Walmart Highlights Progress in Creating Shared Value in Tenth Annual Global Responsibility Report," Walmart, April 20, 2017, https://corporate .walmart.com/newsroom/2017/04/20/walmart-highlights-progress-in-creating -shared-value-in-tenth-annual-global-responsibility-report.

4. "Change the World," *Fortune,* September 21, 2020, https://fortune.com /change-the-world/.

5. "Business Roundtable Redefines the Purpose of a Corporation to Promote 'An Economy That Serves All Americans,'" Business Roundtable, August 19, 2019, https://www.businessroundtable.org/business-roundtable-redefines-the -purpose-of-a-corporation-to-promote-an-economy-that-serves-all-americans.

6. Larry Fink, "Larry Fink's 2021 Letter to CEOs," BlackRock, accessed May 18, 2021, https://www.blackrock.com/corporate/investor-relations/larry -fink-ceo-letter.

7. Michael E. Porter, George Serafeim, and Mark Kramer, "Where ESG Fails," Institutional Investor, October 16, 2019, https://www.institutionalinvestor.com /article/b1hm5ghqtxj9s7/Where-ESG-Fails.

8. CoPeace, "The Dramatic Growth of Impact Investing," SRI Conferences & Community, April 13, 2020, https://www.sriconference.com/blog/the-dramatic -growth-of-impact-investing.

9. Mark R. Kramer, Rishi Agarwal, and Aaditi Srinivas, "Business as Usual Will Not Save the Planet," *Harvard Business Review,* June 12, 2019, https://hbsp .harvard.edu/product/H05oAC-PDF-ENG?Ntt=kramer+corporate+commitme nt+to+sdgs*&itemFindingMethod=Search.

10. For example, European utilities that ignored the shift to renewables destroyed over $550 billion in shareholder value; ExxonMobil is trading at less than half of its value a decade ago.

5

Green Swans

The Coming Boom in Regenerative Capitalism

JOHN ELKINGTON, RICHARD ROBERTS,
AND LOUISE KJELLERUP ROPER

CURRENTLY, CAPITALISM IS OUR BEST HOPE of achieving anything like sustainability, circular economies, and systemic regeneration—but capitalism itself is under a dark cloud and deservedly so. "Capitalism is under threat," concludes American economist Irwin Stelzer. Yet the growing calls for systemic change, he says, are too often ignored by capitalists who fail "to hear the sound of approaching tumbrils." Over half of Americans aged twenty-three to thirty-eight "would prefer to live in a socialist (46%) or communist (6%) nation."[1]

Unfortunately, many capitalists who do understand at least some facets of this growing threat to the system upon which their wealth depends still limit themselves to what Stelzer defines as "virtue-signaling," including calls for modest increases in their tax burdens and increased philanthropy. Without fundamental changes to such things as inheritance taxes, immigration, free trade rules, executive compensation, median pay for all employees, and the repricing of things like carbon and biodiversity—in short, without the enablers of true systemic change—capitalism will come off the rails.

In stark contrast, the green swan is a symbol of radically better times to come. It's also a template for exponential change toward the distant goal of a sustainable future for all. Getting from here to there will be no trivial task, however. Times of disruptive change upend market and political pecking orders, creating political shockwaves that can last for decades—even generations.

After briefly surveying the shifting landscapes of risk and opportunity, we spotlight key elements of tomorrow's business agenda by summarizing what we have learned through our work at Volans in recent years. We will explain why we issued a "product recall" of the triple bottom line, a concept one of us (John) introduced back in 1994. We will set out the key conclusions to date of our ongoing tomorrow's capitalism inquiry and the work we have done with partners like the World Business Council for Sustainable Development, UNEP FI, and Climate-KIC. We will zero in on the key role of finance, with a brief look at the Bankers for NetZero initiative that Volans coleads. And, finally, we will introduce our evolving Green Swans Observatory, designed to identify, map, analyze and support green swan market dynamics around the world. But first a few words about swans.

SWANSPOTTING

Astute readers will quickly spot some of our influences, among them the work of Lebanese-American author, risk analyst, and former options trader Nassim Nicholas Taleb. In his 2007 book, *The Black Swan*, Taleb provides a series of timely lessons about the "impact of the highly improbable," as his subtitle put it. His timing was impeccable, as the global economy descended that same year into a financial meltdown few had seen coming.

Early on in his book, Taleb noted that he was sticking his neck out, in claiming that "against many of our habits of thought . . . our world is dominated by the extreme, the unknown, and the very improbable (improbable according to our current knowledge)—and all the while we spend our time engaged in small talk, focusing on the known, and the repeated."[2]

Rather than sticking tightly to Taleb's definitions, though, we will riff off his metaphor of the "black swan," referring to unpredicted—and generally unpredictable—events driven largely by negative exponentials, in whose wake nothing is the same. Just as the world's most populous nation vaunts "socialism with Chinese characteristics," we have been investigating aspects of capitalism, democracy, and sustainability with either black or "green swan characteristics"—and sometimes a combination of both.

To the now reasonably well-defined categories of black and gray swans, the gray variety involving predicted surprises, we have added two other concepts: those "green swans," which are positive exponential shifts (in markets, technology, politics, or elsewhere), that ultimately could take us to a regenerative future, and "ugly ducklings," organizations, technologies, ventures, and concepts/mindsets that have not yet reached their full potential of driving green swan shifts.

We soft-launched the green swans agenda at a business summit in Copen-
hagen during 2019, hosted by Dansk Industri (Confederation of Danish
Industry)—and attended by the country's new prime minister, Mette Frederik-
sen, various committed royals from Denmark and Sweden, and 1,300 CEOs and
business leaders. An appropriate setting given that one of Denmark's most famous sons is Hans Christian Andersen, author of "The Ugly Duckling."

But what truly blew us away that day was how the Danish government, the
country's leading industry federation, and the wider business community were
working together to drive an ambitious green transformation. A green swan
economy in the making? We hope so. Certainly, their timing looks exquisite.

Our work suggests that the world has entered some sort of U-bend, well
beyond a single, normal recession, where the established macroeconomic and
political order goes down the tubes, and new ones surface. As we head deeper
into the bottom of the U-bend, we enter a period of maximum confusion and
uncertainty. Historically, too, this is often the point where major conflicts occur.

KEEPING CEOS AWAKE

Capitalism is partly in the spotlight because it has embedded pernicious forms
of myopia in our economies, which now threaten to crash the global biosphere.
As capitalism has reshaped democracy, so it has aggravated wider systemic crises. Unfortunately, our default setting is to deny the very possibility of collapse. Denial, however, cannot mask the pace at which we are destabilizing the
climate, unraveling the web of life, acidifying the oceans, and creating teeth-
rattling wealth divides. Indeed, the evidence suggests that the 2020s will see
flocks of proverbial chickens coming home to roost—with the prevailing scientific and economic paradigms shifting at unprecedented speed.

American-style capitalism has opened up immense wealth divides that are
spurring intense concern and criticism. As a result, the business media have
been running full-page articles with titles like "Capitalism Keeps CEOs Awake
at Night." Ray Dalio, an American investor worth almost $17 billion by Bloom-
berg's estimates, who has embraced capitalism since he was a precocious
12-year-old, took to warning his followers on social media: "I'm a capitalist,
and even I think capitalism is broken."[3]

Students of long-term economic cycles may conclude that the likeliest outcome is a future in which key elements of capitalism crash and burn, and some
then rise again from the ashes—something that has happened many times
before. A future of dark and bright phoenixes, you might imagine, rising from

the smoking debris of our economies, societies, and most tragically for the deep future, our natural environment.

Establishing this point does not make an individual either pro- or anticapitalist but rather an observer of what it is that capitalism does, how it behaves, and how it impacts the wider world. Like nature, capitalism goes through energetic cycles, what popular economists would call "booms" and "busts." In our economies, these are periods of intense excitement shading into "irrational exuberance," driven by new forms of innovation that ride up and down the hype cycle, with a rising backbeat of investment and growth. Typically, booms are followed by various forms of bust, profound unravelings, triggering adaptations, and if things go well, ultimate recovery.

As F. Scott Fitzgerald concluded, "The test of a first-rate intelligence is the ability to hold two opposed ideas in mind at the same time and still retain the ability to function."[4] We make no claims for our three intelligences, or for our brains' ability to function under stress, but our work depends on a constant struggle to make sense of two radically opposed ideas.

The first idea is this: we are headed into a hellish world of systemic breakdowns. Key elements of our climate, biosphere, economies, and societies will come apart at an accelerating rate. Startup entrepreneurs talk of their "burn rate," the speed at which they spend other people's money. Viewed as a startup, the subspecies of postindustrialization *Homo sapiens* that some call *Homo economicus* and others *Homo industrialis* has burned through the planet's resources at a dizzying rate—and is now entering a very different reality, what some call the "age of consequences," others "the Anthropocene."

This future, where a single species has a global impact akin to geological forces, is a world first. As the process continues, the world will be plagued by malign flocks of Nassim Nicholas Taleb's black swans, understood here to be challenges that get exponentially worse in ways that most of us struggle to understand, let alone tackle and solve. Black swans are dramatic events that are outliers—beyond the realm of normal expectations—have a major impact and yet are often poorly understood after the event, even with the benefit of hindsight. In simple terms, that means we fail to learn from our mistakes, unwittingly heading into the jaws of the next round of disasters.[5]

In what follows, we will take a slightly looser approach, with the black swan label signaling that an event came as an existential shock to many people, if not all of them. Hyperinflation in Germany after the First World War, for example, set the scene for the rise of Nazism—so you could argue it was part of a black swan unforeseen by those imposing punitive reparations on a defeated enemy. Reparations of this sort were standard practice at the time, practiced by the Germans, too, but the longer-term consequences were beyond the imaginations of most of those putting pen to paper in 1919.

Similarly, some might argue that climate change is a gray swan, given that we have been talking about the risks for decades. But the climate-induced societal collapses that are likely to follow our crossing of the two degrees of warming threshold will likely include true black swans. Our surprisingly fragile economies, societies, and natural environment could well unravel at hitherto unimaginable speeds.

The second, radically opposed idea to hold in mind is that some parts of the world are now heading toward some sort of positive breakthrough future and that more could soon follow in their wake. This world is one of extraordinary creativity, innovation, and enterprise. The environmental and natural resource burn rate of many key players here is shrinking, often at an accelerating pace. This could be a radically different future, and one increasingly characterized by green swans, defined as follows:

> A **Green Swan** is a profound market shift, generally catalyzed by some combination of Black or Gray Swan challenges and changing paradigms, values, mind-sets, politics, policies, technologies, business models, and other key factors. A Green Swan delivers exponential progress in the form of economic, social, and environmental wealth creation. At worst, it achieves this outcome in two dimensions while holding the third steady. There may be a period of adjustment where one or more dimensions underperform, but the aim is an integrated breakthrough in all three dimensions.[6]

Green swans are extraordinary—in the sense of out-of-the-ordinary—forms of progress, driven and shaped by positive exponentials. In a counterintuitive pairing, they often rise phoenix-like out of the ashes left by black swans. Think of the way nature can recover and flourish after a volcano erupts or after destructive fishing pressure is removed. Generally, however, green swans are less likely to take us by surprise, as we generally have to work toward them assiduously over considerable periods.

Be very clear, though: black and green trajectories are not either-or scenarios. They are parallel realities, already emergent and slugging it out all around us. Some black swans will sport green feathers, and vice versa—as when electric vehicles require raw materials linked to human rights or ecological issues. Much as we may want people to be nicer to one another, the struggle between the black and green sectors of the economy has been, is, and will always be brutal. It is a Darwinian struggle for existence. People rarely surrender what they see as their birthright and future without a fight, even if their efforts threaten to crash the future for other people or other species.

That said, we often misunderstand nature, assuming it only uses competition to spur evolution, whereas the truth is that the natural world is largely concerned with collaboration—symbioses. They also sit at the heart of almost all green swan solutions.

Finally, to stretch our brains still further, there is a fourth key term alongside black, gray, and green swans that needs explanation here: ugly ducklings. In the fairy tale of the same name, the ugly duckling is a baby swan dismissed by its peers for looking unlike any of the other birds around—all of them ducks. Similarly, our future often looks alien when we first spot it. So here is what we mean by the term:

> An **Ugly Duckling** is an early-stage concept, mind-set, technology, or venture with the potential to be a driver of a Green Swan shift. Its potential future evolution is very hard to detect early on, unless you know what you are looking for. Tomorrow's breakthrough solution often looks seriously weird today. The net result is that we give them significantly less attention and resources than they need—or than the future of the 2030s and beyond would want us to in hindsight.[7]

We see growing numbers of ugly ducklings as critical to any sort of green swan future. So, in that spirit, here are five initiatives we have been working on.

1. RECALLING THE TRIPLE BOTTOM LINE

How often are management concepts subjected to product recalls by the people who coined them? It is hard to think of a single case. By contrast, if an industrial product like a car fails in a well-run market, the manufacturer pulls it back, tests it, and reequips it if necessary. In case manufacturers grow careless, governments regulate and run periodic road safety tests to ensure that public safety is being accounted for.

Management concepts, by contrast, operate in poorly regulated environments where failures are often swept under boardroom or faculty carpets. Yet poor management systems can jeopardize lives in the air, at sea, on roads, or in hospitals. They can also put entire businesses, sectors, and economies at risk.

With this in mind, we announced the first-ever recall of a management concept via the *Harvard Business Review*.[8] With 2019 marking the twenty-fifth anniversary of the "triple bottom line," a term one of the authors (John) coined back in 1994 to mean a sustainability framework that examines a company's social, environmental, and economic impact,[9] we announced a recall to do some reengineering.

It turned out that we had dodged a bullet, even if that was no part of our intention. A few months later, Anand Giridharadas published his provocative book, *Winners Take All*. With a reputation for skewering plutocrats, Giridharadas argues that the wealthy are using philanthropy to pretend they are changing the world while maintaining the status quo. Even such well-received interventions as BlackRock CEO Larry Fink's letters to shareholders, encouraging greater action on ethical, social, and environmental matters, can be seen as an evasive tactic as long as BlackRock continues to hold shares in climate-destabilizing companies like ExxonMobil. Nor did Giridharadas have much time for the triple bottom line, at one point quoting our recall of the concept.[10]

We worked to reframe the triple bottom line approach during our subsequent Tomorrow's Capitalism Inquiry,[11] arguing the need to use the 3D value concept in the context of a necessary—and rapidly evolving—shift from responsibility to resilience and regeneration.

2. TOMORROW'S CAPITALISM INQUIRY

Intense interest in the recall spurred the launch of the inquiry. This has been driven by a growing sense that the failings of modern capitalism cannot be solved simply by individual companies working with their supply chains, or even in concert with other committed companies. Such approaches are crucial in exploring the limits of the possible, no question, and in coevolving solutions to global challenges. But, ultimately, the challenges now facing us are *political*.

The inquiry explored how companies could become catalysts for systems change. The rationale: our economic system, as currently configured, is undermining the social and environmental systems on which we all rely. Twenty-five years of corporate sustainability has not halted, let alone reversed, this trend. It is time, we concluded, to think—and act—differently.

The imperative to act responsibly within the constraints of today's system has not gone away; indeed far from it, and it is no longer remotely sufficient. In an increasingly exponential world, the risks associated with business-as-usual, and government-as-usual, are escalating fast. Now businesses face the additional challenge of proactively contributing to the emergence of a more resilient and regenerative economy.

Since resilience and regeneration are systemic properties, the implication of this for corporate leadership is a shift in priorities from internal process optimization to nurturing external relationships that bring opportunities to transform markets to better serve people and the planet. Functions like procurement and government affairs are therefore central to the story of how business plays a role in positive systems change.

It is increasingly clear that some companies have been shaping the "rules of the game" to benefit themselves for decades, but the process has been uneven, dominated by those with most to lose from effective political action on issues like climate change. Now the challenge is for the "silent majority" of companies that are more worried by the impact of runaway climate change than a rising carbon price on their business to organize and lobby effectively enough to tilt the balance in favor of policies that correct market failures and, even, "tilt the playing field" toward outcomes that benefit people and the planet. In other words, all companies must now become positive policy activists.

We launched some of these findings at our Tomorrow's Capitalism Forum in early January 2020. The event was subtitled: "Step Up—Or Get Out Of The Way."

3. THE TRANSFORMATION AGENDA

Throughout this time, Volans has continued to work with a wide range of partners to test and improve our thinking. In the second stage of the inquiry, for example, we worked with the World Business Council for Sustainable Development (WBCSD) to examine the structural transformations of capitalism necessary to make WBCSD's Vision 2050 ("9+ billion people living well within the means of the planet") and the role of business in bringing those transformations about. The resulting report, "Reinventing Capitalism: A Transformation Agenda," argues the case for radical reform:

> Capitalism, and its consequences for society and the environment, are very much in the spotlight. Even committed capitalists are beginning to argue that capitalism, in its current form, is unsustainable—socially, environmentally, and economically. Yet capitalism's core features of private enterprise and competitive markets are essential to addressing our greatest societal challenges and unleashing the transformations required to meet the Sustainable Development Goals (SDGs).[12]

"Reinventing Capitalism" synthesized the best available thinking on why capitalism needs to be reinvented if it is to create the conditions for long-term business success, and the actions that business, investors, and policy makers can take today to drive transformation. A key message of the work is that "now is the time for companies and investors to enter—*and lead*—the debate, not just about why capitalism needs to change, but about how we go about transforming it."

The capitalism we need rewards true value creation—not value extraction as today's model does. Specifically, this means that all social and environmental costs and benefits should be internalized and reflected in the relative price of goods and services, and in companies' profit and loss statements, costs of capital, and market valuations.

The report argues that if we are to get to such a version of capitalism, we need to realign the incentives that drive businesses' and investors' behavior, adopting new and better ways of measuring performance, and tackle failures at the market and institutional level that favor financial value extraction over true value creation. A reinvented model of capitalism that addresses these failures will be characterized by five features: stakeholder-oriented, impact-internalizing, long-term, regenerative, and accountable.

Reinventing capitalism along the lines suggested will require complementary action from businesses, investors, and policy makers, with voluntary action from the private sector and changes to law and regulation going hand in hand. Business, therefore, has a critical role to play in shifting capitalism, involving:

- "Walking the talk"—adapting and aligning business models, decision-making processes, governance models, incentives, and approaches to tax, remuneration, reporting, and accounting with a vision of capitalism that pursues true value as experienced and appreciated by citizens.

- Leveraging its relationships with other stakeholders—from suppliers and customers to policymakers and civil society—to influence the norms and rules that shape capitalism as a whole.

- Reeducating investors by rethinking the metrics and key performance indicators that define their performance.

4. BANKERS FOR NET ZERO

It is clear that the transition to a resilient and regenerative economy will not happen unless it is financed—and given the likely quantities of money required, that finance will need to come from both public and private sector actors. Despite significant inflows into "ESG-linked" funds and the like, the financial system as a whole has scarcely begun to grapple with what the transition to a stable climate means for the flows of finance that drive the global economic system.

With this in mind, in 2020, Volans (along with the All Party Parliamentary Group (APPG) on Fair Business Banking, and Re:Pattern, a strategy consultancy specializing in sustainable finance) launched Bankers for Net Zero. The initiative aims to find positive solutions for accelerating progress toward a net-zero world, encouraging the banking sector to play a proactive role in financing a green recovery and net-zero transition across the UK economy.

By collaborating across business, finance, and government, Bankers for Net Zero is exploring how finance for the net-zero transition can be unlocked at scale when policy, regulation, and private sector practices are properly aligned.

5. GREEN SWANS OBSERVATORY

Our book, *Green Swans*, was published in April 2020, with over 100 virtual keynotes in more than 30 countries by the end of 2020 alone. We were continuously asked for more information and case studies linked to people's sectors, markets, and challenges. The online observatory is our response, designed to provide constantly updated intelligence on exponential solutions to some of the world's greatest challenges.

We look forward to a future world turned upside down, with our species in service of life rather than vice versa. At a time when many problems are going exponential, we conclude that we urgently need exponential solutions. So the observatory spotlights exponential shifts in mindsets, markets, technology, politics, and cultures that, directly or indirectly, can enable a "regenerative economy." Shifts we call "green swans."

Launching with a Green Swans Day event in 2019, our linked change agenda took wing at the 2020 Tomorrow's Capitalism Forum we cohosted with Aviva Investors. The idea here is easily stated: a five-year campaign to ensure regeneration is firmly on the board and C-suite agenda by 2025.

We are in the midst of a planetary, multigenerational reeducation process. Education, at all levels, is among the best investments our societies make, with extraordinary (if not always predictable) long-term returns. The ultimate green swan pursuit, perhaps.

NOTES

1. Quotes from John Elkington, *Green Swans: The Coming Boom in Regenerative Capitalism* (New York: Fast Company, 2020), 15.

2. Nassim N. Taleb, *The Black Swan: The Impact of the Highly Improbable* (London: Allen Lane, 2007), xxvii–xxviii.

3. Andrew Edgecliffe-Johnson, "Why American CEOs Are Worried about Capitalism," *Financial Times*, April 22, 2019, https://www.ft.com/content /138e103a-61a4-11e9-b285-3acd5d43599e.

4. Quote Investigator, s.v., "The Test of a First-Rate Intelligence . . . ," accessed May 18, 2021, https://quoteinvestigator.com/2020/01/05/intelligence/.

5. Taleb, *The Black Swan*.

6. Elkington, *Green Swans*, 9.

7. Elkington, *Green Swans*, 11.

8. John Elkington, "25 Years Ago I Coined the Phrase 'Triple Bottom Line.' Here's Why It's Time to Rethink It," *Harvard Business Review*, June 25, 2018, https:// hbr.org/2018/06/25-years-ago-i-coined-the-phrase-triple-bottom-line-heres-why -im-giving-up-on-it.

9. John Elkington, *Cannibals with Forks: The Triple Bottom Line of 21st Century Business* (Mankato, MN: Capstone, 1997).

10. Anand Giridharadas, *Winners Take All: The Elite Charade of Changing the World*, reprint ed. (New York: Vintage, 2019).

11. "Tomorrow's Capitalism Inquiry," Volans, November 2, 2020, https://volans .com/tomorrows-capitalism-inquiry/.

12. "Reinventing Capitalism: WBCSD Lays Out a Transformation Agenda for Business," WBCSD, November 11, 2020, https://www.wbcsd.org/Overview /About-us/Vision-2050-Refresh/News/Reinventing-capitalism-WBCSD-lays -out-a-transformation-agenda-for-business.

6

Contemplating a Moonshot?
Ask Yourself These Three Questions:
Why This? Why Now? Why Me?

NAVEEN JAIN WITH JOHN SCHROETER

IF WE'RE GOING TO CREATE A SUCCESSFUL next-generation architecture of business, we first have to break with the mindset that produced the one we're replacing. That is, we're going to need a new model for how we think and operate in a world that has fundamentally changed and is no longer responsive to "the way we've always done it." The good news is that this is a good thing. Difficult, but good. Let us offer an illustration—one that many here might find to be counterintuitive, if not a little uncomfortable, given our conditioning over the years.

The old cliché, "We can't solve problems by using the same kind of thinking we used when we created them" is true, indeed. But we would add that neither will we be able to solve problems that surface in the future as a consequence of today's solutions! And particularly solutions based on well-meaning initiatives like . . . sustainability.

Wait . . . what?

That's right. Uncomfortable as such ideas might be, in this new "postnormal" world, we must become friends with contradiction, the counterintuitive and the counterfactual.

The fundamental problem with sustainability—indeed, its fatal flaw—is that it serves to reinforce the value of scarce resources. Consequently, the mindset that manifests sustainability initiatives only fortifies an economy based on and driven by scarcity. This gives rise to another problem: in the face of a rising population and growing demand, sustainability is not sustainable!

The fact is, we're going to need a whole lot more of everything, and we're going to need it soon. By 2050, we're going to need at least *twice* as much as we consume today. Twice as much water, twice as much food, twice as much energy, twice as much land, twice as much healthcare, and twice as much education. No amount of conservation, renewables, or design for sustainability will ever be sufficient to meet the overwhelming demands that we continue to lay upon spaceship *Earth*.

Solving these kinds of problems calls for a radically different kind of thinking—disruptive, revolutionary, mind-bending, and paradigm-smashing; the kind of thinking that can yield truly surprising outcomes. Let us tell you why—and what this will mean to you as you reimagine the very concept of business and its agency in the world.

We are rapidly approaching the point on the graph where the demand for resources takes a giant hockey stick turn upward, shooting above and beyond the line that plots the slowing growth rate of readily available resources, renewable or otherwise. And if demand is growing at an exponential rate against limited, linear supply, then sustainability runs out of gas pretty fast. It doesn't take a rocket scientist—much less an economist—to forecast this obvious outcome and the global crisis it will precipitate. Consequently, we have to create *more of what we need* rather than consume *less of what we have*. To do that, we're going to have to adopt a fundamentally different way of operating. In other words, we're going to need to get out of Flatland. By that, we mean escaping the confines of the two-dimensional thinking that dominates the current discourse—left, right; X, Y; black, white. We have to enter the "Z dimension."

This dimension is the domain of *imagination*, where transcendent perspectives yield novel solutions to global grand challenges that are waiting to be transformed into massive opportunities—by you! In dedicating yourself to meeting these opportunities, you will discover the many unexpected ways we can exponentially expand humanity's creative potential, solve the grandest of grand challenges, and empower every person to experience a life of abundance.

This is the very essence of the emerging new theory of business: "full-spectrum flourishing" is the creation of a world where businesses can excel, all persons can thrive, and nature can flourish. But this vision is not without its challenges. Foremost among the challenges is that people—even a great many very smart business people—tend to get caught up in seeing the world only *as it is* and not imagining what the world *could be*. If you focus only on what the world is, then you are resigning yourself to a particular destiny, one that is constrained by the familiar; just another version of the anxious world we know today. Recognizing this Flatlandish default condition is the start of the needed change in mindset that can yield the "new" right answers we desperately seek.

We can tell you that the promise of abundance will never be fulfilled with short-sighted visions, linear thinking, or incremental solutions. Our objective here is to open the world to new possibilities. If we can start with the ends in view and work backward, it will become abundantly clear that what is called for are solutions that are not only bigger but *exponentially* bigger. This is nothing short of a radical reshaping of our future reality. We create the future *from* the future, not the past. And this is entirely a function of mindset.

It all begins with an individual believing in the possibilities and creating a movement that ultimately changes the mind of society. That is the moment when the tectonic plates shift. But a society, strictly speaking, doesn't have a mind; *individuals* have minds. And to the extent that the ways of society change, those changes happen one individual at a time. So let's make this personal. And in the process, let's see just how practical a simple shift in mindset can be in bringing about a better, more prosperous world.

—ɯ—

Irrespective of the industry, whenever we contemplate starting a new venture—or even an audacious initiative within an existing company—we ask ourselves these three simple questions:

1. Why *this*?
2. Why *now*?
3. Why *me*?

Don't be fooled: these are deceptively deep, soul-searching questions that have the power to completely realign your life, amplify your purpose, and impact the lives of many people. Let's take them in turn.

WHY *THIS*?

It is a perennial observation that we live in revolutionary times. But when has the human race ever *not* been in some form of upheaval, boiling over with contradictions and chaotic forces running amok?! So given these forces, what is one to attack first? Disease? Pestilence? Hunger? Illiteracy? Substance abuse? Environmental crises? Economic opportunity? Clean water? Safety, security, and well-being? Corruption? Poverty? Chronic illness?

Every one of these issues impacts billions of people globally each day. Certainly, there is no shortage of problems in need of solutions. There is an *overabundance* of problems. And every problem comes prepackaged with opportunities for new solutions, yielding a never-ending stream of opportunities— and never-ending reasons for hope and optimism. Indeed, our fundamental thought pattern is that *everything* is possible, and the bigger the problem, the bigger the opportunity. So ask yourself, if your venture was to be successful, would it help a billion people live better lives in one way or another? Because if it doesn't move the needle, then it doesn't matter.

This brings us to the very essence of moonshot thinking—that vital component of our "new theory of business"—*thinking big*. Now, in thinking big, what is the best way to create a $100 billion company? Answer: help a billion people live better lives. Launching a moonshot, while certainly challenging, can actually *be easier* than starting a smaller company based upon a less ambitious goal. What's more, what many people dismiss as "crazy" might be well within reach. History is replete with examples.

The fact is every breakthrough starts in life as a crazy, impossible idea—until it is done. As Niels Bohr once said to fellow physicist Wolfgang Pauli, "We are all agreed that your theory is crazy. The question that divides us is whether it is crazy enough to have a chance of being correct!"[1] If people don't think your idea is crazy, then that's a clue that you're not operating in the moonshot arena.

What, then, is the industry that *you* want to disrupt? What part of the future state of the world do you want to own now? And what will be the future state of that world if you do *not* act? Either way, your decision will impact the future. So what will it take for you to flip the switch that sets the dream in motion? Many massive market opportunities are simply waiting for someone like you to wake up one day and make a decision that you'll do *something* about just one of them.

If you approach global challenges with this kind of mindset, then you'll begin to think about solutions in very different ways. You will begin to see the possibilities of impacting a billion people rather than affecting a few hundred thousand or even a million people. And that lifts everybody.

WHY NOW?

Think back on just the past couple of years and take stock of the amazing technological advances that have happened. Now flip the scope and look ahead to the next few years. What can we expect to see that will enable the kinds of solutions to grand challenges that we couldn't even contemplate just a decade ago? Here's a paradox: we can begin to "use" the technologies of tomorrow to solve today's problems through the very surprising and deceptive nature of exponential technologies.

Our minds are generally geared to think *linearly*, and consequently, we miss out on the impact of exponential advances over time. Even a relatively short period. The effect of doubling a technological advance over 30 years will produce a *billion*-fold increase in capability. The point is that technology is available to us *right now* to create, leverage, and deploy the technologies of tomorrow that will solve the world's great problems in innovative ways and impact billions of people. Consider yet another example of aligning business plans to trajectories of future technology developments.

Siri was the first AI-driven, conversational personal assistant deployed commercially at scale. It was an outgrowth of DARPA's CALO project, which was managed by SRI International. CALO was defined as a five-year program that launched in 2003 with a total budget of $200 million and involved 400 scientists and engineers. The program's chief architect, Adam Cheyer, described the program's goal as an ambitious effort to bring together all the stove-piped aspects of artificial intelligence into an "integrated, human-like system that could learn in the wild."[2] It was so ambitious that he came to think of it as AI's Manhattan Project. In 2008, upon completion of the program, the resulting technology was spun out as Siri with $24 million in venture funding. The Siri team had long targeted the smartphone as the preferred platform for the service, but at the time of the company's founding, the smartphone technology was not yet mature enough to support it. But they knew it would be, soon enough. And sure enough, the introduction of the iPhone 3GS in June 2009 provided both the requisite processing power *and* the wireless bandwidth to enable Siri to work. A year later, Siri was acquired by Apple.

Likewise, concerning my (Naveen Jain's) company, Viome, a world free of illness is not something we ever thought we could do in a year or even 10 years. We started Viome with an unequivocally audacious mission to make illness optional by preventing and reversing chronic diseases. To address such an ambitious challenge we needed to do three things: (1) *digitize* the human body, (2) *decode* the human body, and (3) *decipher* the human body. Now, for digitization and decoding to be feasible, the cost of sequencing had to come down significantly. When we started, sequencing the human genome was a $1,000 proposition. We expected it to drop to $100 over the next few years. Today, we can do it for just $10. So while we anticipated that the technology would improve and the cost would drop, it turned out that we were 10X pessimistic!

After digitization, the next challenge was the cost of decoding these massive troves of digital data. We were certainly aware of the advances in cloud computing, but we were still paying close to $40 to process the digitized information for every individual. We expected the cost of decoding the data to drop to $10 over the next few years. What surprised us again was that the cost came down to about $1. And once again, even our optimistic outlook turned out to be 10X pessimistic. This is largely thanks to the dramatic drop in the cost of computing, a rate of improvement that has outpaced Moore's law. What very recently required a supercomputer to execute at great expense can now be done cheaply on networked desktops.

But here's the point: even in the early going, we had everything we needed to get the ball rolling. So we got started. Yes, there were still many unknowns, still much research to do, and we needed additional technologies that did not yet exist. But we knew where this was headed, which allowed us to project the point at which the necessary technologies would intersect so that we'd be there to meet them when they did. That was enough for us.

As Goethe famously wrote, "Whatever you can do or dream you can, *begin it*. Boldness has genius, and magic and power in it. *Begin it now.*"

WHY *ME*?

The old saying is everybody wants to be unique—just like everybody else. But the fact is, you *are* unique. That uniqueness, if activated, can be your secret sauce. And when that quality is mated to a possibility-driven mindset and vision-driven value system, that uniqueness is amplified all the more and to great effect.

Taken together, this collection of attributes that defines a very unique *you* also translates to a very unique response to grand challenges—and the kinds of questions *only you* will ask when thinking about them. And the crazier the questions, the better. Let us give you a couple of examples.

Moon Express is my (Naveen Jain) private enterprise venture to create a multiplanetary society. The reasons are myriad, not the least of which is that the resources available to us on the moon alone could solve the entire world's energy problems. Yet when we talk about building lunar outposts, everyone asks the same question: "How are we going to grow food on the moon?" Well, let's flip this with a very different kind of question. A "crazy" question. Rather than asking how we'll grow food, instead, we should ask, "Why do we *need* food?"

Here's the import—and the power—of this approach: if we ask only the first question, then every potential solution is directed toward finding ways to grow food in a hostile environment. If, on the other hand, we ask the second question, innumerable possibilities are suddenly available. Even radical possibilities. Let's follow this through.

We eat food because we need energy and nutrition. So let's reframe the issue from how we will *grow* food to what it is we *need*. We know, for example, that radiation exposure is harmful to humans. We also know that a great many bacteria can live quite comfortably in highly radioactive areas. So let's connect this up with not only providing our bodies with the energy and nutrients it needs but at the same time, address the general issue associated with living in a lunar habitat.

One of the solutions NASA is investigating involves digging underground habitats, which would protect lunar astronauts from both cosmic radiation and the intense cold. But living underground would be pretty confining, and who would want to go all the way to the moon, let alone Mars, only to live sequestered in a cave? Maybe there's a better way—a *crazy* way. Could we possibly genetically modify our bodies to make them radiation-tolerant? What if that were possible? With the nascent CRISPR gene-editing technology, this solution appears to be on the horizon. But how? Where would we find radiation-resistant genes to splice into our own, and would they work?

It turns out that there are microbes that are not only able to survive radiation exposure but also thrive in it, actually consuming radioactive waste as their energy source! They eat radiation for breakfast. Among them is the *deinococcus radiodurans*—the world's toughest extremophile bacterium. So let's think about this. If you could insert any gene from another organism into your DNA, what would it be? Well, if you happen to be an astronaut—or aspire to become one—you might want to choose the tardigrade *Dsup* protein. Tardigrades, if you don't recognize them by that name, are also known as water bears—the near-microscopic animals that look like a cross between a flea and a manatee. Tardigrades are tough little critters, surviving temperatures down to near absolute zero. They also exhibit extraordinary tolerance to radiation and other physical extremes. To learn just how tough they are, in 2007, the European Space Agency sent tardigrades into low Earth orbit, where they survived for 12 days—*on the outside of the capsule.* That's tough! Might their DNA be just what the lunar doctor ordered?

Before you dismiss this as one jumped shark too far, recall that the technology behind CRISPR was likewise pure fantasy just a few short decades ago.

Now, let's bring this kind of thinking and questioning back down to Earth. First, challenging the status quo begins with daring to ask, "What if?" Now, when *you* ask a big "What if?" question, what you are asking is *fundamentally different* from what everyone else is asking. And that difference makes all the difference.

When I began to think of the company that became Viome, I said to anyone who would listen, "Imagine if there were a world where illness is optional. *What if* that world could be created? Wouldn't you want to be part of creating that world? I'm not saying that I am doing it, or how I would do it; I'm just suggesting that it's possible." So there's no argument here. You simply ask, could such a world be possible? And if you believe that such a world *is* possible—and that you can visualize it—why can't it also be created? If, on the other hand, I start the conversation from the viewpoint of a specific technology or particular solution to the problem, people will immediately begin to argue with me—they simply won't believe. But I don't go there. If I ask them only to imagine the possibility, 9 times out of 10, they'll come around and agree that yes, it actually could be possible. Once we've established that the possibility exists, the only question is how to get there. But it begins with me simply asking a very different—a very *unique*—question.

Again, my experience with Viome illustrates the point. When we surveyed the competitive landscape, we discovered that everyone in the space was addressing the problem by asking essentially the same questions about (1) one's DNA and (2) the composition of the microorganisms in the gut. In other words, by the questions they're asking, they seek to understand what organisms exist in people who suffer from chronic diseases, and what organisms exist in those who don't. In short, their questions assume an equation of genetics and microbiota with illness.

It turns out that these are the wrong questions. Why? Well, absent CRISPR interventions, one's DNA never changes! Our genes don't change when we become obese; they don't change when we become depressed or diabetic or develop heart disease or Alzheimer's or any number of autoimmune diseases. But because we also know that people develop chronic diseases, we ask, could the mechanism be not the genes, but gene *expression*? If that were true (it is), then you could be loaded up with all the bad genes in the world, but if they're not expressed, it wouldn't matter! And if you could prevent them from ever being expressed, then the presence of these "bad" genes really would be irrelevant to one's health.

It's easy to see, then, how this "unique" perspective completely reframes the issue. If our mission is to prevent and reverse chronic diseases, then we need to look at what *does* change: gene expression. The right question to ask then, is what genes are being expressed in the human host as it begins to develop chronic disease? Here is where we hit on something vital related to the microbiome, which comprises over 100 trillion microorganisms that live in and on us, including over 10,000 species of bacteria that enable our metabolic and immune systems. The question we asked was what genes are the microbes expressing, rather than simply identifying what they are. It turns out that this "forgotten organ" is the wellspring of our well-being—and, on the shadow side, the source of many of our diseases, particularly chronic ones. Interestingly, its role in our health has been largely overlooked until very recently, and our unfolding understanding of the microbiome is on the cusp of revolutionizing healthcare.

The questions we ask, then, go to the very consensus-driven foundations of what everyone else has simply taken for granted. You might be surprised at just how many cracks have formed in these foundations. On this point, Michael Crichton put it best when he said, "The work of science has nothing whatever to do with consensus. Consensus is the business of politics. . . . In science consensus is irrelevant. What is relevant is reproducible results."[3]

BREAKING WITH CONSENSUS—AND CONCLUSIONS

Indeed, the greatest scientists in history are great precisely because they broke with the consensus. As such, let me encourage you to take nothing in hand without deliberate purpose—your very unique purpose. To this end, as Marcus Aurelius wrote in his Meditations, "A man's true delight is to do the things he was made for. He was made to show goodwill to his kind, to rise above the promptings of his senses, to distinguish appearances from realities, and to pursue the study of universal Nature and her works."

What, then, were you made for? What is it that gives you the strongest sense of sailing true north? If it is something that resonates strongly with that sense, then it is a good thing and may be your thing, a calling—the very unique calling you answer with your life. Do you know what it is? If you are unable to answer that question just now, don't worry. All it means is that you have an exciting time of discovery ahead of you. But you do need to be deliberate about it. To be on this journey is the greatest thing you can do for yourself and others. And only you can do it.

Finally, there's one other important component to the "Why me?" question, and that concerns your dedication to solving your chosen grand challenge. And it is yet another challenge to the idea of conventional wisdom. It goes like this: How many times have you been told to "follow your passion"?

I'm here to say: forget passion. No amount of passion will work to reinvent the world. What this grand challenge requires is nothing short of obsession. Now, the word *obsession* has gotten a bad rap. But here's the problem with that. Passion is merely a catalyst—an agent that increases the rate of a chemical reaction without itself undergoing any permanent chemical change. In other words, while passion may precipitate an event, it is not the event itself. Put another way, you can think of passion as the primer that ignites the propellant that ultimately puts the muzzle velocity behind your idea—the great armor-piercing projectile you launch into the world. It's the latter part of this metaphor that defines obsession; passion alone won't project anything. Obsession is "passion squared." Passion is the start; obsession requires grit for the long haul. Passion peters out; obsession presses on. Obsession asks what you are willing to die for but then demands that you choose to live for it. To such audacious ends, passion is passé. Obsession, though, is an exceptionally rare quality. And we need to learn to cultivate it.

We close this chapter with a bonus question. When you're satisfied with your answers to the first three, ask finally, *Why not?* Indeed, the harvest is great, but the workers are few. So if not you, then who?

NOTES

Adapted from Naveen Jain, *Moonshots—Creating a World of Abundance* (Bainbridge Island, WA: Abundant World Institute, 2018).

1. Edward Frenkel, "The Holy Grail of Quantum Physics on Your Kitchen Table [Excerpt]," *Scientific American*, September 27, 2013, https://www .scientificamerican.com/article/the-holy-grail-of-quantum-physics-on-your -kitchen-table-excerpt/#:%7E:text=As%20Niels%20Bohr%2C%20one%20 of,a%20chance%20of%20being%20correct.%E2%80%9D.

2. Danielle Newnham, "The Story behind Siri and the Man Who Made Her," LinkedIn, October 31, 2015, https://www.linkedin.com/pulse/story-behind-siri -man-who-made-her-danielle-newnham/.

3. Mark Perry, "Michael Crichton Explains Why There Is 'No Such Thing as Consensus Science,'" American Enterprise Institute, December 15, 2019, https:// www.aei.org/carpe-diem/michael-crichton-explains-why-there-is-no-such -thing-as-consensus-science/.

**PART
TWO**

NET POSITIVE = INNOVATION'S
NEW FRONTIER

7

Net-Positive Business and the Elephants in the Room

PAUL POLMAN AND ANDREW WINSTON

IF THE LAST FEW YEARS have taught us anything, it's that the world is a deeply interconnected network. Humans share one immune system—risk to one is risk to all. We have one planet with interdependent systems that supply us resources, food, clean air and water, and a stable climate.

The world will succeed or fail together, and there's no way we get there without significant engagement and action by the business community. The private sector is the dominant driver of GDP, capital flows, and jobs. What it means to be a business will have to change; this will mean reinventing our organizations to become agents of world benefit.

It's hard to ignore the scope of the problems we face as a species. The existential challenges are, in essence, deep inequality, global warming, and the decline of biodiversity. The data is not in our favor.

While hundreds of millions of people have come out of dire poverty in recent decades, COVID has stalled or reversed that progress—up to 150 million people may have slipped backward.[1] Poverty is not solely a developing world issue. Up to 50 percent of workers at America's 1,000 largest public companies (the Russell 1000) were not making enough to support a family of three, even with a partner working part time.[2] Overall inequality has accelerated for years. For half a century, the large majority of the wealth and income gains in the developed world have flowed to the top 1 percent (and within that to the top 0.1 percent).

Companies have made the situation worse. As of 2018, 466 of the S&P 500 companies have been public for the previous decade. Over those years, 92 percent of their profits went to shareholders or executives through buybacks and dividends.[3] And CEOs now make 320 times the average employee, up from 61 times in 1989.[4]

71

On the environmental side, the climate situation continues to deteriorate. The volume of storms, floods, and fires is growing and we're still projected to warm much more than the 1.5°C that we can afford. Even if countries hit their Paris climate accord commitments, the world is still on track to reach a devastating 3.0°C increase.[5]

At the same time, the natural world has experienced a shocking 68 percent decline on average in mammal, fish, bird, reptile, and amphibian populations in less than five decades.[6] Some call it the sixth great extinction. We have cut down half the world's rainforests in a century. Since nature provides services worth around $125 trillion a year, it would make good sense for us to take better care of it.[7]

MOVING TOWARD A NEW MODEL

It should be getting clearer by now that there is no infinite growth on a finite planet. Anything we can't do forever is by definition unsustainable. If we continue on this path, ultimately we reach a point of system collapse. We might be at a tipping point in more than one sense. Since COVID, the failings and weaknesses of our systems have become more transparent. Some 90 percent of executives believe that the COVID-19 crisis will fundamentally change the way they do business over the next five years.[8]

We see growing evidence that shareholder primacy, the current prevailing business model in Western economies, is a failed doctrine that destroys our natural environment, funnels wealth upward, and undermines social cohesion. If we want capitalism to survive, we have to start with quantifying stakeholder value, and that includes the planet, fellow citizens, and future generations.

A longer-term, multistakeholder model is increasingly more attractive and profitable. Companies will be competing more on trust, responsibility, and creating and maintaining deep relationships with stakeholders—all rooted in shared truths and values. A growing number of organizations understand that profit should not come from creating the world's problems but from solving them.

The progress of business toward more sustainable practices in the last decade has been substantial, and it is speeding up. A decade ago, effectively zero large companies had carbon reduction goals in line with science. The biggest companies also had no quantitative goals for social performance on issues like gender parity or diversity and inclusion. Fast forward to the fateful year of 2020, and virtually all of the largest 500 companies have some form of sustainability reporting or have public carbon or energy targets.

Going Positive

Why has the level of commitment to sustainability accelerated? There are many reasons, including the fact that climate change is no longer a debate about the future but a real problem today. Companies see it, experience the costs of it, and feel pressure from a range of stakeholders to do something about it. In addition, the economics of acting on climate change have gotten radically better, with the costs of clean energy and technologies plummeting. Thus, in many ways, the battle to convince businesses to take some responsibility for their broader impact is over. We're at the end of the proverbial first inning.

For years, we've been transitioning from executives worrying solely about a company's direct impacts—its own "four walls"—to considering how the company's choices affect the full value chain of suppliers and consumers (which, in climate terms, is so-called scope 3 emissions). Companies are also rapidly committing to get to zero on many operational dimensions, such as waste, carbon emissions, and safety. These are important advancements, but given the speed of change in natural and human systems, it's not remotely good enough. As the news about our greatest challenges gets worse, the horizon we're shooting for is moving away from us. We have to broaden our sights and go much faster and much bigger.

Given this dual reality that there's more action, but it's not enough, it's time to reset what it means to be a good business. It isn't enough anymore to just reduce carbon emissions, manage water use effectively, cut waste, ensure employee safety, demand more of suppliers on their environmental and social performance, and so on. Companies must pursue something greater than doing incrementally better. We need companies to improve the world, repairing and regenerating as they go.

In our new book *Net Positive: How Courageous Companies Thrive by Giving More Than They Take*,[9] we make the case for companies to move much quicker toward a new horizon. Businesses, and especially multinationals, need to be thinking about going well beyond "zero" and into positive territory. We define *net positive* for business in our book in this way: "a business that improves well-being for everyone it impacts and at all scales—every product, every operation, every region and country, and for every stakeholder, including employees, suppliers, communities, customers, and even future generations and the planet itself.... The core question is whether the world is better off because your business is in it."

This is a north star, not a short-term plan. No company—including global leader Unilever, which one of us led for a decade—can claim to be net positive.

Some leaders are getting close in aspects of the business. IKEA, for example, generates more renewable energy than it needs for operations—in electricity, it is net positive. For most business leaders though, shooting for all facets of a business to serve stakeholders first, above itself and shareholders, is a big lift. After decades of Milton Friedman dogma on the purpose of business being business, it can seem too daunting to take on.

We can go faster and think bigger. The whole world, and business in particular, learned something in 2020. The pandemic not only opened us up to how connected we are, but it also showed us that we can move very fast if we have to.

Business Can Pivot Fast

When COVID swept through the world, every institution was caught off guard. Experts had warned of a pandemic for years, but no government or business had truly prepared. A lot went wrong as we discovered how little resilience was built into our health systems and supply chains. Entire distribution pathways that efficiently brought goods to hotels, restaurants, cruise ships, and other service businesses shut down. The other channels to the home were overloaded.

But something amazing happened. Businesses and other organizations discovered they could pivot much faster than they thought; in fact, they had no choice. Companies shifted production globally and many offered help by manufacturing things they never had before—auto companies made ventilators, luxury goods companies produced hand sanitizer, and more. Unilever took a small hand sanitizer business and increased production 14,000-fold in six weeks. Of course, the most impressive move was the pharma industry pulling off a miracle and developing multiple effective vaccines within months.

The pandemic accelerated trends that were already in the works. Trane Technologies makes Thermo-King refrigeration units for trucks carrying perishable food. Speaking about their business during the early months of the pandemic, Paul Camuti, SVP Innovation and chief technology officer, said, "This is the biggest disruption in the flow of food we've ever seen—there were some long term-trends we were getting ready for . . . and we had to change how we do business in *days*."[10] Trane was not alone. A large range of products and services found they had to innovate quickly. Restaurants became more take-out focused and created outdoor spaces; the at-home grocery business expanded rapidly; live business events became Zoom and Microsoft Teams meetings with different formats for speaking and sharing information; the arts moved outside, with shows appearing in parks and six-foot spacing laid out for the audience. Some of these trends will revert, but many were in the works already and will continue to a large degree.

The pandemic was a historic test of our humanity and our systems. But in the intense opening to the 2020s (which seem many years long already), it was not the only dramatic stressor. The rise of Black Lives Matter, #MeToo, and threats to democracy have shaken society to its core. We hit tipping points. The murder of George Floyd took the United States in particular over some mental edge. Suddenly organizations of all stripes felt the need to have a position on systemic racism.

Through these massive shifts in societal norms, including awareness of sexual harassment in business and government, companies have increasingly spoken out and taken a stand on these and other challenges. And on top of all that, the global populist movements—which included the terrifying moment when the world's oldest democracy faced an insurrection attempt—have destabilized so much of what we once took for granted.

And business has reacted to it all quicker than most thought possible.

EMBRACING ELEPHANTS IN A VUCA WORLD

The good news is that a volatile, uncertain, complex, and ambiguous (VUCA) world holds potential. A time of accelerating change is a great opportunity to challenge paradigms and dogmas. On some level, the pandemic has been a painful opening act for even larger challenges we face as a species. As we contemplate the existential threats of climate change, inequality, and biodiversity—and all the related problems that stem from these intertwined challenges—we know we'll need to shift how we do business in fundamental ways. We're primed to expand the role of business in society.

We could explore what net positive means operationally for a business around its core products and services. In our book, we look at how to build an organization around purpose and collaboration and go deep into the kinds of partnerships we need to get there. In the context of the "Business as an Agent of World Benefit" events and publications at the Fowler Center for Business at Case Western Reserve, the work to make an enterprise more sustainable in its operations and supply chains is well-covered territory.

So, here we'll discuss other critical topics that a net-positive company needs to address, going well beyond its value-chain footprint. These are the proverbial "elephants in the room" that people avoid talking about but, if left unaddressed, will continue to drive the world toward instability and away from a thriving future.

The Travesty of Executive Pay

In 2020, the hedge fund billionaire Stephen Schwarzman made $610 million.[11] Many private equity and hedge fund executives made tens of millions as well, the majority of it in dividends or capital gains, which are taxed at 20 percent instead of the top income tax rate of 37 percent. As Warren Buffet has said, these wealthy investors pay lower taxes than their assistants. From his epic haul, Schwarzman paid the lower rate on $524 million.[12] As this data went public, the U.S. Congress was debating a $1.9 trillion COVID relief package and could not get enough support to include an increase to the minimum wage to $15 per hour.

To earn as much as Schwarzman, someone making the current minimum wage of $7.25 per hour, for 40 hours a week, 50 weeks a year would need to work for more than 42,000 years. Wages should be much, much higher. An Economic Policy Institute study calculated that if the minimum wage had grown with total economy productivity over the last 50 years, it would be $21.69 today.[13]

Hedge fund executives are the extreme case, and they make corporate executives look like rank amateurs in hoarding money. But CEOs and the C-suite are doing just fine. Over 40 years, CEO compensation rose more than 1,100 percent, while the typical worker saw wages rise by just 14 percent.[14] CEOs are even making more than other very wealthy people—six times the average of the top 0.1 percent of wage earners, a ratio that has also accelerated.[15] While global and national inequality rose, the leaders in the business and finance communities have been taking an accelerating portion of income and wealth.

This elephant in the room here is overpaying executives and investors and thereby reducing social cohesion and trust. This level of inequality is destabilizing. Executive pay is an issue that leads to mistrust of institutions and "elites." The amount of money flowing to top executives and investors increases economic inequality and exclusion of entire groups from opportunity locks in racial and gender inequality.

It also drives warped behavior in companies. The increase in executive pay is largely due to the use of stock options as bonus compensation. This shortened time horizon undermines the work to make a business more sustainable, which requires patience and consistency. How can a short-term obsessed company invest in developing more sustainable products, increasing wages in the supply chain to living wage levels, or working in partnership to improve community health and well-being? The value of these efforts compound over time, but only if a company invests.

There are no easy answers to the problem. But we believe net-positive companies will be more innovative about their pay structures to make executives long-term owners, reduce the games with options, and build an internal bench of talent as a defense against pay inflation for outside hires. They will also look at *all* salaries closely and improve wages. Part of the CEO ratio problem is in the denominator—how much average workers make. So a net-positive company will increase its minimum wages, or give employees more ownership and stock of their own. They will also support living wage laws that raise the level for all.

This is just one example of a tough issue that executives avoid. A net-positive company has to stare down and help solve these uncomfortable problems.

The Herd of Elephants

In *Net Positive* we describe nine big elephants (including overpaying executives). All of them play a core role in the economic system that has created our existential crises. They contribute to the hoarding of power and wealth and drive the system toward short-term focus and long-term ruin. Let's look quickly at the other issues companies avoid and how they contribute to our challenges:

- *Paying taxes.* Dozens of the largest companies regularly pay zero in tax. Paying a fair share of taxes sounds like a legal or public relations issue, but it's at the core of how a company engages with the world. If you don't pay taxes, how can you claim you're fully contributing to the society around you? Philanthropy and CSR are often poor substitutes for this simple responsibility.

- *Corruption.* Companies drawn into bribery, theft, and other forms of corruption not only risk their brands but are active contributors to a system that sucks more than $1.2 trillion from developing countries annually.[16] Corruption also raises the cost of doing business and reduces morale (of both company and community).

- *Paying the wrong shareholders.* The $7 trillion the S&P 500 companies spent buying back stock and issuing dividends in the 2010s could have gone toward investing in the businesses themselves, making them more sustainable, and creating value over time.[17]

- *Unprepared boards.* Recent surveys of large company board members show an astounding lack of knowledge on environmental, social, and governance (ESG) issues. A small percentage have relevant knowledge, and more than half of board members surveyed said the attention on sustainability issues is "overblown."[18] A lack of diversity of all kinds on these boards is holding companies back and degrading short-term thinking.

- *Human rights and labor standards.* Modern slavery is still at the core of many global supply chains. A global benchmark of large-company performance on human rights shows a profound "head in the sand" view—more than half of the multinationals do zero due diligence on what's going on in their supply chains. No amount of employee well-being efforts will make up for the horrible conditions in supply chains.

- *Trade association lobbying.* Companies that set aggressive sustainability goals but lobby for policies that undermine progress are hypocritical at best. Few companies directly contradict themselves, but a large majority belong to trade associations that then argue on their behalf, going against their stated interests. This disconnect dramatically slows progress on policy and can move us backward.

- *Money and influence in politics.* Companies wield enormous influence over legislators through political donations. It's a global issue, but far more intense in the United States where the rules are so lax, we are observing legalized corruption. The companies with the most influence are generally not only using it to stop progress on climate change in particular but also on minimum wages and social safety nets. The fossil-fuel sector has used influence to fight climate action for decades.

- *Broader diversity and inclusion.* While efforts to expand inclusion in business have accelerated, there's a long way to go. Women have half the entry-level jobs in the United States, but 21 percent of C-suite roles.[19] There are only four Black CEOs in the *Fortune* 500.[20] Less than a third of those with disabilities are employed.[21] This represents an incredible waste, as more diverse companies outperform their peers. A system that locks out entire groups is not moving toward a thriving future.

CONCLUDING THOUGHTS

Companies are accelerating efforts to manage their environmental footprint and improve their social impact. Sustainability is firmly on the agenda. But the scale of effort needed today eclipses what business can do alone. Systems need to change in fundamental ways, and business has no choice but to play an active role in fixing those systems.

The issues we've talked about have been willfully ignored because they're uncomfortable, or companies believe it's not in their short-term interest to deal with them. There's some fear as well; leaders don't want to put themselves out there and take criticism. Some CEOs have stuck their necks out, like the ones who pulled back on political donations after politicians in the United States (all from one party) supported the attempted coup in January 2021. Some have embraced real inclusion efforts and collaborative work to reduce human rights violations. But for the most part, these elephants have not been addressed. That can't continue, as there's no way to be a net-positive company while participating in these drains on shared well-being. They stand in the way of collective action against our largest challenges.

We can envision what business and society might look like if we embrace these issues and work together to fix them. Eliminating the corrupting influence of money in politics will allow companies to embrace net-positive advocacy and help bring about policies that serve all. Wealth more broadly shared will bring more people out of poverty and into a stable middle class, and they will add to the economy. An inclusive business world will thrive and represent all people better.

When we face these systemic hurdles head on, we can create net-positive businesses that serve the world.

NOTES

1. "COVID-19 to Add as Many as 150 Million Extreme Poor by 2021," World Bank, October 7, 2020, https://www.worldbank.org/en/news/press-release/2020/10/07/covid-19-to-add-as-many-as-150-million-extreme-poor-by-2021.

2. Paul Tudor Jones and Dan Schulman, "CEOs, Make Sure Your Employees Aren't Struggling to Get By," CNN, September 22, 2020, https://edition.cnn.com/2020/09/22/perspectives/employees-financially-secure-paypal/index.html.

3. William Lazonick, Öner Tulum, Matt Hopkins, Mustafa. E. Sakinç, and Ken Jacobson, "Financialization of the U.S. Pharmaceutical Industry," Institute for New Economic Thinking, December 2, 2019, https://www.ineteconomics.org/perspectives/blog/financialization-us-pharma-industry.

4. "CEO Pay Increased 14% in 2019, and Now Make 320 Times Their Typical Workers," Economic Policy Institute, August 18, 2020, https://www.epi.org/press/ceo-pay-increased-14-in-2019-and-now-make-320-times-their-typical-workers/.

5. "National Climate Action under the Paris Agreement," World Resources Institute, September 30, 2020, https://www.wri.org/ndcs.

6. Niall McCarthy, "Report: Global Wildlife Populations Have Declined 68% in 50 Years Due to Human Activity [Infographic]," *Forbes*, September 10, 2020, https://www.forbes.com/sites/niallmccarthy/2020/09/10/report-global-wildlife -populations-have-declined-68-in-50-years-due-to-human-activity-infographic/ ?sh=51b675d7180f.

7. Sean Fleming, "How Much Is Nature Worth? $125 Trillion, According to this Report," World Economic Forum, October 30, 2018, https://www.weforum .org/agenda/2018/10/this-is-why-putting-a-price-on-the-value-of-nature-could -help-the-environment/.

8. Jordan Bar Am, Laura Furstenthal, Felicitas Jorge, and Erik Roth, "Innova-tion in a Crisis: Why It Is More Critical Than Ever," McKinsey & Company, June 17, 2020, https://www.mckinsey.com/business-functions/strategy-and -corporate-finance/our-insights/innovation-in-a-crisis-why-it-is-more-critical -than-ever.

9. Paul Polman and Andrew Winston, *Net Positive: How Courageous Compa-nies Thrive by Giving More Than They Take* (Boston: Harvard Business Review Press, 2021).

10. Paul Camuti (Trane Technologies), in conversation with authors, May 19, 2020.

11. Chibuike Oguh, "Blackstone CEO Schwarzman Took Home $610.5 Million in 2020," Reuters, March 1, 2021, https://www.reuters.com/article/us -blackstone-group-ceo-compensation-idUSKBN2AT2V7.

12. Oguh, "Blackstone CEO Schwarzman."

13. Thea Mei Lee, "Our Deeply Broken Labor Market Needs a Higher Mini-mum Wage: EPI Testimony for the Senate Budget Committee," Economic Policy Institute, February 25, 2021, https://www.epi.org/publication/our-deeply -broken-labor-market-needs-a-higher-minimum-wage-epi-testimony-for-the -senate-budget-committee/.

14. Economic Policy Institute, "CEO Pay."

15. Economic Policy Institute, "CEO Pay."

16. Sean Fleming, "Corruption Costs Developing Countries $1.26 Trillion Every Year—Yet Half of EMEA Think It's Acceptable," World Economic Forum, December 9, 2019, https://www.weforum.org/agenda/2019/12/corruption-global -problem-statistics-cost/.

17. Lazonick et al., "Financialization of the U.S. Pharmaceutical Industry."

18. "Running the Risk: How Corporate Boards Can Oversee Environmental, Social and Governance (ESG) Issues," CERES, November 20, 2019, https://www .ceres.org/resources/reports/running-risk-how-corporate-boards-can-oversee -environmental-social-and-governance.

19. Sarah Coury, Jess Huang, Ankur Kumar, Sara Prince, Alexis Krivkovich, and Lareina Yee, "Women in the Workplace 2020," McKinsey & Company, September 30, 2020, https://www.mckinsey.com/featured-insights/diversity -and-inclusion/women-in-the-workplace.

20. Ellen McGirt and Aric Jenkins, "Where Are the Black CEOs?" *Fortune*, February 4, 2021, https://fortune.com/2021/02/04/black-ceos-fortune-500/.

21. Accenture, AAPD, and Disability:IN, "Getting to Equal: The Disability Inclusion Advantage," Accenture, 2018, https://www.accenture.com/_acnmedia /PDF-89/Accenture-Disability-Inclusion-Research-Report.pdf.

8

Accountability for All

*There Is No Stakeholder Capitalism Without
Stakeholder Governance*

BART HOULAHAN AND ANDREW KASSOY

INTRODUCTION

Our economic system is not meeting its promise to produce a positive impact for all while creating significant negative impacts on human well-being and the planet we inhabit. Whether we focus on the environmental crises, accelerating wealth inequality, or structural racism (or the way each of these deepens the impacts of the others), our economic system, with business at its center, is generating externalities that are limiting the collective good. If it wasn't obvious before, 2020 became our proof point. The global pandemic and a globalized reaction to racial injustice have laid bare the inequities of a current economic system that is simply not resilient enough—at least not for the many.

Both democracy and capitalism are in crisis—in tandem. The reaction to these ranges from violent to inspiring. But in all cases, people are demanding a system that witnesses them, creates opportunity for them, and protects the planet they live on. And that requires an economic system that works for everyone.

Unfortunately, the current economic system is simply not designed to do that. From Paris to Santiago, from London to Lebanon, from Hong Kong to Portland, citizens have taken to the streets to demand change. Though the manifestations of these protests have been different, the commonality they share is a growing, visceral frustration with the system that defines our present working reality.

Both the culture and the legal structure of the private sector drive businesses to create value for one constituency, shareholders, while dismissing all other stakeholders as costs to be minimized or externalized. This has certainly been true for 50 years since Milton Friedman popularized the idea of shareholder primacy in his 1970 *New York Times* essay on the social responsibility of business, although many would say this has been baked into our system for 400 years since the earliest businesses in the colonies traded in human beings. The demand for change was already building, but the chaos of the past four years and the calamity of 2020 have created historic momentum for economic systems change.

Systems change requires two things: systems failure and a viable alternative. Today there is a surge in demand from across a spectrum of consumers, workers, policy makers, media, investors—all calling for change and seeking that viable alternative. The twin crises of the current climate emergency and accelerating wealth inequality have created an existential threat for the private sector. With the last six years as the warmest on record,[1] the top 1 percent now controlling 44 percent of the world's wealth,[2] and a sense that government has failed to address many (or any) of these problems, business leaders are facing unprecedented pressure to be the agents of and advocates for systemic change. There is evidence that the business community is beginning to listen.

A CULTURAL SHIFT

To move our economy toward a more inclusive and equitable system will require behavioral change, structural change, and cultural change. Perhaps the culture change—what we expect of our business leaders and how we define business success—must come first. We need to embrace a broader definition of value creation: an economic system that drives value for all stakeholders, not just shareholders.

The good news is that this larger cultural shift accelerated dramatically in 2019. On August 19 of that year, the Business Roundtable published a statement calling for a new "purpose of a corporation."[3] One hundred and eighty-one CEOs of many of the largest companies in the world (i.e., Amazon, Apple, J. P. Morgan, BlackRock, GM) committed to "lead their companies for the benefit of all stakeholders—customers, employees, suppliers, communities and shareholders." Following this pronouncement, in December 2019 the World Economic Forum similarly published the new Davos Manifesto, proclaiming, "The purpose of a company is to engage all its stakeholders in shared and sustained value creation. In creating such value, a company serves not only its shareholders, but all its stakeholders—employees, customers, suppliers, local communities and society at large."[4]

Both of these declarations represent an important cultural moment, recognizing the rising threats facing the current economic system. This cultural transformation is a result of more than 50 years of focused efforts, beginning with the corporate social responsibility movement of the 1970s and 1980s to the sustainability and impact investing initiatives of today. Momentum has been driven not only by the external dangers of climate change and accelerating inequality but also by meaningful market pressures from important business constituencies. Whether it be the growing consciousness of global consumers (80 percent of who now expect companies to "solve society's problems"[5]), or the shifting interests of millennial workers (86 percent of whom would be willing to take a pay cut to work at an organization with purpose[6]), or the rapidly growing sustainable investing marketplace (representing one in four dollars under professional management in the United States[7]), what began five decades ago as a small but vocal progressive social responsibility movement has grown to become the defining business trend of the early twenty-first century, embraced by the CEOs of Bank of America and General Motors.

The pandemic of 2020 has only accelerated this cultural shift, with 90 percent of consumers demanding that companies must "protect the well-being and financial security of their employees and their suppliers, even if it means suffering big financial losses until the pandemic ends."[8] The historic shift from an economy focused on shareholder return to one that balances the interests of stakeholders is well underway and accelerating.

Importantly, however, though declarations, pronouncements, and principals are important indicators of a cultural shift, too often they are simple exercises in public relations. Without legal accountability and requisite transparency, there are no structural mechanisms to ensure these cultural milestones result in a meaningful shift in behavior. In October of 2020, Columbia Business School conducted a study of the 181 companies whose CEOs signed the BRT statement. The study concluded that the signatories were falling short of their commitments. "Relative to within-industry peer firms, signatories of the BRT statement have higher rates of environmental and labor-related compliance violations (and pay more in compliance penalties as a result), despite the BRT statement's specific reference to employees and the environment. Moreover, the higher rate of environmental violations may be associated with our finding that BRT signatories have higher levels of carbon emissions (in terms of total emissions), even relative to similar-sized within-industry peers."[9] Relatedly, a study financed by the Ford Foundation and conducted six months into the global pandemic by KKS Advisors and TCP investigating the BRT signatories' performance during the crisis concluded, "Since the pandemic's inception [the BRT Statement] has failed to deliver fundamental shifts in corporate purpose in a moment of grave crisis when enlightened purpose should be paramount."[10]

A cultural shift without structural reform is unlikely to produce lasting change because everyone is still playing by the old rules of the game. *Long term, there can be no stakeholder capitalism without stakeholder governance, where companies and investment fiduciaries are accountable for the common good, not just talking about it.* Seemingly acknowledging that they'd like to change the culture but are unwilling to be accountable for changing behavior, the BRT explicitly stated, in a follow-up memo to their letter, that while they were declaring shareholder primacy dead, they did not believe their fiduciary duties should change accordingly.[11] Fortunately, a viable alternative exists.

A VIABLE ALTERNATIVE

In 2010, the state of Maryland in the United States was the first state to pass legislation recognizing a new corporate form: the benefit corporation. This legislation (and other similar forms promoting stakeholder governance) has since been passed in 43 states and seven countries. The legislation creates legal permission for companies to balance the interests of stakeholders and shareholders while creating clear accountability and transparency requirements for those who adopt this new corporate structure.

The core components of the legislation include (1) expanding the corporate purpose of business beyond maximizing shareholder value to create general public benefit; (2) creating accountability for directors to consider the impacts of their decisions on both shareholders and stakeholders; and (3) requiring transparency for this expanded purpose. The effect of the legislation is to upend the principal tenet of corporate law for the last century—shareholder primacy.

Shareholder primacy is the corporate governance theory, rooted in corporate law and normative behavior, that the ultimate goal of corporate directors is the delivery of shareholder return. Under this theory, any consideration of stakeholders is in service of creating shareholder value and "derivative of the duty to stockholders."[12] Though there have been legal debates regarding whether corporate law mandates shareholder primacy, there is little doubt that practically all corporations have embraced this doctrine over the last 50 years since

Milton Friedman's seminal essay published in 1970. Friedman famously wrote, "There is one and only one social responsibility of business—to use its resources and engage in activities designed to increase its profits so long as it stays within the rules of the game, which is to say, engages in open and free competition without deception or fraud."[13]

Colin Mayer, former dean of the Saïd Business School at the University of Oxford, and Leo Strine, the former chief justice of the Delaware Supreme Court, recently wrote on the fiftieth anniversary of the Friedman essay, "Half a century later, it is clear that this narrow, stockholder-centered view of corporations has cost society severely. Well before the COVID-19 pandemic, the single-minded focus of business on profits was criticized for causing the degradation of nature and biodiversity, contributing to global warming, stagnating wages, and exacerbating economic inequality."[14]

And they are not alone in this evolving criticism of shareholder primacy. Political leaders on both the left and right have also decried the negative impacts on society of shareholder primacy. When introducing the Accountable Capitalism Act, Democratic Senator Elizabeth Warren stated, "There's a fundamental problem with our economy. For decades, American workers have helped create record corporate profits but have seen their wages hardly budge. To fix this problem we need to end the harmful corporate obsession with maximizing shareholder returns at all costs, which has sucked trillions of dollars away from workers and necessary long-term investments."[15] The Accountable Capitalism Act proposes that all companies above $1 billion in revenues must adopt a corporate form similar to that of the benefit corporation.

Similarly, in the summer of 2019, Marco Rubio, Republican senator from Florida, released a white paper entitled "American Investment in the 21st Century" in which he criticized shareholder primacy. According to Senator Rubio, "Shareholder primacy theory is a driving cause behind this shift of American business away from the traditional role expected of it in our economy. Rising out of the economic stagnation of the 1970s, shareholder primacy theory refocused corporate management's understanding of economic value as a financial return to shareholders. This theory tilts business decision-making towards returning money quickly and predictably to investors rather than building long-term corporate capabilities, reduces investment in research and innovation, and undervalues American workers' contribution to production."[16]

Upending shareholder primacy is not a partisan issue. To that end, for the last 10 years, the legislation to create the benefit corporation has passed *unanimously* in the United States more than 30 times.

A GROWING MOVEMENT

The benefit corporation legislation began as a vehicle for companies principally seeking certification as a B Corporation. Founded in 2007, a certified B Corporation is a corporate certification for businesses that have met the highest standards of social and environmental performance, accountability, and transparency. Unlike most other environmental or social certifications, it is comprehensive and plural in its approach, rather than focusing on a particular product or practice. To qualify for the certification, a company must (1) take and pass an assessment of its impact on all of its stakeholders; (2) amend its corporate governing documents to balance the interests of shareholders and stakeholders; and (3) share its social and environmental performance transparently. As of the end of 2020, there were 3,800+ certified B Corporations in 70+ countries across 150+ industries.[17]

The legal requirement of the certification is intended to embed the company's commitment to its stakeholders in the DNA of the business. The amendment fundamentally changes fiduciary duty, moving stakeholder consideration from an option to a requirement with legal accountability. There was, however, a catch: in several states, including the home of American corporate law, Delaware, amending a company's articles to include stakeholder consideration would not be upheld in a court of law. As a result, B Lab, the nonprofit behind the B Corporation movement (and the organization that the authors cofounded along with Jay Coen Gilbert), crafted legislation to create this new corporate form.

Early concerns about the legislation included anxieties regarding increased liability, third-party rights of action, and negative impacts on fundraising. To address these anxieties, written into the legislation was a prohibition of monetary damages, with remedies limited to injunctive relief and specific performance (which served the underlying purpose of the statute—to ensure that companies pursue and create the impact they say they want). Additionally, accountability for benefit corporation performance is limited to actions brought by shareholders—wherein stakeholders have no standing.

Unsurprisingly, capital-raising concerns have been less easily resolved from a policy perspective. By adopting this new corporate form, traditional investors are accepting a new fiduciary duty whereby their financial interests are no longer the exclusive legal obligation of the company. Further, in many of the statutes, including the Delaware version (the public benefit corporation [PBC]), the law specifically requires directors and executives to "balance" financial and societal interests. The DE law explicitly states that "a public benefit corporation shall be managed in a manner that balances the stockholders' pecuniary interests, the best interests of those materially affected by the corporation's conduct, and the public benefit or public benefits identified in its certificate of incorporation."[18]

Focusing on investor education, B Lab began a campaign to alleviate investor concerns regarding this form, beginning with venture capitalists and private equity investors. As the certification has grown in popularity, so have the number of traditional investors that have invested in either a B Corporation or a benefit corporation. From KKR to Kleiner Perkins to Founders Fund, private investors are growing increasingly comfortable with this new structure. Currently, certified B Corporations have raised more than $2 billion in the private capital markets,[19] including significant offerings by companies like Allbirds, Culture Amp, Ripple, and Revolution Foods.

As might be expected, the public markets were slower to accept or encourage companies interested in the adoption of the new corporate form. The year 2017 proved to be pivotal. Laureate Education was first to undertake an IPO as a certified B Corporation, with a Delaware Public Benefit Corporation legal structure, raising $490 million in a successful offering.[20] Before this IPO, only Natura, a multibillion-dollar publicly traded cosmetics company in Sao Paulo, had pursued a shareholder vote to amend their articles to include stakeholder interests in 2015. The initiative passed with an affirmative vote of 99 percent.[21]

These companies were largely alone until 2020 when Lemonade and Vital Farms both had successful IPOs as public benefit corporations; Amalgamated Bank and Veeva Systems converted as existing public companies, and Broadway Bank and City First Bank merged following a shareholder vote to form a publicly traded benefit corp. The big coup came in July 2020, when Danone Group in Paris converted to an Entreprise à Mission, the French equivalent of a benefit corporation, receiving a 99 percent positive shareholder vote.[22] The tide has shifted in the public markets.

THE CHALLENGES OF MAKING ACCOUNTABILITY AN OPTION

These pioneers have created a pathway for others to follow and a foundation upon which to build a new, more equitable, and inclusive structure for corporations. But mainstream adoption of the benefit corporation will continue to be slow as long as stakeholder consideration remains optional; institutional impediments in the capital markets are simply too powerful. Following the BRT's announcement about the new purpose of the corporation, the Council of Institutional Investors (CII) released a statement on the same day proclaiming, "Accountability to everyone means accountability to no one." They went on to write, "While it is important for boards and management to have and articulate long-term vision, and sustain focus on the long-term strategy where they have strong conviction, a fundamental strength of the U.S. economy has been and continues to be efficient allocation of equity capital. If 'stakeholder governance' and 'sustainability' become hiding places for poor management, or for stalling needed change, the economy more generally will lose out."[23]

On August 25, 2019, six days following the CII statement, the Business Roundtable responded with a Q&A on their medium page stating:

> Are Business Roundtable CEOs abandoning shareholders? No. The new Statement could not be clearer that companies need to generate "long-term value for shareholders, who provide the capital that allows companies to invest, grow and innovate." What it pragmatically reflects is the reality that for corporations to be successful, durable, and return value to shareholders, they need to consider the interests and meet the fair expectations of a wide range of stakeholders in addition to shareholders, including customers, employees and the communities in which they operate.[24]

It took six days for the BRT to reaffirm shareholder primacy. Six days.

THE WAY FORWARD: RAISING THE FLOOR
OF ACCOUNTABILITY FOR ALL

In September of 2020, the Stakeholder Commons and B Lab released "From Shareholder Primacy to Stakeholder Capitalism," a policy vision for the U.S. economy in which they call for stakeholder governance, or benefit governance, to be required for both companies and investors. "Laws and regulations must be changed to require businesses and financial institutions to look beyond their own financial returns and take responsibility for the impact they have on the social and ecological systems on which a more just, equitable, and prosperous economic system depends. Our policy proposal would require that all companies and institutional investors must adopt benefit governance, consisting of revised fiduciary considerations that extend beyond responsibility for financial return, because accountable benefit governance is the foundation of Stakeholder Capitalism."[25]

The addition of investors to this call for benefit governance is critical. The laws and regulations that govern the capital markets are designed to protect the shareholder. They have resulted in a decoupling of the capital markets from productivity and societal benefit. The separation of profit from productivity has resulted in the externalization of costs, exploitation of human and natural resources, and the financialization of the markets (see the GameStop phenomenon of early 2021[26]). According to Mayer and Strine, "Although corporations can opt in to become a PBC, there is no obligation on them to do so and they need the support of their shareholders. It is relatively easy for founder-owned companies or companies with a relatively low number of stockholders to adopt PBC forms if their owners are so inclined. It is much tougher to obtain the approval of a dispersed group of institutional investors who are accountable to an even more dispersed group of individual investors. There is a serious coordination problem of achieving reform in existing corporations."[27]

The proposal to shift the legislation from an option to a requirement is not unique to the United States. Similar proposals are being considered in the European Union, Brazil, and the UK. As an example, the "System Upgrade" initiative in the United Kingdom supported by 166 companies has crafted the Better Business Act, which proposes to amend Section 172 of the Companies Act, requiring all companies in the UK to adopt and report on stakeholder governance, explicitly calling on directors to advance the interest of all stakeholders.

CONCLUSION

The year 2020 will be remembered as a year of historic devastation driven by the worst global pandemic the world has confronted in a century. As the virus has ravaged communities, killing more citizens in the United States than World War I, World War II, Korea, and Vietnam combined, the inequitable effects of the growing calamity across marginalized populations have been laid bare. The pandemic has dramatically impacted communities of color at far higher rates than others.

As we look forward to the end of this pandemic, global leaders are no longer calling for a return to normal. They are looking for a new normal: an economic system that works for everyone. The shift from an economy exclusively focused on the creation of private wealth for a few to a system that balances the interests of all is our collective way forward. It will not be a reality, however, without a governance structure that changes the rules, demands different outcomes from the private sector, and delivers a more equitable, inclusive, and regenerative economy. Without clear accountability and transparency, declarations, pronouncements, and principles will be insufficient to address the existential challenges facing the private sector and the economic system as a whole with urgency.

As offered by our advocates Mayer and Strine, "We are calling for the universal adoption of the PBC (Public Benefit Corporation) for large corporations. We do so to save our capitalist system and corporations from the devastating consequences of their current approaches, and for the sake of our children, our societies, and the natural world."[28]

NOTES

1. Robert Rohde, "Global Temperature Report for 2020," Berkeley Earth, January 14, 2021, http://berkeleyearth.org/global-temperature-report-for-2020/#:%7E:text=Over%20land%2C%202020%20was%20 unambiguously,%C2%B0C%20observed%20in%202016.

2. "Global Inequality," Inequality.Org, February 3, 2021, https://inequality .org/facts/global-inequality/#global-wealth-inequality.

3. "Business Roundtable Redefines the Purpose of a Corporation to Promote 'An Economy That Serves All Americans,'" Business Roundtable, August 19, 2019, https://www.businessroundtable.org/business-roundtable-redefines-the -purpose-of-a-corporation-to-promote-an-economy-that-serves-all-americans.

4. Klaus Schwab, "Davos Manifesto 2020: The Universal Purpose of a Company in the Fourth Industrial Revolution," World Economic Forum, December 2, 2019, https://www.weforum.org/agenda/2019/12/davos -manifesto-2020-the-universal-purpose-of-a-company-in-the-fourth-industrial -revolution/.

5. "Edelman Trust Barometer Special Report: Brand Trust in 2020," Edelman, June 25, 2020, https://www.edelman.com/research/brand-trust-2020.

6. Nina McQueen, "Workplace Culture Trends: The Key to Hiring (and Keeping) Top Talent in 2018," LinkedIn, June 26, 2018, https://blog.linkedin .com/2018/june/26/workplace-culture-trends-the-key-to-hiring-and-keeping -top-talent.

7. "Why SRI/ESG," SRI Conferences & Community, accessed May 20, 2021, https://www.sriconference.com/.

8. Edelman, "Edelman Trust Barometer Special Report."

9. Aneesh Raghunandan and Shivaram Rajgopal, "Do Socially Responsible Firms Walk the Talk?" SSRN, April 1, 2021, https://papers.ssrn.com/sol3/papers .cfm?abstract_id=3609056.

10. "COVID-19 and Inequality: A Test of Corporate Purpose," KKS Advisors, September 2020, https://c6a26163-5098-4e74-89da-9f6c9cc2e20c.filesusr.com /ugd/f64551_a55c15bb348f444982bfd28a03ofeb3c.pdf.

11. "Redefined Purpose of a Corporation: Welcoming the Debate," Business Roundtable, August 25, 2019, https://bizroundtable.medium.com/redefined -purpose-of-a-corporation-welcoming-the-debate-8f03176f7ad8.

12. Cydney S. Posner, "So Long to Shareholder Primacy," Harvard Law School Forum on Corporate Governance, August 22, 2019, https://corpgov.law .harvard.edu/2019/08/22/so-long-to-shareholder-primacy/.

13. Milton Friedman, "A Friedman Doctrine—The Social Responsibility of Business Is to Increase Its Profits," *New York Times*, September 13, 1970, https:// www.nytimes.com/1970/09/13/archives/a-friedman-doctrine-the-social -responsibility-of-business-is-to.html.

14. Colin Mayer, Leo E. Strine Jr., and Jaap Winter, "50 Years Later, Milton Friedman's Shareholder Doctrine Is Dead," *Fortune*, September 13, 2020, https:// fortune.com/2020/09/13/milton-friedman-anniversary-business-purpose/.

15. "Warren Introduces Accountable Capitalism Act," U.S. Senator Elizabeth Warren of Massachusetts, August 15, 2018, https://www.warren.senate.gov /newsroom/press-releases/warren-introduces-accountable-capitalism-act.

16. "Rubio Releases Report on Domestic Investment," U.S. Committee on Small Business & Entrepreneurship, May 15, 2019, https://www.sbc.senate.gov /public/index.cfm/2019/5/rubio-releases-report-on-domestic-investment.

17. "A Global Community of Leaders," Certified B Corporation," January 1, 2021, https://bcorporation.net/.

18. "Delaware Public Benefit Corporations: Choosing a Specific Benefit," Benefit Corporation, January 1, 2016, https://benefitcorp.net/sites/default/files /Delaware%20Public%20Benefit%20Corporations_%20Choosing%20A%20 Specific%20Benefit%20FINAL_6_3_0.pdf.

19. "The Decline of the Single Bottom Line and the Growth of B-Corps," Rapid Transition Alliance, August 16, 2019, https://www.rapidtransition.org /stories/new-economics-the-rise-of-the-b-corp/.

20. "Laureate Education Announces Pricing of Its Initial Public Offering," Laureate Education, January 31, 2017, https://www.laureate.net/laureate -education-announces-pricing-of-its-initial-public-offering/.

21. Jay C. Gilbert, "New Business Trend: An Authentic Commitment to Purpose," *Forbes*, July 18, 2019, https://www.forbes.com/sites/jaycoengilbert /2019/07/18/new-business-trend-an-authentic-commitment-to-purpose/?sh =76f6fc1324d5.

22. Leila Abboud, "Danone Adopts New Legal Status to Reflect Social Mission," *Financial Times*, June 26, 2020, https://www.ft.com/content/1eff9241 -ef11-4a38-8b5c-bb825fa108ca.

23. "Council of Institutional Investors Responds to Business Roundtable Statement," Council of Institutional Investors, August 19, 2019, https://www.cii.org/aug19_brt_response.

24. "Redefined Purpose of a Corporation."

25. Frederick Alexander, Andrew R. Kassoy, Holly Ensign-Barstow, and Lenore Paladinao, "From Shareholder Primacy to Stakeholder Capitalism," Harvard Law School Forum on Corporate Governance, October 26, 2020, https://corpgov.law.harvard.edu/2020/10/26/from-shareholder-primacy-to-stakeholder-capitalism/.

26. Howard Smith, "Why GameStop Stock Continues to Run Up," Motley Fool, March 10, 2021, https://www.fool.com/investing/2021/03/10/why-gamestop-stock-continues-to-run-up/.

27. Mayer, Strine Jr., and Winter, "50 Years Later."

28. Mayer, Strine Jr., and Winter, "50 Years Later."

9

The Business of Business Is the Future

RAJ SISODIA

A PARADIGM SHIFT

We are living through an unprecedented confluence of events—a perfect storm of existential challenges. Like a churning ocean, the events of 2020 have brought to the surface massive problems that have long existed. Now they have risen from the depths to confront us, and we are rightly terrified.

We inhabit an ailing planet whose many life-giving eco subsystems are under severe strain; we have already damaged some beyond their ability to recover. The human footprint on the planet is enormous, growing, and overwhelmingly negative. Our collective global impact is now comparable to that of geological forces.

The existential threat of climate change needs no elaboration here. Partly because of climate change, we are living through the fifth mass extinction in the planet's history, the first one primarily caused by human activity. According to the UN, up to 1 million species are currently threatened with extinction: "The health of ecosystems on which we and all other species depend is deteriorating more rapidly than ever. We are eroding the very foundations of our economies, livelihoods, food security, health and quality of life worldwide."[1]

Another monumental challenge we face is extreme and growing levels of social inequality. This is contributing to an epidemic of rising anxiety, depression, and suicide, made far worse by the isolation and economic devastation caused by the pandemic. Startlingly, 25.5 percent of Americans suffered from an anxiety disorder, 24.3 percent from depressive disorder, and 10.7 percent reported serious suicide ideation during June 2020; among 18 to 24-year-olds, a heart-breaking 25.5 percent seriously considered suicide.[2] Think about that: a

94

quarter of our young people, born into a free society with so much to live for, feel that life is not worth living. That is a brutal indictment of the business and political leadership that has brought us to this point. What kind of world have we created? How can we change it?

Rising inequality and long-stagnant worker pay have given rise to populist movements in many countries. These have resulted in the election of extremist candidates who have opportunistically ridden the waves of discontent but offered few to no meaningful solutions capable of arresting the malaise.

With so much suffering in the world, the need for healing is paramount and urgent. We need to heal ourselves, our families, and our communities. We need to heal our companies and our countries. We need to heal our planet and its ability to sustain life. With so much at risk, this is the time to reinvent the systems and structures that have given rise to all this suffering. As Winston Churchill said, "We shape our buildings, and then our buildings shape us." The greatest task of leadership today is to devise *systemic* rather than symptomatic solutions to our many challenges.

Toward the end of the U.S. Civil War, Abraham Lincoln said, "The dogmas of the quiet past are inadequate to the stormy present. The occasion is piled high with difficulty, and we must rise with the occasion. As our case is new, so we must think anew, and act anew." That applies today even more than it did then. We need to rethink everything: what it means to be human, why we exist, what we do, how we do it, who we are as leaders, our definition of success, and our time horizon. This is true for every part of society, especially business. What do we need to do to ease the very real and consequential anxieties of our time? It starts with recognizing that bad ideas matter more than bad people. Humanity has been in thrall to too many bad ideas for too long. We have allowed our higher capacities to atrophy, silenced our better angels, and are mindlessly stampeding toward collective self-destruction.

The pressing need of the hour is for better ideas.

Perhaps the most consequential idea we have ever had is capitalism; it is undeniably the greatest system for human cooperation that has ever existed. If capitalism functions well, it can enable all of us to live lives of meaning and purpose and manifest the gifts we were born with to deliver to humanity. If it doesn't, it can lead us toward social despair and planetary desolation—as we are experiencing. Whether capitalism exacerbates our problems or eases them depends on which theory of business we use: the one we have had for the past two centuries or a new one that reflects where we are and what we face at this critical juncture of the human journey.

THE PERILS OF BUSINESS-AS-USUAL

Nothing is as dangerous to a business, to our shared future, and for the planet as "business as usual." Using a profit-centered operating system, businesses collectively have shown a stunning level of ecological heedlessness to date. We are the only species that is on a suicidal path of systematically destroying its own habitat. Too many of us suffer from a kind of dissociative disorder; we come *from* this planet, not into it, yet we act as though we exist outside of nature. We are as much a part of nature as a tree or a boulder, but we have separated ourselves, like a vital organ trying to exist outside the body. In our mindless mania to produce more, sell more, acquire more, and waste more, we are committing matricide—killing Mother Earth, the source of all life.

The Supreme Court jurist Oliver Wendell Holmes Jr. said, "I would not give a fig for the simplicity this side of complexity, but I would give my life for the simplicity on the other side of complexity." Traditional businesses operate with a simplistic mindset: their purpose is to maximize profits, and profit equals revenue minus cost. They thus seek to maximize revenue by selling as much and charging as much as they can, whether customers need what they are selling or not. They minimize costs by paying employees as little as possible, squeezing their suppliers, and externalizing as many of the true costs of doing business on to society and the environment as they can.

Such businesses are more like parasites than real businesses capable of generating and trading their way to betterment in any given domain: instead of creating value, they primarily extract value from employees, customers, suppliers, communities, and the environment. Many traditional businesses use aggressive marketing to encourage compulsive and excessive consumption by customers, disregarding the physical, mental, and emotional consequences. They ignore the well-being of their employees and their families. Work matters in our lives; it can be a source of joy, meaning, and fulfillment. But most work is meaningless and joyless, engaging a tiny fraction of our extraordinary capacities. This is tragic; billions of highly intelligent, conscious, creative, caring beings are engaged in mindless, draining work. We have never wasted as much human potential as we are doing today, evidenced by Gallup's research showing global employee engagement levels hovering around 15 percent for years.[3]

We must strive for the "simplicity on the other side of complexity," creating businesses that operate as a finely honed system of interconnected parts that individually thrive and collectively contribute to the flourishing of the business, society, and the planet. For if we don't reform, we will surely perish. We need to rethink the definition, role, purpose, and domain of business. If we do not elevate capitalism, we will decimate it—taking humanity and the planet down with it.

Business should reflect and amplify the best of what it means to be human, not our basest and most primitive qualities. We must forever disavow corrosive mantras such as "greed is good." The actor and podcaster Russell Brand puts it beautifully:

> Why are our systems not more representative of the divine purer truth that we can access through spirituality—an infinite world made out of love and understanding? That level of consciousness exists. Our systems—athletic, entertainment, economic, political, social—should be as close as possible to that feeling. Isn't it odd that we are able to experience this sense of oneness, this love that seems to transcend our personal form and every-thing we believe in—and yet when it comes to our systems for organizing this plane that we live on, the material plane, the choices we make are not about that love and understanding. They are about resources and elitism and our monkey need for survival.[4]

The future of humanity, the survival of millions of species of plant and ani-mal life, and the health of the planet depend on the awakening of business to this new consciousness. Businesses need to wake up, grow up, and show up: be engaged in the dominant issues of our day, alleviate the anxieties of our times, and be a part of the solution rather than deepening the problem.

BEING HUMAN

The editors of this volume articulated a beautiful vision: "A world where busi-nesses can excel, all persons can thrive, and nature can flourish, forever." Mak-ing this vision a reality requires full alignment among people, society, the planet, and business. Nothing short of that will suffice.

We need to start with a deeper understanding of what it means to be a human being today. For too long, we have accepted the caricature that econo-mists created of humans as purely selfish beings who seek only to maximize their self-interest. It is a grotesque distortion to suggest that self-interest alone drives humans, even if economists have tried to finesse that in recent years by broadening the definition of self-interest. Self-interest is indeed essential to our survival. But a three-dimensional view of human beings also needs to rec-ognize our *innate need to care* and our *growing drive to purpose*.

Our need to care is even greater than our drive for self-interest, as any parent could attest. We increasingly hunger for meaning and purpose; it is no surprise that the bestselling book of the past several decades is *The Purpose Driven Life.*[5] When the primary energy driving business is one of pursuing self-interest, it causes suffering in the world. People live in a constant state of insecurity and fear. We fight over money. We become anxious, depressed, sick, even suicidal. We feel anger, guilt, and shame. We become isolated, greedy, and ruthless. We end up sacrificing what is beautiful and divine and magical about human existence at the altar of things that are transient, illusory, and ultimately irrelevant.

A NEW THEORY OF BUSINESS

We humans are the only species with free will, imagination, and a moral compass. Everything we do, including business, must reflect these defining characteristics of what it means to be human. The standard definition of business is "the production, distribution and sale of goods and services for a profit."[6] Everything in that definition builds to that last word; profits are unquestionably at the center of the traditional business universe. In this understanding of business, people matter only if they contribute to greater profits.

In the seventeenth century, Nicolaus Copernicus showed that Earth was not the center of the universe. Today, we need a new Copernican revolution, to recognize that profits do not belong at the center of the business universe. We need to put the life-affirming essentials—human and planetary flourishing—at the center. Everything else, including profits, must revolve around and serve those transcendent goals.

We must remember that in free societies, governments do not take care of most of our needs; we give businesses the opportunity and the responsibility for sensing and meeting those needs. We base the new theory of business on the premise that we human beings are here to express our unique selves and take care of each other; business is a way we can do that at scale. Business enables us to serve and meet each other's needs in economically and ecologically viable ways.

The goal is to create a market-based economy in which we derive joy and meaning by meeting the genuine needs of our fellow living beings. Rather than compete to be the largest or most profitable, companies compete to have the largest positive impact on humanity and the planet's future. They seek to do more good, to heal more profoundly, and to restore and rejuvenate all planetary systems. They play an infinite game (in which the aim is to continue the game forever) instead of a finite game with a limited time horizon, few winners, and many losers. "Humans are very bad at understanding statistical trends and long-term changes," according to political psychologist Conor Seyle, director

Table 9.1. Contrasting theories of business

CURRENT THEORY OF BUSINESS	NEW THEORY OF BUSINESS
Human beings are motivated by self-interest.	Human beings are motivated by self-interest, the need to care, and a search for meaning and purpose.
We are here to serve ourselves and use others to achieve success, which means accumulating as much wealth and power as possible.	We are here to express ourselves and serve others.
Business is a way to use others and serve yourself (to fulfill your needs, wants, and desires) at scale.	Business is a way to express yourself and serve others at scale.
Everyone should pursue their self-interest "to the hilt." We pretend to care for stakeholders to earn their loyalty and trust.	Humans have a sincere desire to serve. Business enables us to do that in a way that nourishes us and the recipient.
"The business of business is business." (Alfred P. Sloan)	"The business of business is people— yesterday, today and forever." (Herb Kelleher)
Business exists as an engine of profit making and wealth generation for business owners and society.	Business exists as a vehicle of service through fulfilling human needs at multiple levels on Maslow's hierarchy.
Business and society are best served by the direct pursuit of a singular aim: profits. Therefore, businesses must do whatever it takes (while staying within the law) to maximize profits.	Businesses should do the right things for the right reasons. Profits are essential to the health of the business, but profits cannot be pursued, they ensue (just like happiness) as a consequence of serving a higher purpose, genuinely caring for people, and growing from adversity.
We operate with a "limited liability" mindset.	We operate with a "full accountability" mindset.
Financial outcomes are the only ones that matter.	The human, social, and natural consequences are as important as financial outcomes— sometimes more so.

Table 9.1. *continued*

CURRENT THEORY OF BUSINESS	NEW THEORY OF BUSINESS
"Collateral damage" from the pursuit of profits is inevitable and acceptable.	Collateral damage is unnecessary and unacceptable. We must account for and internalize all externalities (unless they are positive ones).
Trade-offs are essential to running a business.	Rejecting trade-offs stimulates caring, creativity and uncovers sources of synergy.
We make all decisions with specific objectives in mind and with the lens of "economic value-added."	We are not attached to a "cherished outcome." We engage in "right actions," trusting that they will lead to the right outcomes, economic and otherwise.
Human suffering (anxiety, depression, stress, fear, insecurity) is unrelated to the business model.	The business model exacerbates or eases suffering.
Prosperity equals financial abundance.	Genuine prosperity is holistic and multifaceted.
In the competitive world of business, there are a few winners and many losers.	There is no win without a win-win. Everybody matters and everybody wins.
Dealing with stakeholders is a zero-sum game. If one gains, another loses.	To win-win-win, we must give-give-give. The more we give, the more we receive. But if we try to take as much as we can from the system, the system eventually dies.
We operate with a meritocratic, "sink or swim" mentality.	We have an egalitarian culture that affords respect and dignity for all. Everybody can grow and develop in their own unique way. There is no "caste system" separating white collar and blue collar, college educated versus not, full time versus part time.
We operate with a linear economy mindset.	We operate with a circular economy mindset.

Table 9.1. *continued*

CURRENT THEORY OF BUSINESS	NEW THEORY OF BUSINESS
Business is a finite game with a limited time horizon, exit strategies, winners, and losers.	Business is an infinite game, with the primary goal of being able to continue the game indefinitely.
The business operates with short time horizons, typically spanning the tenure of the leader or a few years more.	The business operates with long time horizons, extending beyond the leader's tenure and even beyond his/her lifetime.
Efficiency is king. Human and planetary considerations are secondary.	Efficacy is king. Human and planetary considerations are front and center.
Business is a mercenary career choice—a means to make money.	Business is a noble path of contribution and service.
If a business can generate profits, it deserves to exist (e.g., hedge funds).	If a business does not add value to society, it does not deserve to exist (e.g., high-frequency trading).

of research at One Earth Future Foundation.[7] Cognitive biases including things like hyperbolic discounting (perception that the present is more important than the future), bystander effects ("someone else" will deal with the crisis), sunk-cost fallacy (biases toward "staying the course" even in the face of negative outcomes) are all part of the pain points to the emergence of new behaviors and indeed a new theory. Table 9.1 summarizes the key differences between the traditional theory of business and the one we are proposing here.

MANY KINDS OF WEALTH

Profits are important. Indeed, profit is a social good; it is socially irresponsible for a business *not* to be profitable in free-market societies. In a free society, governments do not create wealth; they can only tax and spend the wealth generated by a profitable business. Without profits, we don't have taxes, and without taxes, there is no infrastructure, no public education, or any of the other essential elements of a functioning society. In a sense, taxes are profits that accrue to society to enable continued investments in public goods and promote overall well-being. They are essential to the healthy functioning of the system that enable businesses to generate wealth. Unfortunately, many companies spend more on tax attorneys than they do paying taxes.

Profits are not thus just beneficial for shareholders. They also allow companies to invest in better goods and services for people, add more innovation to the market, create more jobs, contribute to the competitiveness of economies and thus to the well-being of society. Profits matter, but it matters even more *how* a business generates profits. It can do so by squeezing people and the planet, or it can simultaneously have a positive impact on both. Evidence shows that businesses that conform to this new paradigm are far more profitable over the long run than traditional businesses.[8]

TOWARD A MORE BEAUTIFUL WORLD

The profit-maximizing approach to business gave us dramatic gains in per-capita incomes, extraordinary technological advances, and significant increases in longevity. But the relentless and single-minded pursuit of profits and efficiency also resulted in the dehumanization of work. We treated people as costs to be minimized and resources to be exploited. That mindset was directly responsible for the rise of militant unions, followed by Marxism, socialism, and communism. Those social movements and ideologies arose as responses to the abuses that were sanctioned and justified under the old theory of business where central rent-seeking interests destroyed all kinds of other potential value. It divided the world and created unfathomable amounts of suffering.

The environmental and planetary consequences have been even worse. We treated this finite and fragile planet as an infinite source and an infinite sink, resulting in devastated ecosystems, deforested landscapes, polluted air and water, overfished oceans, and the destruction of countless species. We instituted systems of unconscionable cruelty in factory farming systems in pursuit of efficiency and profits. We forgot what we could learn about distributed models and decentralization from nature and the synchrony, elegance, and simplicity of biomimetic organizations. We are individually and collectively responsible for all the suffering we have wrought in the pursuit of profits. It is time to atone, heal, and elevate to a better way of doing business.

We do not need to choose between profits and people or between success and suffering. Adopting a new human and planetary-centered approach to business gives us access to the upsides of capitalism to an even greater extent than before, with none of the downsides. Practiced along these lines, business becomes noble, heroic, and beautiful. The authors of "The Purposeful Company" expressed it well:

> Great firms are precious economic and social organizations. They are the originators of wealth generation, offering solutions to human dilemmas and wants at scale, and are thus agents of human betterment. They are enabled by the pursuit of clearly defined visionary corporate purposes, which set out how the company will better peoples' lives. Those purposes are binding commitments on the whole enterprise that generate trust and enable increasingly sophisticated forms of value creation.[9]

As William Gibson said, "The future is already here—it's just not very evenly distributed."[10] Many companies already function with this mindset today. We need to recognize, celebrate, and learn from these companies. We need to teach the millions of students who graduate from business schools around the world every year that this is how we need to do business in the future.

If we do not do this, we will have failed at the greatest responsibility ever borne by humans. Future generations will forever remember those now in positions of power and influence as the callous, myopic, and complacent overseers of a disintegrating system. We are stewards who need to finally awaken to our stewardship. Our planet has existed for 4.5 billion years, but we have destroyed a substantial portion of its life-giving capacity in just a couple of hundred years. Earth can sustain a stunning diversity of life forever, but the ignorant and mindless way in which we have lived and led means that people alive today can vividly foresee the devastation of human society and the extinguishing of most other life forms in their lifetimes.

Yet, this future is far from inevitable. We have agency. We can influence and alter the trajectory of life on our planet. The levers are in our hands. If we exercise them with care and consciousness, we can set human society and the planet back on a life-sustaining path. It starts with a fresh approach to business. Most businesses act as though the future doesn't exist or does not matter; this is unconscionable, myopic, and suicidal. Every business should consider the future as its biggest stakeholder. We must reject any action that does not contribute to the creation of a vibrant future for life on the planet and the life of the planet.

It is time for us to wake up from our collective trance. It is time to remember who we are: the apex species whose sacred duty it is to steward the planet with wisdom and foresight for the continued flourishing of life. It is time to elevate to a new understanding of what business is really about.

NOTES

1. "UN Report: Nature's Dangerous Decline 'Unprecedented'; Species Extinction Rates 'Accelerating,'" United Nations Sustainable Development, May 6, 2019, https://www.un.org/sustainabledevelopment/blog/2019/05/nature -decline-unprecedented-report/.

2. Mark É. Czeisler, Rashon I. Lane, Emiko Petrosky et al., "Mental Health, Substance Use, and Suicidal Ideation During the COVID-19 Pandemic—United States, June 24–30, 2020," *Morbidity and Mortality Weekly Report 69*, no. 32 (August 14, 2020): 1049–57, DOI: http://dx.doi.org/10.15585/mmwr.

3. Annamarie Mann and Jim Harter, "The Worldwide Employee Engagement Crisis," Gallup Workplace, January 7, 2016, https://www.gallup.com/workplace /236495/worldwide-employee-engagement-crisis.aspx.

4. Pete Holmes, "Russell Brand," July 3, 2019, in *You Made It Weird*, produced by Katie Levine, Apple podcast, MP3 audio, 2:04:00, https://podcasts.apple.com /us/podcast/russell-brand/id475878118?i=1000443510504.

5. Wikipedia, s.v., "List of Best-Selling Books," last modified May 18, 2021, 20:57, https://en.wikipedia.org/wiki/List_of_best-selling_books#More_than_100 _million_copies; and R. Warren, *The Purpose Driven Life Journal* (Grand Rapids, MI: Zondervan, 2020).

6. "What Is Business?" EFL Burkina, https://efl.elearning-burkina.com/index .php/texts-test/g1-g2-h-series/645-what-is-business#.

7. Matthew Wilburn King, "How Brain Biases Prevent Climate Action," BBC, March 7, 2019, https://www.bbc.com/future/article/20190304-human-evolution -means-we-can-tackle-climate-change.

8. For example, see Raj Sisodia, Jagdish Sheth, and David Wolfe, *Firms of Endearment: How World-Class Companies Profit from Passion and Purpose*, 2nd ed. (Upper Saddle River, NJ: Pearson FT Press, 2014); and Alex Edmans, *Grow the Pie: How Great Companies Deliver Both Purpose and Profit* (New York: Cambridge University Press, 2020).

9. Big Innovation Centre, "The Purposeful Company: Interim Report," Purposeful Company, May 2016, http://faculty.london.edu/aedmans/PCP.pdf.

10. "William Gibson," https://en.wikiquote.org/wiki/William_Gibson.

10

Stakeholder Capitalism

Three Generations, One Voice

R. EDWARD FREEMAN, JOEY BURTON,

AND BEN FREEMAN

INTRODUCTION

Every generation leaves behind a set of challenges for subsequent generations to solve. This is especially true when we consider the role of business in society. Since the post–World War II Greatest Generation, we have seen numerous transformations of our underlying narrative about business take place. We are currently on the cusp of a new narrative about business that has the potential to transform society for the better. It goes by several names. We will designate it as "stakeholder capitalism." Others have called it "conscious capitalism," "inclusive capitalism," "just capitalism," "ESG or impact investing," or many other terms that are currently rising in popularity and visibility.

In section 2 we will convey this story in terms of some key ideas that are fundamental to any version of this new story of business and stakeholder capitalism in particular. In sections 3, 4, and 5 we will give a brief "generational view" of business, from the standpoint of boomers, Gen Xers, and millennials, the three generations to which the authors belong. We will argue that stakeholder capitalism responds to some of the concerns of all three. Finally, in section 6 we will look at the implications of stakeholder capitalism for society and outline the work that remains to be done.

As this new narrative gains traction, it needs to speak to multiple generations of citizens simultaneously. Business needs to be a critical part of the solutions to the issues of our day, including global warming, racial inequity, globalization, new technology that challenges our ethics, and a fractured political system.

THE FIVE KEYS TO STAKEHOLDER CAPITALISM

The old story of business is fast becoming obsolete; it rests on the idea that fundamentally, business is primarily about making profits for shareholders or other owners. Recently, Freeman, Martin, and Parmar (2020) have argued that there are many proposals for the reform of capitalism, and there are five ideas that underlie most of these proposals. Any new version of capitalism or narrative about business must deal with at least five issues that are often seen as dichotomies but need to be seen as working together in harmony. Successful businesses in the twenty-first century will need (1) purpose and profits; (2) value creation from stakeholders and shareholders; (3) attention to societal and market forces; (4) attention to our full humanity as well as our economic interests; and (5) ethics and business.

There are thousands of businesses being created around the world by boomers, Gen Xers, and millennials that are consistent with this new story of business. For instance, the phenomenon of "social entrepreneurship" is now strong in many countries. In the United States, we have seen the rise of companies such as Whole Foods Market, the Container Store, the Motley Fool, and others that have grown up with high purpose and stakeholder orientation. In addition, companies such as CarMax have placed ethics front and center to their business, and in so doing they have subsequently disrupted an industry. Large global enterprises such as Danone and Unilever have rediscovered their sense of purpose and deepened their commitment to creating value for stakeholders and addressing issues such as global warming. And, there are established companies such as New York Life that have been managed along the lines of stakeholder capitalism for many years.

In truth, this so-called new story of business is not very new. While many are in the grip of the "shareholder primacy" narrative, even those executives and pundits realize that good business leadership doesn't ignore customers, suppliers, employees, and society/community. Stakeholder capitalism acknowledges that all five of these stakeholders (and maybe others as well) are important, allowing businesspeople the freedom to improve the value creation process for all. There is growing evidence that taking care of stakeholders (including shareholders) leads to better performance (see Freeman, Martin, and Parmar 2020; and chapter 10).

This new story is consistent with at least three generations, each of which has had a somewhat ambivalent relationship with business. These three have often been depicted as quite different from each other, and we suggest that while that may be true, there are also important similarities that are spoken to via stakeholder capitalism.

STAKEHOLDER CAPITALISM AND BOOMERS

"Marriage is the only thing that scares me," says one. "Religion is for old people who have given up living," says another. "The only thing you've got over [adults is] the fact that you can mystify and worry them," says another. "[We] want to hit back at all the old [people] who tell us what to do" (Deverson and Hamblett 1964, 28). Then another adds, "I'd prefer to do something for the good of humanity" (130).

Who is talking? Your answer probably depends on your age. Baby boomers probably hear the voices of millennials in the dissatisfaction with the prior generation's institutions, and their desire for their life's work to benefit society. Generation X probably hears the voices of their children—Generation Z, or zoomers—in their open criticism of older people, in their affirmative attempts to "worry" their parents, and in the naïve entitlement of, "I'd prefer to do something for the good of humanity."

The voices, however, belonged to teenagers in 1965. Speaking to journalists trying to understand postwar teens—those we'd now call boomers—these kids expressed feeling neglected by the prior generation, feeling unmoored from the institutions that had given prior generations stability and social cohesion, and having less loyalty to wisdom received from before. The interviewers named the teens Generation X because, without their investment in the social institutions they had inherited, it wasn't clear yet what they would become and what role they would play in society.

We have since reappropriated Generation X to describe the children of the boomers, but even that was because of the similarities between the two generations as youth. Every generation grows up. Age comes with different challenges, interests, and priorities. It is interesting, though, that the boomers started where millennials and Generation Z are now: "I want to do something for the good of humanity."

Boomers have always had a skeptical view of business. Recall those rants in college about "the establishment," "the military-industrial complex," and even the conspiracy theories about global corporations ruling the world—the so-called trilateral commission. President Eisenhower's 1961 warning, while specific to military-adjacent industries, reads today very similar to how our public discourse treats big technology companies. "The total influence—economic, political, even spiritual—is felt in every city, every statehouse, every office of the federal government," Eisenhower said. "We recognize the imperative need for this development. . . . Our toil, resources and livelihood are all involved; so is the very structure of our society. In the councils of government, we must guard against the acquisition of unwarranted influence, whether sought or unsought" (Eisenhower 1961).

It should not be surprising, notwithstanding their initial skepticism about business, that some of our greatest entrepreneurs were boomers, such as Steve Jobs, Bill Gates, and John Mackey, three men who changed the world and how business, governments, and other societal institutions interact.

The 1970s and 1980s, as boomers were coming of age, was the time of Wall Street madness, financial manipulation, and innovation; it was also the time of Milton Friedman's (1970) famous dictum that the only responsibility of a businessperson was to maximize profits for shareholders.

Lest we forget, this was also the age of corporate social responsibility, socially responsible investment funds, and shareholder activism to force social change. As much as boomers led the charge for greater shareholder control over business operations, they also led multiple movements for market reforms globally that lifted millions out of poverty and gave whole populations access to a quality of life that had previously been observed only in the wealthiest countries.

Stakeholder capitalism, with its five key ideas, is friendly to the concerns of present-day boomers. Worried about retirement income, boomers should be happy that study after study is now showing that paying attention to stakeholders leads to better financial results. And those idealistic boomer values that led to the brink of a revolution are back in fashion for businesses to undertake solutions to societal problems.

STAKEHOLDER CAPITALISM AND GEN XERS

The so-called Generation X—the children of boomers, born between 1965 and 1979—were described as slackers, loners, and irreligious sexual deviants given to near-tribal cliquishness and very loud music. Generation X's hallmark became introversion. Referred to as "latchkey kids" for the keys they wore on chains around their necks, they were the first generation raised to a great degree by both working mothers and working fathers in households with two stable incomes; and alternatively, they were the first generation who as children experienced large-scale divorce and single-parent-headed households. Unlike the boomers before them and the millennials after, Gen X wasn't associated with a particular ideology, a particular view of society, or social institutions.

However, they now fill social roles that, like other generations, have key consequences for the new story of business. Gen X became "stealth fighter parents," neither helicoptering nor staying too long—surgically striking on behalf of their children (Howe 2021). They have become reliable voters in both major political parties (Pew Research Center 2018). They express similar degrees of religiosity to the previous cohort (Pew Research Center 2021). They have more education than previous generations (Bialik and Fry 2019). About half of business leaders are Generation X, having invested their careers in corporations learning traditional management; a similar proportion of Gen Xers as millennials use technology well, consuming more media (including social media) than millennials (Neal and Wellins 2018).

Beyond business leadership roles, Generation X's social function is often misunderstood. As the parents of the largest living generation and the children of the oldest living generation, Generation X is increasingly likely to be caretakers for both children and parents or grandparents (Parker and Patten 2013; Calhoun 2020). An estimated 20 percent of charitable giving comes from Generation X (QGiv 2020). And while they will be compensated, they'll increase their worth by about $17 trillion over the next decades; millennials will only increase theirs by a projected $11.6 trillion (Holger 2019), though millennials stand to inherit triple that within three decades from boomers (Hall 2019).

Owing to their propensity to work in corporate jobs with good benefits, including managed retirement savings, and to the expansion of aggressive 401K management during their lifetimes, Generation X is the only generation to have made back what they lost in the financial crisis of 2008–2009 (Fry 2018). As such, they are often thought of as much more risk-tolerant than either their parents or millennials, who are twice as likely to keep their savings in cash as Gen X and half as likely to use credit (Krishna 2019).

Despite taking on these significant social roles, millennials are widely understood to be more socially conscious than Gen X. That is changing. While a reported 78 percent of wealthy millennials had ESG investments in their portfolios in 2018, they were over twice as likely as wealthy Gen Xers that year to invest in businesses and funds that expand the diversity of business leadership, support environmental sustainability, and bear a socially beneficial purpose. By the end of 2020, primarily Gen X investors (and the asset management funds where Gen X retirement savings are invested) have driven a 42 percent increase in socially responsible investing, including funds that track business' climate change, environmental, labor, gender diversity, and racial diversity practices, to reach over $17 trillion in managed funds or about 33 percent of the total funds invested in the United States (Holger 2019). While they may originally have been seen as directionless slackers, Gen X has proven themselves to be not only *responsible* caretakers for other generations but also *socially responsible* in their investments.

In the future, as the share of business leaders, especially in senior roles made up by Gen Xers increases, it would not be inconsistent either with their corporate training, their risk appetite, or with their values to observe Generation X changing how business, and especially big business, operates to further social goals. Speculative as it is, they are the last generation with deep ties to the corporate-driven capitalist institutions of the past, and are, by their age, now poised to take them over. Generation X will be an important driver of stakeholder capitalism in the coming two decades.

STAKEHOLDER CAPITALISM AND MILLENNIALS

Born in the 1980s and 1990s, millennials grew up during a period of unprecedented global connectedness, technology advancement, and wealth; and an era of global financial volatility, increasing environmental degradation, global insecurity, and heightened global awareness of increasing inequality. While the previous generation observed the stagnation and lower productivity of nonmarket-driven economies, millennials, assisted by technology, have observed the human toll of a version of capitalism that is unmoored from purpose and stakeholders' needs. Perhaps because millennials had greater access to technology, and to the instant publication of their views on social media, millennials have had the most to say about who they are and the most actual power in defining their narrative concerning business. This narrative is more complicated than "millennials are socially aware" (see the Pew Research Archive for more information on millennials, especially Huang and Silver 2020).

For example, millennials are skeptical of big business but are very likely to be entrepreneurs. About one-third of millennials run a business or an independent "side-hustle" compared to about one-fifth of the previous generation. They have an affinity for markets—they just think that markets should be fairer and more inclusive (Locke 2019).

This viewpoint heterogeneity enabled by technology gives millennials an unprecedented diversity of choices about their future and about how they will integrate business into their worldview. As social media has made apparent, there is more within-group variation in millennials' views on capitalism and business than there is variation across generations—especially when their attitudes are compared with past generations' attitudes at a similar age. Society is diverse, and millennials are especially so. In the United States, millennials are more likely than other generations to be immigrants or ethnic minorities (Fry and Parker 2018). They are less likely to hold centrist political views (Parker, Graf, and Igielnik 2019). They are less likely to have children at every age. And they have, because of various factors economic and social, delayed the life stages experienced by previous generations—they started forming households, rearing children, working, saving for retirement, and owning homes at later ages (Bialik and Fry 2019).

Despite the extreme discourse of "greed is good" and shareholder value maximization on one side, and "capitalism is evil" and "big business sucks" on the other, millennials' viewpoint diversity will allow them to essentially mix and match what works in capitalism and business to create something more sustainable and inclusive.

Millennials view themselves as having a *stake* in issues outside of their immediate circle, and the idea of using business to do good is more commonplace. Customers have become much more knowledgeable about how their products are made and about who makes them. They are more selective in the age of social media about which companies they support based on their values. Millennials do not view themselves as consumers; rather, they view themselves as supporters of values, people, policies, and stakeholders, and technology has given them unprecedented power to use their dollars to do it.

Millennials grew up in global online communities, with a more direct, personal understanding of the world. Foreign countries do not seem so foreign when you know Tang from Vietnam, Ish from Pakistan, and Martin from Germany all from playing and learning about poker together online. Even having never met in person, millennials know people around the world well enough to consider each other friends. Just by having access to people from these countries millennials have been exposed to much more diversity than was ever possible before. Millennials have created inclusive, diverse online communities, based less on their locations than on common interests. This may afford them a deeper understanding and real connection to world affairs, whereas previous generations more commonly saw the world as faraway places on TV.

This global connection extends to humanitarian efforts and socially conscious business endeavors. The well-being of global economies, businesses, and workers seems just as important to millennials as helping people in their backyards because the globe is virtually the only backyard they have known. If a company is providing shoes, socks, or glasses to people around the world who desperately need them, millennials are likely to see it as a company worth supporting. Whereas previous generations might have hired the local lawn care company that sponsors a little league team because their community is important to them, the millennial view is defined by the sheer scale of their community.

Not only are millennials skeptical and conscious consumers—or as they see it, supporters—they are entrepreneurs. Millennials are the "side hustle" generation. Working multiple jobs is not new, but millennials are much more likely to have a side hustle than Gen Xers or boomers. This habit is partially due to joining the workforce during or just after the housing and financial crises and also because the internet expanded opportunities and created the gig economy. Millennials have come of age along with the internet, which has given them an advantage of seeing these entrepreneurial possibilities mushroom.

Websites like Etsy gave millennials the freedom to lead the charge to create products and start businesses by creating a global virtual market and by reducing the time-consuming aspects of running a business. Aided by technology, the biggest concern for such entrepreneurs is purely creating the actual goods, making it infinitely easier to have a side hustle that is worth their time.

Watching the experiences of previous generations who had been perhaps falsely taught that they could depend on a company's loyalty as reciprocal opened millennial workers' eyes. Millennials are much leerier of depending on employers—and especially big corporations—than previous generations. They have experienced factory closures, financial busts, entire industries decimated, and long-time employees left with inadequate retirement savings, remnants of outmoded capitalism.

Millennials' approach to work has centered on turning a hobby or interest into a legitimate entrepreneurial enterprise. Most millennials want to start their own business, and by 2016, about half of millennials had a second job or entrepreneurial endeavor (Alton 2021). This entrepreneurial and thoroughly millennial approach to business in a more global community is defined partially by providing a social good as part of companies' purpose, not just as a byproduct of success. Fundamentally, millennials do not view social good as incompatible with business activity or with financial success. Companies may not solve famine, climate change, dictatorships, or anything else, but they will provide socks, shoes, and other necessities for needy people. As millennials continue to grow their share of the global economy, their entrepreneurial instincts will have a measurable impact on the world's problems. And they will make a profit while doing it.

MAKING STAKEHOLDER CAPITALISM WORK

While we are optimistic about the future, given our argument about the three generations and stakeholder capitalism, we believe that more can be done to enhance the ability of this new story to take hold in society. First, we see the role of government as one of facilitating value creation (Freeman and Burton 2019). Governments, primarily at the state and local levels, can sponsor incubators, accelerators, classes, and mentors to help entrepreneurs without a lot of bureaucracy. This is especially important for those groups who have not been able to participate in the business economy. Jeff Cherry's Conscious Venture Lab in Baltimore is an iconic example (Cherry 2020).

Second, we should consciously try to become a nation of entrepreneurs, with programs in our schools at all levels to encourage even more business start-ups, more side hustles, where extant businesses could take the lead here under the guise of building stronger communities. Encouraging cross generational mentorship is an important way of building more unity concerning stakeholder capitalism.

Third, there are probably changes in the laws of corporations that may facilitate stakeholder capitalism. This is a large question, and we note it and leave it for further discussion.

Finally, we simply celebrate those companies that are actively engaged in value creation for stakeholders. We need to lift entrepreneurs and side hustlers who are trying to make the world better through their businesses. Of course, they need to get paid, and of course, they need to create value for their stakeholders. This is difficult in practice, but until we recognize that practicing stakeholder capitalism is what most entrepreneurs and executives intentionally or unintentionally do, we can't make much progress.

We need to be the generations that make business better; that take on and find solutions to the problems and issues left to us and that we have created. We must be the generations that create a better world for those to follow.

REFERENCES

Alton, Larry. 2021. "Why Millennials and Gen Z Are Going to Take the Small Business World by Storm." May 13. https://www.inc.com/larry-alton/why-millennials-gen-z-are-going-to-take-small-business-world-by-storm.html.
Bialik, Kristen, and Ron Fry. 2019. "Millennial Life: How Young Adulthood Today Compares with Prior Generations." Pew Research Center, January 30.

https://www.pewresearch.org/social-trends/2019/02/14/millennial-life-how
-young-adulthood-today-compares-with-prior-generations-2/.

Calhoun, Ada. 2020. "Gen-X Women Are Caught in a Generational Tug-of-War."
Atlantic, January 7. https://www.theatlantic.com/family/archive/2020/01
/generation-x-women-are-facing-caregiving-crisis/604510/.

Cherry, Jeff. 2020. "Musings about Work, Equality, Social Justice, and Capitalism." Medium, September 13. https://jcherry26.medium.com/whats-on-my
-mind-4b90a889686e.

Deverson, Jane, and Charles Hamblett. 1964. *Generation X*. New York: Fawcett
Publications.

Eisenhower, Dwight D. 1961. "Military Industrial Complex Speech, Dwight
David Eisenhower, 1961." Yale Law School, Lillian Goldman Law Library.
https://avalon.law.yale.edu/20th_century/eisenhower001.asp.

Freeman, R. Edward, and Joseph Burton. 2019. "Should Businesses Fight for
Democracy?" MIT Sloan Management Review, August 19. https://
sloanreview.mit.edu/article/business-in-society/.

Freeman, R. Edward, and Ben Freeman. 2020. "Is There a Generation Gap in
Business?" MIT Sloan Management Review, March 26. https://sloanreview
.mit.edu/article/is-there-a-generation-gap-in-business/.

Freeman, R. Edward, Kristen E. Martin, and Bidhan L. Parmar. 2020. *The Power
of And: Responsible Business without Tradeoffs*. New York: Columbia University Press.

Friedman, Milton 1970. "A Friedman Doctrine: The Social Responsibility of
Business Is to Increase Its Profits." *New York Times*, September 13. https://
www.nytimes.com/1970/09/13/archives/a-friedman-doctrine-the-social
-responsibility-of-business-is-to.html.

Fry, Ron. 2018. "Gen X Rebounds as the Only Generation to Recover the Wealth
Lost after the Housing Crash." Pew Research Center, July 23. https://www
.pewresearch.org/fact-tank/2018/07/23/gen-x-rebounds-as-the-only
-generation-to-recover-the-wealth-lost-after-the-housing-crash/.

Fry, Ron, and Kim Parker. 2018. "Early Benchmarks Show 'Post-Millennials' on
Track to Be Most Diverse, Best-Educated Generation Yet." Pew Research
Center, November 15. https://www.pewresearch.org/social-trends/2018/11/15
/early-benchmarks-show-post-millennials-on-track-to-be-most-diverse-best
-educated-generation-yet/.

Hall, Mark. 2019. "The Greatest Wealth Transfer in History: What's Happening
and What Are the Implications." *Forbes*, November 11. https://www.forbes
.com/sites/markhall/2019/11/11/the-greatest-wealth-transfer-in-history-whats
-happening-and-what-are-the-implications/?sh=669cee094090.

Holger, Dieter. 2019. "What Generation Is Leading the Way in ESG Investing? You'll Be Surprised." *Wall Street Journal*, September 10. https://www.wsj.com /articles/what-generation-is-leading-the-way-in-esg-investing-youll-be -surprised-11568167440.

Howe, Neil. "Meet Mr. and Mrs. Generation X: A New Parent Generation." AASA. Accessed May 16, 2021. https://www.aasa.org/SchoolAdministrator Article.aspx?id=11122.

Huang, Christine, and Laura Silver. 2020. "U.S. Millennials Tend to Have Favorable Views of Foreign Countries and Institutions Even as They Age." Pew Research Center, July 8. https://www.pewresearch.org/fact-tank/2020 /07/08/u-s-millennials-tend-to-have-favorable-views-of-foreign-countries -and-institutions-even-as-they-age/.

Krishna, Mrinalini. 2019. "Millennials Are Risk Averse and Hoarding Cash." Investopedia, June 25. https://www.investopedia.com/news/millennials-are -risk-averse-and-hoarding-cash/.

Locke, Taylor. 2019. "Here's How Much Extra Money Young People Make from Side Hustles." CNBC, September 19. https://www.cnbc.com/2019/09/19 /survey-how-much-millennials-gen-x-make-from-side-hustles-on-average .html.

Neal, Stephanie, and Richard Wellins. 2018. "Generation X—Not Millenni- als—Is Changing the Nature of Work." CNBC, April 11. https://www.cnbc .com/2018/04/11/generation-x--not-millennials--is-changing-the-nature-of -work.html.

Parker, Kim, Nikki Graf, and Ruth Igielnik. 2019. "Generation Z Looks a Lot like Millennials on Key Social and Political Issues." Pew Research Center, January 17. https://www.pewresearch.org/social-trends/2019/01/17 /generation-z-looks-a-lot-like-millennials-on-key-social-and-political-issues/.

Parker, K., and E. Patten. 2013. "The Sandwich Generation Rising Financial Burdens for Middle-Aged Americans." January 30. http://www.pewsocial trends.org/2013/01/30/the-sandwich-generation/.

Pew Research Center. 2018. "Trends in Party Affiliation among Demographic Groups." March 20. https://www.pewresearch.org/politics/2018/03/20/1 -trends-in-party-affiliation-among-demographic-groups/2_6-10/.

Pew Research Center. 2021. "Religious Landscape Study." Accessed May 17, 2021. https://www.pewforum.org/religious-landscape-study/.

QGiv. 2020. "Generational Giving Report." Accessed May 17, 2021. https://www .qgiv.com/blog/resources/generational-giving/.

11

Transforming Business, Transforming Value

GILLIAN M. MARCELLE AND JED EMERSON

INTRODUCTION: REIMAGINING THE DREAM

A world of "full-spectrum flourishing" where businesses work and excel in collaboration with other stakeholders, where all persons thrive, and where nature flourishes is desirable. This vision can be achieved with a facilitative institutional system (laws, organizations, infrastructure) that enables smooth supply responses to policy prescriptions and advocacy. In this world, enterprises are well-resourced and fully capable of making changes over time by investing in new technological systems, educational institutions, and labor markets; they engage with citizens for the common good.

While we affirm this optimistic vision, we eschew the mainstream starting point; *Homo economicus cannot* be the default point of reference for all things financial and economic (Persky 1995). Creating a sustainable, regenerative world as embodied in that vision requires reimagining the dream by taking a critical and inclusive posture to both our current assessment of the world and shaping of possible futures. In so doing, we draw on political economy, critical management studies,[1] feminist economics, and critical realist philosophy, among other traditions. We bring the marginalized, oppressed, and excluded to the center, rather than leave them on the wings of the stage, appearing in the mist as seemingly permanent shadows. We refute the assumption of perfect markets and include in our concerns the real world as experienced by the global majority around the planet. We are not preoccupied with convenient abstractions.

Business functions differently around the world based on diverse paths of development, culture, and societal systems. Our vision of a flourishing world expands beyond dominant Western European perspectives, and this offers fresh wellsprings of insight and knowledge. Our effort does not seek to produce a single answer or unified framework, but it changes the "frame" by centering our arguments around a conceptual framework introduced below,[2] explicitly incorporating theoretical frames drawn from African American and Global South scholars, and applying feminist and decolonization praxis. As the poet Audre Lorde said, "The Master's tools will never dismantle the Master's house" (Lorde 1984).

We regard current efforts to move from Shareholder to Stakeholder Capitalism as steps in the right direction (Schwab and Vanham 2021), but we see these efforts as insufficient for deeper systemic transformation, as they do not incorporate alternative understandings of value and stewardship that emanate from ancient African, Asian, and indigenous traditions whose wisdoms have been relegated to the fringes of our global economic system. This is particularly important in light of the global pandemic and trends of growing inequality. This chapter outlines an agenda that fills these lacunae.

FIVE LEVERS FOR TRANSFORMATION

Our project for transformation includes a vision and strategy that can tackle the multiple crises facing the world, and it outlines a role for business acting with other actors by drawing on five levers and exploring each in turn:

1. Innovation as an organizing principle
2. Interrogation of the purpose of capital
3. Application of the Triple B framework, to mobilize multiple forms of capital
4. A focus on dignity and well-being
5. Restructuring of economic systems.

Innovation as an Organizing Principle for Societal Change

One of the most important conceptual and practical levers for change is innovation. In theoretical work, Marcelle (2017) has argued that it is important to conceive of innovation as a knowledge and learning process rather than as a technocentric performance obsessed with novelty. In this framing of innovation, the positive outcomes for the world arise out of actively seeking solutions in as wide a space as possible. Innovation-centered transformation involves optimizing the process of generating and organizing knowledge and the search for solutions from a wide and ever-increasing variety of sources. Within this framework, investors search for innovators and solutions, and are proactive and intentional about creating shared meanings, blended value, as well as mutually beneficial outcomes that are equitably distributed among various groups in society. Businesses along with governments and communities as innovators play an important role by expanding the solution space and harnessing the intensity of a crisis (Marcelle 2020b).

The Purpose of Capital

A clear understanding of the purpose of capital is central to our collective ability to finance innovation and sustainability in future markets. Many in the West tend to begin and end with the presumption that the purpose of capital is to seek its highest and best use as defined by optimizing financial return alone. This notion is the aberration from humanity's experience over centuries and one taken to scale within the framework and practices of modern financial capitalism; at the same time, it is also one that stands in sharp contrast to a large number of other cultural and historic traditions.[3] It is up to each generation and culture to reflect upon and refine its definition of capital's true purpose.

Bottlenecks, Blind Spots, and Blended Finance—the Triple B Framework

Devising strategies to mobilize and activate all forms of capital is critically important to our proposed agenda. To achieve this, we recommend the application of the Triple B framework, an approach that consists of three components and seeks to solve for sluggishness in capital growth as well as improvements in allocation decision making. This framework draws on Douglas North's (1992) institutional economics thinking and emphasizes the role of structures, processes, and cultural rules and norms in behavior and outcomes. At the foundation of this framework is an understanding that context matters and that social structures are racialized and gendered (Crenshaw 1989).

The Triple B conceptual framework consists of three dimensions: (1) bottlenecks, (2) blind spots, and (3) blended finance. It is an approach for activating assets and creating equitable societal benefits. Implementing investment strategies using this approach involves taking meaningful steps toward removing bottlenecks and reducing blind spots that inhibit the development of flourishing economies and societies.

Bottlenecks are defined as barriers that slow down or hinder capital mobilization and deployment processes; these are categorized as structural, processual, and cognitive. Zinica Group and Bitt are two examples of successful enterprises that have directly addressed structural bottlenecks in Caribbean capital markets by developing regulated digital currencies, in the case of Bitt, and an expanded "digital" stock exchange in the case of Zinica.[4]

Blindspots arise out of the behavior and attitudes of human parties in the system. Drawing on psychology, including work on bias, we posit that blindspots often result in misalignment of capital mobilization systems and related processes, resulting in negative effects on human well-being and natural ecosystems. Cognitive blindspots, such as the "group-think" that arises out of persistent gendered, racial, and ethnic homogeneity present a major bottleneck to change. This is particularly true in the finance and investment sectors; for example, in the U.S. investment industry, leaders still generally do not appear to believe that a diversity dividend exists and have not accelerated efforts to widen the racial, gender, and economic status breadth of their talent pools.[5] As a result, finance and investment firms have truncated processes of innovation and limited problem-solving capabilities. By including a focus on behavioral and psychological features of capital markets, the Triple B framework adds explanatory and prescriptive power. Work along these lines is already taking place—Illumen Capital is a prominent example of an investment company that has embraced removing biases and blindspots as central to their business model.[6]

Blended finance, as the final component of this framework, is defined as an investment strategy that deploys financial capital in combination with other forms of capital—intellectual, political, social, cultural, network, and relationship—through the application of systematic processes. The strategy aims to produce an optimal level of beneficial services from assets, recognizing that these may be held either by individual or collective owners.

A distinct advantage of the Triple B framework approach, and in particular its definition of blended finance, is that it allows for consideration and remediation of settings where business and capital market ecosystems are weak. In such contexts, nonfinancial forms of capital may even be more important than financial capital, and injections of knowledge capital should be sequenced first. Under these circumstances, catalysts and activators will be required to play critical roles. Ecosystem builders deploying nonfinancial forms of capital help to align the supply-and-demand side of capital markets and reduce friction in the supply chain response. Individual business champions, ecosystem builders, and facilitating institutions are a critical priority. Our transformation agenda suggests that this deserves much more attention, and its absence explains the persistent gap in SDG financing.

A particularly important aspect of a project to facilitate human flourishing will be to include considerations of the effects of human beings on natural capital.[7] We note there have been strides in this direction—for example by taking into account the negative effects of human beings on our planet (anthropomorphic climate change) and increasing the use of tools and techniques to derive benefits from natural capital (e.g., blue/green bonds, coastal zone and conservation finance, funds specializing in renewable energy, regenerative systems, and circular economies). The Triple B framework has been applied in this arena.

Focus on Dignity and Well-Being

As part of the agenda proposed in this volume, we recommend moving in the direction of centering upon human dignity and flourishing rather than defaulting upon reliance on market forces to deliver benefits indirectly through distribution mechanisms. The contributions of philosophers Andersson and Richards (2015), Richards and Andersson (2021), and Lindner (2012, 2020) and their work that focuses on redirecting policy from individual market-based employment opportunities and livelihoods are particularly salient. This work, based on critical realism, provides a radical set of propositions for directly addressing humans' innate needs for connection, belonging, and dignity (Richards and Andersson 2021). In this schema of unbounded organizing, business and individual entrepreneurs seek to maximize opportunities to facilitate and improve human well-being. Within such a gestalt, a project between business and other interest groups in society would completely decenter profit and surplus maximization as the overriding goal.

Restructuring of Economic Systems

The logic of the prevailing economic system produces substantial wealth and positive livelihoods for the few at the expense of increasing inequality and environmental degradation. Late-stage capitalism is characterized by systemic exclusion and injustice; therefore, without a fundamental recalibration of the purpose and nature of economic systems, and a reckoning with the limitations of late-stage capitalism, the full spectrum flourishing envisaged here will not be possible. This concern for restructuring an economic system that (re)produces inequality on a scale that has steadily increased over recent decades is shared and growing. For example, the Green Economy Coalition addresses the negative effects of late-stage capitalism on humans, other species, and the planet.[8] Others like Oxfam International and other INGOs have advocated for shifting the nature and purpose of capitalism. At the other end of the spectrum, major investment firms and the World Economic Forum have argued for a shift in capitalism as opposed to a root-and-branch restructuring of the economic system itself.[9] We pick this up in the next section.

ECOSYSTEM FOR SUCCESS

The aforementioned five levers of transformation proceed at multiple levels: the individual, the organizational, and the broader society. The agenda is nested in culture and institutions that provide an ecosystem for success.

At the individual level, the first step involves heightened awareness to fully understand one's connection with the larger ecosystem of which one is a part; in order for systems to change, there must first be a shift in individual awareness and consciousness. While we have witnessed many changes in how mainstream discussions within the business community have evolved over recent decades, they are rooted in the reality of growing numbers of individual business people coming to recognize the importance of moving from success in business to purpose in the world and the global community.

Embedded within certain Buddhist and Asian traditions is the notion of the illusion of separation, by which is meant embracing an awareness that a focus upon the individual (whether a person or company) is flawed. Within those same traditions is the idea that an individual may not achieve nirvana (or, in Christian traditions, salvation) in the absence of any other individual, or by extension his/her community, attaining its next level of nirvana, salvation, or heightened consciousness. Such focus on human existence as a collective is a prominent feature of African cosmology, known in written representations as Ubuntu.[10] Various Western authors (indeed, philosophical and religious traditions) have explored this insight, but the importance of such a shift in the individual awareness of today's business and community leaders is central to the possibility of achieving future success.[11]

At an organizational level, business exists in engagement with other interest groups within a single country, which in turn exists within wider regional and global ecosystems. In 2020, there appears to have been an important inflection point globally concerning the mental model that applies to the purpose of business.[12] These developments have been greeted with great optimism regarding how stakeholders (often defined as workers, consumers, citizens, and the planet itself) might benefit from business, while not sacrificing a focus on financial returns. It remains to be seen how the issue of pecuniary benefits in the form of ownership and profit distribution will play out in this context. We are more sanguine about this trend, because many features of business as an institution have remained unaltered.

Our critical reading suggests that transformation needs to embrace an engagement with business's history of exploitation through extractive practices that draw value from the Earth and communities (largely in the Global South) for the benefit of a small set of shareholders (historically largely located in the Global North). Repositioning business is therefore nontrivial and will require much more than the exhortations of influential actors. Business leaders will need to transcend managerialism and rhetoric using evidence-based approaches, reconfigured incentives, and a shift in mental models to produce the desired change.

Moving to action to transcend the performative will require a reckoning with the past and the blind spots of the current mental model and an intentional embrace of alternatives. Business leaders should demonstrate a willingness to change the fabric of their organizations because it means their betterment. Boards and leadership teams must include persons from diverse backgrounds and subject area expertise in fields that are required to tackle the crises facing humanity. We must see transparency in all aspects of business operation, including compensation and adherence to rules that aim to reward performance rather than validate status. Businesses will need to become truly accountable, moving beyond gestures intended to draw attention in a news cycle and social media rather than aiming for any long-term changes.

These changes and the aforementioned personal transformations will be extremely challenging as they will disrupt existing systems of privilege and require trust and the development of new relationships across communities, generations, gender, and race. These are difficult journeys to undertake and require guides and tools, champions, and unequivocal and principled leadership. This is a whole of society effort, rather than one for business leaders acting on their own.

CONCLUSION

Building our common future will require the largest businesses in the world and their most influential voices to be convinced of the benefits of a different operating status quo. This chapter has only begun this conversation. Because of the power of size and the dominance of the prevailing mental models, it will take a long-term program of exploration and intentional engagement for change to be embedded. Influential business leaders will need to seek out examples of human flourishing outside of their own cultures and geographies by widening the solution space; they will need to, with the help of trusted guides, engage deeply with entrenched blind spots and to contemplate the negative consequences of not making the changes outlined here. Shaping an ethical and just future will require new approaches. When applied by practitioners, our proposed mapping of key issues may help reduce bottlenecks, illuminate blind spots, and mobilize capital. We call on the readers of this volume to join us in this movement of transforming business by extending our frames of reference and a joint reimagining of what constitutes value and purpose.

NOTES

1. Critical management studies (CMS) as a distinct field has developed to address the lacunae in the discipline of management. Interested readers are referred to Adler, Forbes, and Willmott 2007; Adler 2008; Ruggunan 2016; and Faria, Ibarra-Colado, and Guedes 2010.

2. The Triple B© framework provides the conceptual guidance for the work of Resilience Capital Ventures in its capital raising, advisory, and advocacy work. See Marcelle 2021; Marcelle 2020a.

3. For more on this history and these concepts, please see free eBook and readers guide formats at Emerson 2018.

4. Zinica Group, https://www.zinica.com/; Bitt, https://www.bitt.com/.

5. Data on the U.S. investing industry found in an empirically robust study funded by the Knight Foundation (Lerner et al. 2019) and an oft-cited study on how race influences professional investors' financial judgments by leading Stanford scholars (Lyons-Padilla et al. 2019). A more recent account of widespread racial discrimination often accompanied by sexual harassment is Holgado 2020. In early 2021, the U.S. Senate pushed back at proposals to include proactive consider-ations of diversity in the investment industry, arguing against market leaders that diversity would not enhance financial performance. This recent empirical study on diversity and resistance to change in corporate settings is Prieto and Phipps 2021.

6. Illumen Capital, https://www.illumencapital.com/.

7. Marcelle 2021. Triple B framework has been applied to understanding mobilization of capital for the transition to green economies.

8. A global movement for green and fair economies. Green Economy Coalition, https://www.greeneconomycoalition.org/.

9. Oxfam International, https://www.oxfam.org/en; and World Economic Forum, https://www.weforum.org.

10. These pieces provide philosophical discussion of the historical develop-ment of the Ubuntu Discourse in Southern Africa (Gade 2011), the application of these principles in nation building (Tutu 2000), and in management (Khomba 2011, chapter 4: The African UBUNTU Philosophy).

11. There is both a historic and contemporary body of literature exploring these ideas in greater depth, including Emerson 2018; Hutchins 2014; and Wheatley 2006.

12. Influential proponents of shifts in business include Larry Fink of Blackstone, one of the world's largest investment firms (2020, 2021); Klaus Schwab of
the World Economic Forum (WEF) (2017, 2021), and the Business Roundtable
(2018).

REFERENCES

Adler, Paul S. 2008. "CMS: Resist the Three Complacencies!" *Organization* 15,
no. 6: 925. https://doi.org/10.1177/1350508408097912.
Adler, Paul S., Linda C. Forbes, and Hugh Willmott, 2007. "3 Critical Manage-
ment Studies." *Academy of Management Annals* 1, no. 1: 119–79. https://doi.org
/10.5465/078559808.
Andersson, Gavin, and Howard Richards. 2015. *Unbounded Organizing in
Community.* Dörzbach, Germany: Dignity Press.
Business Roundtable. 2018. "Embracing Sustainability Challenge." Accessed
May 16, 2021. https://www.businessroundtable.org/policy-perspectives
/energy-environment/sustainability.
Crenshaw, Kimberlé. 1989. "Demarginalizing the Intersection of Race and Sex:
A Black Feminist Critique of Antidiscrimination Doctrine, Feminist Theory
and Antiracist Politics." *University of Chicago Legal Forum* 1989, no. 1: 139.
Emerson, Jed. 2018. *The Purpose of Capital: Elements of Impact, Financial Flows,
and Natural Being.* San Francisco, CA: Blended Value Group Press.
Faria, Alex, Eduardo Ibarra-Colado, and Ana Guedes. 2010. "Internationaliza-
tion of Management, Neoliberalism and the Latin America Challenge." *Critical Perspectives on International Business* 6 (2–3): 97–115. http://doi.org/10.1108
/17422041011049932.
Fink, Larry. 2020. "BlackRock's 2020 Letter to Clients." BlackRock. https://
www.blackrock.com/corporate/investor-relations/2020-blackrock-client
-letter.
Fink, Larry. 2021. "Net Zero: A Fiduciary Approach." BlackRock. https://www
.blackrock.com/corporate/investor-relations/blackrock-client-letter.
Gade, Christian B. 2011. "The Historical Development of the Written Discourses
on Ubuntu." *South African Journal of Philosophy* 30, no. 3: 303–29. https://
doi.org/10.4314/sajpem.v30i3.69578.
Holgado, Ray. 2020. "Performative Philanthropy and the Cost of Silence."
NCRP's Journal (November). https://bjn9t2lhlni2dhd5hvym7llj-wpengine
.netdna-ssl.com/wp-content/uploads/2020/11/RP-Nov2020-Holgado.pdf.
Hutchins, Giles. 2014. *Illusion of Separation: Exploring the Cause of our Current
Crises.* Edinburgh: Floris Books.

Khomba, James K. 2011. "Redesigning the Balanced Scorecard Model: An African Perspective: The African UBUNTU Philosophy." PhD dissertation, University of Pretoria. UPSpace Institutional Repository.

Lerner, Josh, Ann Leamon, Richard Sessa, Rahat Dewan, and Samuel Holt. 2019. "2018 Diverse Asset Management Firm Assessment. Final Report." Bella Private Markets, January. https://naicperformancesurvey.com/wp-content /uploads/2019/10/2018-DiverseAssetManagementFirmAssessment.pdf.

Lindner, Evelin. 2012. *A Dignity Economy: Creating an Economy That Serves Human Dignity and Preserves Our Planet*. Oslo: Dignity Press.

Lindner, Evelin. 2020. "From Humiliation to Dignity: For a Future of Global Solidarity: The Corona Pandemic as an Opportunity." https://humiliation studies.org/documents/evelin/FromHumiliationtoDignityCorona2020.pdf.

Lorde, Audre. 1984. "The Master's Tools Will Never Dismantle the Master's House." In *Sister Outsider: Essays and Speeches*, 110–14. Toronto: Crossing Press.

Lyons-Padilla, Sarah, Hazel R. Markus, Ashby Monk, Sid Radhakrishna, Radhika Shah, Norris A. "Daryn" Dodson, and Jennifer L. Eberhardt. 2019. "Race Influences Professional Investors' Financial Judgments." *Proceedings of the National Academy of Sciences* 116, no. 35: 17225–30. https://doi.org/10.1073 /pnas.1822052116.

Marcelle, Gillian M. 2017. "Science, Technology and Innovation Policy That Is Responsive to Innovation Performers." In *Research Handbook on Innovation Governance for Emerging Economies*, edited by Stefan Kuhlmann and Gonzalo Ordonez-Matamoros, 59–86. Northampton, MA: Edward Elgar Publishing.

Marcelle, Gillian M. 2020a. "Mobilizing All Forms of Capital." Medium, October 11. https://medium.com/@gillianmarcelle/mobilizing-all-forms-of -capital-for-sustainable-development-c3e08bff6380.

Marcelle, Gillian M. 2020b. "Innovation Possibilities in Times of Crisis." Resilience Capital Ventures, April. https://www.resiliencecapitalventures .com/thought-leadership/innovation-possibilities-in-time-of-crisis.

Marcelle, Gillian M. 2021. "Bottlenecks, Blind Spots and Blended Finance: Towards a New Financing Framework for People and Nature." Green Economy Coalition, March 22. https://www.greeneconomycoalition.org /news-and-resources/bottlenecks-blind-spots-and-blended-finance.

North, Douglass C. 1992. "Institutions and Economic Theory." *American Economist* 36, no. 1: 3–6. https://journals.sagepub.com/doi/10.1177 /056943459203600101.

Persky, Joseph. 1995. "The Ethology of Homo Economicus." *Journal of Economic Perspectives* 9, no. 2: 221–31. https://doi.org/10.1257/jep.9.2.221.

Prieto, Leon C., and Simone T. A. Phipps. 2021. "Reconfigure Your Board to Boost Cooperative Advantage." *MIT Sloan Management Review*, February 16. https://sloanreview.mit.edu/article/reconfigure-your-board-to-boost -cooperative-advantage/.

Richards, Howard, and Gavin Andersson. 2021 forthcoming. *Economic Theory and Community Development*. Oslo: Dignity Press.

Ruggunan, Shaun D. 2016. "Decolonising Management Studies: A Love Story." *Acta Commercii* 16, no. 2, 103–38. http://dx.doi.org/lo.4102/ac.v16i2.412.

Schwab, Klaus. 2017. *The Fourth Industrial Revolution*. Sydney: Currency.

Schwab, Klaus, and Peter Vanham. 2021. *Stakeholder Capitalism: A Global Economy That Works for Progress, People and Planet*. Malden, MA: Wiley.

Tutu, Desmond. 2000. *No Future without Forgiveness*. London: Ebury Publishing.

Wheatley, Margaret. 2006. *Leadership and the New Science: Discovering Order in a Chaotic World*. San Francisco: Berrett-Koehler Publishers.

12

The Problem with Removing Humanity from Business Models

ROGER L. MARTIN

ONE FOR THE BAFFLING ITEMS BIN

In August 1984, I got a call from a friend to let me know he had just fired my youngest brother about three weeks before the planned end of his summer job doing research work for my friend's startup consulting company. At the end of the call, in what appeared to be a bid to reassure me, he told me, "This isn't personal; it's business." The attempted reassurance baffled me. Apparently, I was supposed to feel better that it wasn't "personal." As with many such things, I simply file them away in the back of my brain waiting for sense to emerge. Over three decades later, I realized that my friend was using a particular form of flawed model found frequently in business. In addition, I realized that the world of business needs to understand the structure of that flaw as well as ways to avoid falling prey to it.

But before I get into the flaw and protections against it, a little background is in order. I met my friend at business school. After he graduated, he cofounded a business and let me know he needed a researcher for the summer of 1984. By happy coincidence, my youngest brother had just finished his junior year at college and wanted to stay in that city for the summer. I served as matchmaker, and my brother agreed to a 12-week stint as a research assistant for my friend's company. The compensation centered around free board for my brother in the attic space of a big, old house that my friend lived in, worked out of, and was renovating in stages. He was paid a modest wage that took into account the free accommodation.

My friend's justification for the termination was the poor quality of my brother's work, which didn't seem entirely plausible. My brother was a top student at his Ivy League school, diligent enough in his work to be accepted a few months later into a top-tier PhD program. He graduated from that program and in due course wrote a book that made him a star in the field and has enjoyed a long career as a chaired professor at an Ivy League University, hardly the career of a dummy or slacker!

I immediately checked on the situation with my brother, and his story was that my friend had decided that he wanted to start the renovation of my brother's floor with about three weeks to go in the agreed-upon tenure and asked my brother to vacate immediately. My brother refused, arguing that my friend had no right to unilaterally change their agreement in a way that dramatically inconvenienced him. In response, my friend fired him.

I will never know for certain which story is true. But it struck me as incredibly strange that my friend could imagine that I would treat the matter as 100 percent business and not personal. For what is business if not a series of interactions between persons? It is personal when someone fires your kid brother—whether for really good or somewhat dubious reasons. Can one hypothetically get beyond the personal? Certainly. But to declare the matter as devoid of a personal dimension was sufficiently odd that I just filed it away in my brain's "baffling items" bin.

HOW TO BUILD A FLAWED MANAGEMENT MODEL

Fast forward 27 years to 2011. I had just published my book, *Fixing the Game,*[1] on the shortcomings of a singular focus on shareholder value maximization. In the book, I argue that it is both ineffective, in that pursuit of it doesn't enhance the chance of it happening, and it creates untold collateral damage in the form of sacrificing employees and customers, plus causing executives to behave in ways that range from unbecoming to unethical to illegal.

Happily, the subsequent decade saw the crumbling of the hegemony of the model of shareholder value maximization. Even early proponent, GE former CEO Jack Welch, denounced it as "the dumbest idea in the world."[2] But its demise raised the questions: How does a dumb management model hold such sway for so long? And, do you have to endure decades of a bad management model before shedding it?

Then it hit me—my friend had the answer way back in 1984. The very best way to create a management model that is plausible enough to take hold but is doomed to the eventual discovery of its ineffectiveness is to create a separation between business and humanity by stripping humanity out of business. Just as my friend had attempted with his logic that "this isn't personal; it's business." This has the effect of simplifying the natural complexities of life, getting rid of the intangible, immeasurable properties of the situation. While it may feel comforting to those, like my friend, performing the simplification, it has its costs.

The case for the singular corporate focus in shareholder value maximization provides an excellent example of how to build a flawed management model in this way. Arguably, that the model building process started with Milton Friedman's seminal 1970 article, "The Social Responsibility of Business is to Increase Its Profits."[3] He framed a model cleverly and intuitively: the business of business is business. Businesses should work to maximize their profits and then ship the resultant dividends to the shareholders—who, after all, own the company—and then if any shareholders want to give their dividends to charity, it is up to them. It is a clever if not distortive construction that takes the humanity out of the lives of business executives. They shouldn't care about the less fortunate, or their community, or anything but making profits: they are unidimensional businesspeople.

The logic of Friedman's model was built upon by Michael Jensen and William Meckling in their influential 1976 article on agency theory, "Theory of the Firm: Managerial Behavior, Agency Costs and Ownership Structure."[4] The article reinforced the logic of the Friedman model that business executives work for shareholders and laid out the dangers that stem from executives deviating from pure service to shareholders—the agency costs to which the title refers.

Interestingly, Jensen and Meckling bring humanity back into the argument, explicitly recognizing the "self-control problems" of executives. However, the task was not to accept humanity but to attempt to stomp it out. The theory enhancement that followed out of this seminal paper was that shareholders could and should bribe executives to suppress their humanity and purely serve shareholder interests by aligning them through the power of stock-based compensation. Proponents used yet another clever logical gambit: that way if shareholders do better, executives do better. As I document in *Fixing the Game,* it turns out not to be the case in practice; executives do well regardless of how well shareholders do.

Jensen would go on to build further on the argument for taking humanity out of business. In his 2005 article, "Value Maximization, Stakeholder Theory, and the Corporate Objective Function,"[5] he argued that without a singular objective function, executives are incapable of making intelligent decisions. The logic was imported from optimization theory, which requires a singular objective function to use a technique like linear programming to optimize a production operation, such as an oil refinery.

Across 31 years, the original logic was built upon to create a plausible if not compelling sounding theory. Owners should be charitable with their dividends and should not have their personal charitable decisions usurped by the executives who run the companies that they own. To encourage executive compliance, provide management with powerful stock-based compensation incentives. And the singular focus on shareholder value maximization is necessary to prevent executives from lapsing into confusion as to how to make daily decisions.

The logic hangs together beautifully, and its strength as an argument is boosted by taking people out of it: managers should be willing to manage for shareholders and not care about anything else; and if they attempt anything else, you can bribe them with stock-based compensation to do so. It is critical to persuade them to adopt such nonhuman compliant behavior because if they are allowed to think independently, they will become confused and incompetent decision makers. Separating humanity is conducive to strengthening the argument. It is a nifty rhetorical sleight of hand. Without humanity, executives influenced by stock-based compensation will maintain the single-minded and clarifying focus on shareholder-value maximization, which is what the shareholders deserve.

But human beings don't spend their lives happily toiling for nameless, faceless people called shareholders, focusing solely on maximizing their benefit because some theory says they should. It is especially the case if those shareholders come and go as they please, selling their shares without giving a rationale or notice. In addition, for most shareholders, the name on the stock register isn't the name of the shareholder but rather of a fiduciary (e.g., Fidelity, Black-Rock) acting on behalf of the real and hidden shareholder. Humans aren't motivated by such an abstract and distant theoretical beneficiary.

While a linear program may be incapable of spitting out a solution unless it has a singular objective function, actual humans spend their entire lives balancing conflicting concerns—between home life and work life, between the short term and long term, between work and leisure, between risk and certainty. They aren't incapacitated by a complex objective function. That is, in fact, a human condition. We have medical terms for human beings who adopt a singular focus and ignore everything else. We call it a pathology with names like obsessive-compulsive disorder (OCD) or hyperfocus, a subcondition of attention deficit hyperactivity disorder (ADHD).

In summary, it helps to make a business model more compelling if humanity is taken out of the model without that fact being explicitly noticed. In this narrow and artificial context, the business model can seem very appealing. But the fact that humanity has been taken out of the model should be a warning sign that the model is going to end badly. In the end, humanity will intervene because the business models involve humans.

EXAMPLES OF BUSINESS MODELS FATALLY FLAWED
BY THE REMOVAL OF HUMANITY

Historically, there have been numerous business models that have been constructed with a central feature being the removal of humanity from them—and all have or will end badly for the world. They include slavery, the assembly line, at-will work, and artificial intelligence.

American Plantation Slavery

Arguably the most nefarious business model in history was slavery, with American slavery being a particularly heinous representation. Of course, it was partially a social model—domestic slaves. But it was substantially a business model in that slaves were inexpensive and compliant labor primarily for southern U.S. plantation farming, beginning in the seventeenth century. The logic of the model only held up to the extent that slaves were not considered human—but rather beasts of burden. That argument ignored that they had language, culture, families, social structures, villages, hopes for their children, and so on. But those human features were removed from the logic of the model to buttress an otherwise untenably depraved model that stood against everything for which the American Constitution stands. In the end, it took a Civil War to extinguish this tragic model.

Like all business models that remove humanity, it had horrible consequences for its victims that will be felt for centuries. These consequences could have been predicted from the onset because the core model removed humanity from the equation to make the flawed logic appear to hold up.

The Assembly Line

Henry Ford was reputed to have exclaimed: "Why is it every time I ask for a pair of hands, they come with a brain attached?" In doing so, he was complaining about humanity creeping back into his business model that required its removal. While the assembly line innovation, which launched with Model T production in 1913, produced a step-function improvement in manufacturing productivity, it required human beings to carry out one simple rote physical task repeatedly for every minute of their shift, each shift every day, every day of the week, every week of the year.[6] For that, Henry Ford wished that they didn't have brains because all he wanted was them to use their hands as non-human robots.

In due course, Ford would get his wish because the modern assembly line features robots often more prominently than humans. But in the meantime, the assembly line created strife between unhappy workers and their employers and severe quality problems spurred by the alienation they felt,[7] a feeling that was captured perceptively and sorrowfully in the Charlie Chaplin classic *Modern Times*.

The assembly line model had a logic that was strong enough to make it a feature of modern times. But the flaw that has dogged its entire existence is that it removed humanity from the equation to make it function.

At-Will Work

In all 50 U.S. states, employment is governed by the legal construct of at-will work, which means that an employer can terminate an employee for any reason without warning and dates from the late nineteenth century.[8] For employers, this is an extremely attractive business model, which affords them flexibility and control. Under at-will, labor is an entirely variable cost, and the employer has an unrestricted ability to control behavior due to the imminent threat of termination.

However, the attractiveness is secured by the removal of humanity from the model. In human relationships, people don't have productive relationships for long periods that they terminate without providing a reason and without any warning. Of course, relationships end. But in normal human relationships, there are warnings and attempts to overcome problems before the severing of a relationship. This would particularly be the case if one member of the relationship depended on the other in some important way—for example, for economic livelihood. If a person treated relationships as "at will," the person would be considered pathologically antisocial. It is not consistent with humanity.

Has at-will employment crumbled yet as a business model? No. But I would argue that it is a significant part of the fundamental dissatisfaction of average American workers with their jobs and their employers.

Artificial Intelligence/Machine Learning/Data Analytics

Perhaps the newest class of nonhuman business model is artificial intelligence (AI) or its friends, machine learning and data analytics. Here the model is explicitly nonhuman. The theory is that better decisions will be forthcoming if the decisions exclude human beings from the decision-making process, allowing machines to make the decisions based on algorithms. Again, once humanity is taken out, it sounds like a plausible if not compelling model. Machines making decisions strictly on the data will be faster, more accurate, and more unbiased than human beings.

We will have to wait for a while to make a robust evaluation of the effectiveness of the business model of using AI to make decisions because the track record isn't nearly long enough. But I am willing to predict here and now that this business model will end badly, like plantation slavery, the assembly line, and at-will work because humanity will eventually undermine systems devoid of humanity.

THE HUMAN FEATURES OF SUSTAINABLE MODELS

How then would one be able to make a judgment in advance as to whether a model is sufficiently infused with humanity to be sustainable over time? I cannot presume at this point in my study of the subject to have a comprehensive list of features and would invite further ideas. But to start the dialogue, I would propose any such model would be built on the foundation of these three principles.

Motivation Is Neither Unidimensional nor Linear

Many nonhuman things are unidimensional and linear. There is a one-to-one relationship between cause and effect, and the response is generally of consistent magnitude. If one presses the gas pedal of a car, it speeds up. If the pedal is pushed a bit, it speeds up a bit; if pressed a lot, it speeds up a lot. Such simple and unidimensional nonhuman relationships can cause one to think that life is and should be that way.

But it simply does not hold for humans. For example, monetary compensation is only one of many aspects of motivation. And the value of another increment of monetary compensation is different under different circumstances. It might be worth a lot more if it represents the funding necessary to expand the home to accommodate the arrival of a second child than if it is simply going to be added to a burgeoning investment account.

The unusual partner compensation model of legendary New York law firm Cravath, Swaine & Moore recognizes this principle. Most of its competitors in the highly competitive, dog-eat-dog world of high-end corporate legal services in New York City pay partners explicitly for performance. More billings and more clients brought to the firm are rewarded with more compensation for the partner responsible—or at least declared to be responsible. That, holds the model, is because the firm will perform better if each partner has the compensation incentive to bill more and sell more; it is simple and clear.

At Cravath, partner compensation is entirely "lockstep," which means that a partner's compensation is determined entirely based on tenure as a partner—that is, all seventh-year partners earn the same compensation regardless of billings or client sales. Why give up entirely the incentive to do two things that are associated with law firm prosperity—selling clients and billing hours? Isn't that crazy? No. Cravath believes that cooperation among partners is the key to the best client service, which in turn is the key to keeping existing clients and earning new ones. And firm success combined with a pleasant and cooperative work environment is what will attract and retain the best partners. Cravath believes that happiness and satisfaction are socially constructed, as do I. Being a valued member of a community that you value and is valued by those outside the community is the "trinity of happiness."[9] For Cravath, motivation is neither unidimensional nor linear, and its business model has been stably sustainable and prosperous for a long time with no let-up in sight.

Relationships Cannot Be Fully Quantified

There is an inexorable drive to quantify every aspect of business, and that includes relationships among members of a given system. Business attempts to quantify the lifetime value of a customer based on purchases per period, profit per purchase, and length of expected times as a customer. Law firms, excluding Cravath, attempt to quantify the value of a partner based on hours billed and revenues brought to the firm.

None of these is a terrible thing to try. It is important in business life to quantify that which can be reduced to quantities. But it is a mistake to believe that the entirety of a relationship with another human being can be quantified. Can you quantify the value or intensity of your love for your spouse, children, or parents? Of course not. Relationships have qualities associated with them as well as quantities. One can measure the quantities involved—for example, this customer has been with us for 17 years. But for the qualities, they can't be measured, only appreciated. For example, in a pinch, this customer will tend to show flexibility and cooperation, more like a friend than a party to a contract.

There Is No Antidote for Unfairness

Many business models assume that they can be unfair to humans in the system in question and still be sustainable. For example, health plans ask members to pay premiums as if they will reimburse members for their covered medical expenses, but then they put so many roadblocks in the way of reimbursement that members give up in disgust. Banks charge hidden fees on all sorts of financial products and point to the fine print that was disclosed but never understood. Companies pay different wages for identical work and think those being paid less—especially women and minorities—will "understand." Centibillionaire owners think it will work out just fine to pay their workers less than a living wage.

But the distaste for unfairness runs deep. This is even the case with capuchin monkeys as demonstrated in a famous experiment where the animals are trained to perform a simple task—returning a small stone to their trainer in exchange for a slice of cucumber, a food they find sufficiently delicious to cause them to contentedly perform the task. But cucumber pales in comparison to grapes, their favorite food. In the experiment, two well-trained monkeys are placed in side-by-side cages. The first monkey is given the task and receives the reward, which it eats happily. The second monkey is given the same task and receives a grape instead of a cucumber slice. The researcher returns to the first monkey who performs the task immediately, undoubtedly believing that the reward ante has been upped to a grape. When the researcher gives the monkey another cucumber slice, the monkey tosses it back at the researcher in anger—and does so in repeated trials with increasing agitation.[10]

There is simply no antidote for unfairness. The hatred runs too deep. What was previously a delicious slice of cucumber became a slap in the face. It is unsustainable. If the business model required that first monkey to perform the task, it would eventually collapse in the face of unfairness. In the cases above, massive hatred from consumers/workers brings government regulation to bear to end the unfair business models. But the consumers will never love their provider/employer when they know the unfairness was reduced or eliminated only through government fiat. In this way, it is typically synergy between citizens and government that brings down unfair business models. It is hard for citizens to make fundamental changes on their own, and governments are less likely to prioritize action without pressure from citizens.

CONCLUSION

If humanity has been removed from a business model, it might work for a while, but it will be doomed to failure as the humans involved in it come to understand the missing humanity and feel its counterproductive impacts. Look instead for signs that humanity is centrally embedded in a business model. Is the motivation assumed in the model multidimensional and nonlinear? Does it assume that relationships have important qualities along with measurable quantitative aspects? Does it pay attention to fundamental fairness to all the parties involved in the business model? If it has these human features, it has a chance of being sustainable. Of course, this is not an all-or-nothing question. There will always be degrees of humanity in any model. Think of humanity as laying in the eyes of the participant. If you are a participant in a business model, does the model feel sufficiently human overall for you to participate in it enthusiastically? If it does, then dive in. If it doesn't, it is your job to work to make it human enough to warrant your and others' participation.

To return for a moment to my friend, he has enjoyed a spectacularly successful professional career. He plies his professional trade as well as anyone in the world. However, the only time he was given a chance to lead an organization rather than just operate as a professional, he failed quickly and absolutely. I believe the reason was that his people didn't want to work for a leader who attempted to remove humanity from the way their business operated. While it is one small example, it both inspired me and provides a warning of the unsustainability of nonhuman business models.

NOTES

1. Roger L. Martin, *Fixing the Game: Bubbles, Crashes and What Capitalism Can Learn from the NFL* (Boston: Harvard Business Review Press, 2011).

2. Francesco Guerrera, "Welch Condemns Share Price Focus," *Financial Times*, March 12, 2009.

3. Milton Friedman, "The Social Responsibility of Business Is to Increase Its Profits," *New York Times Magazine*, September 13, 1970, 122–26.

4. Michael C. Jensen and William H. Meckling, "Theory of the Firm: Managerial Behavior, Agency Costs and Ownership Structure," *Journal of Financial Economics* 3, no. 4 (October 1976): 305–60.

5. Michael C. Jensen, "Value Maximization, Stakeholder Theory, and the Corporate Objective Function," *Journal of Applied Corporate Finance* 14, no. 3 (April 11, 2005): 8–21, https://doi.org/10.1111/j.1745-6622.2001.tb00434.x.

6. Tony Swan, "Ford's Assembly Line Turns 100: How It Really Put the World on Wheels," *Car & Driver*, April 30, 2013.

7. Bob Blauner, *Alienation and Freedom: The Factory Worker and His Industry* (Chicago: University of Chicago Press, 1964).

8. Horace Gay Wood, *A Treatise on the Law of Master and Servant* (Albany, NY: J. D. Parsons, 1877).

9. Roger L. Martin, "The Power of Happiness," *Rotman Magazine*, Spring/Summer 2005, 5–9.

10. Frans de Waal, "Two Monkeys Were Paid Unequally: Excerpt from Frans de Waal's TED Talk," TED Blog Video, April 4, 2013, YouTube video, 2:43, https://www.youtube.com/watch?v=meiU6TxysCg.

PART
THREE

THE ULTIMATE ADVANTAGE:
A LEADERSHIP REVOLUTION THAT
IS CHANGING EVERYTHING

13

Business as an Agent of World Benefit

The Role of Virtuousness

KIM CAMERON

RECENT EVENTS INCLUDING earthquakes, floods, tornadoes, cyberattacks, ethical lapses, wildfires, and the worldwide COVID-19 pandemic have created a confluence of challenges that most of us have not experienced in our lifetimes. Racial injustice, economic devastation, and loss of life have elevated our collective consciousness regarding what is going wrong in our world. Contention, outrage, and violence have become widespread. Extensive economic, emotional, and health effects have changed normal daily activities, relationships, institutions, and even values. The world appears to be in commotion.

In such conditions, when it is natural to focus on the negative, on problems, on disruptions, and on the uncomfortable, the momentum often leads toward sinking ever further into darkness and divisiveness. So how might businesses create world benefits in this kind of environment? How might the positive take precedence over the negative?

My research has uncovered an alternative to this dismal downward motion. This alternative emerged after a decade of research on a wide variety of organizations that were downsizing, retrenching, facing a fiscal crisis, and experiencing high levels of trauma and ambiguity. An overwhelming number of those organizations deteriorated in performance as a result of their strategies for coping with those trying times. Productivity deteriorated, the quality deteriorated, morale deteriorated, trust and ethics deteriorated, and customer and employee loyalty deteriorated.

A few organizations, however, flourished after emerging from these difficult circumstances. In examining these few exceptions, I discovered that they were all characterized by what I refer to as virtuousness. They had institutionalized

virtuous practices such as compassion, forgiveness, dignity, kindness, gratitude, trustworthiness, and higher purpose in their cultures. Their leaders were
described in virtuous terms. Their leaders defied the negativity they faced and,
instead, focused on attributes and behaviors that represented the best of the
human condition and, subsequently, they produced extraordinarily positive
outcomes.

These findings motivated me to investigate how organizations, in general,
can succeed in trying times, how they can produce world benefit, and how
leadership can be developed to counter the negative momentum that predom-
inates in difficult circumstances. In the two decades following that initial research, abundant evidence (Cameron et al. 2011; Cameron and Spreitzer 2012)
has been produced demonstrating that virtuousness in organizations produces
outcomes that far exceed industry averages (e.g., profitability, productivity,
quality, innovation, customer loyalty, employee engagement). In addition, the
virtuousness of these organizations produces a positive impact on the broader
environment.

To explain what I mean by virtuousness and to illustrate its importance as
an agent of world benefit, I first discuss the concept of virtuousness and its
benefits, and then I provide some brief illustrations of its positive impact.

VIRTUOUS ASSUMPTIONS IN ORGANIZATIONS

Whereas studies have shown that virtuousness in organizations is associated
with a positive impact on bottom-line performance, its real importance is not
grounded in these instrumental outcomes. Rather, the key benefit of virtuousness is its association with ennobling behaviors, the excellence and essence of
humankind, the best of the human condition, and the highest aspirations of
humanity (Comte-Sponville 2001; Weiner 1993; Chapman and Galston 1992;
Dent 1984; MacIntyre 1984). These are the defining attributes and benefits of
virtuousness.

In trying times when momentum moves toward contention, dissension, and
dissolution, virtuousness in organizations is less a means to another more desirable outcome than the ultimate end itself. The value of virtuousness is not that
some other suitable outcomes can be produced for virtuousness to be valued.
Rather, virtuousness is its own reward. If the world was characterized by virtuousness, for example, no poverty would exist, no war would exist, everyone would
be well-educated, fairness would predominate, all individuals would flourish,
and the world would benefit irrespective of other bottom-line outcomes.

The intrinsic value of virtuousness in organizations can be explained by its four core assumptions—a *eudaemonic assumption,* an *inherent value assumption,* an *amplification assumption,* and a *fixed-point assumption* (Bright, Cameron, and Caza 2006; Cameron 2011; Cameron and Winn 2012).

The Eudaemonic Assumption

Virtuousness is based on the assumption that an inclination exists in all human beings toward moral goodness (Aristotle 1999; Dutton and Sonenshein 2007). Several authors have provided evidence that the human inclination toward virtuousness is inherent and evolutionarily developed (Tangney, Stuewig, and Mashek 2007; Miller 2007). Inherent virtuousness, or an inclination toward the best of the human condition, develops in the brain before the development of language. Studies of the human brain indicate that individuals appear to have a basic instinct toward morality and are organically inclined to be virtuous (Haight 2006; Hauser 2006; Pinker 1997). Krebs (1987) asserted that human beings are "genetically disposed" to acts of virtuousness from the time they are a few months old, and observing and experiencing virtuousness helps unlock the human predisposition toward behaving in ways that benefit others. Virtuous actions allow people to live together, pursue collective ends, and protect against those who endanger the social order. Virtuousness pursues the ultimate best—eudaemonism—rather than merely avoiding the negative or emphasizing the attainment of alternative material outcomes. Inherently, individuals strive to achieve the best of the human condition or, in other words, virtuousness.

Inherent Value Assumption

Virtuousness in pursuit of another more attractive outcome ceases by definition to be virtuous. If kindness toward employees is demonstrated, for example, solely to obtain a payback or an advantage (e.g., kindness is displayed only if people work harder), it ceases to be kindness and is, instead, manipulation. Virtuousness is associated with social betterment, but this betterment extends beyond mere self-interested advantage. Virtuousness creates social value that transcends the instrumental desires of the actor(s) (Aristotle 1999). Virtuous actions produce advantages to others in addition to, or even exclusive of, recognition, benefit, or advantage to the actor or the organization (Cawley, Martin, and Johnson 2000). Virtuous actions, by definition, produce good for all. If they do not, they are not virtuous.

Amplification Assumption

A third assumption is that virtuousness creates and fosters sustainable positive energy (Cameron 2021). Virtuousness is elevating and self-perpetuating, and it requires no external motivator for its pursuit. Because it is an ultimate end and an intrinsic attribute of human beings, virtuousness produces an elevating effect. That is, virtuousness is amplifying when it is experienced (George 1995).

Fredrickson and Joiner (2002) found evidence that observing virtuousness in others creates upward positive spirals. Compassion begets gratitude, gratitude motivates improved relationships, witnessing good deeds leads to elevation, elevation motivates prosocial behavior, and observing virtuousness fosters even more virtuousness (also see Algoe and Haight 2009; Maslow 1971; Hatch 1999; Sethi and Nicholson 2001). Studies reported by Cialdini (2000) and Asch (1952) support the idea that when people observe exemplary or virtuous behavior, their inclination is to follow suit.

Thus, observing virtuousness creates a self-reinforcing inclination toward more of the same. People never tire of or become satiated with virtuousness, unlike the acquisition of personal rewards or benefits. Thus, there cannot be too much virtuousness because it is self-perpetuating (Fredrickson 2009).

Fixed-Point Assumption

It is commonly acknowledged that the most dominant feature of the current environment is change and turbulence. Unfortunately, when everything is changing, it becomes impossible to manage change effectively (Cameron 2011). Without a stable, constant reference point, direction and progress become indeterminate.

Airplane piloting offers an instructive metaphor. Pilots with no visual or instrumentation contact with a fixed point are unable to navigate. Consider the last flight of John Kennedy Jr., who began flying his private plane up the New England coast at dusk. He lost sight of land and, when it grew dark, the horizon line as well. He lost his fixed point of reference, and the result was disorientation. He flew his plane into the ocean, likely without even knowing he was headed toward the water. He was unable to manage the continuously changing position of his airplane without a standard that remained unchanged.

The same disorientation afflicts individuals and organizations in situations where there are no unchanging referents. When nothing is stable—that is, an absence of fixed points, dependable principles, or universally accepted values—

individuals tend to make up their own rules (Weick and Sutcliffe 2001; Weick 1993). They decide for themselves what is real and what is appropriate based on criteria such as experience, immediate payoff, political expediency, popular polls, personal reward, and so on (March 1994).

Ethical standards, unfortunately, are not the same as virtuousness. Ethical standards often change over time and circumstance, as they are socially constructed. Hence, ethical guidelines serve as inadequate fixed points and may not always identify constant, universalistic standards across different contexts (Caza, Barker, and Cameron 2004; Cameron 2011). Consider segregation in public schools, for example, in which ethical standards have changed markedly between the 1960s and the present time. The same can be said of the ethics associated with financial transactions, accounting principles, environmental policies, sustainability, death, marriage, free speech, and many others.

Virtuousness, on the other hand, can serve as a fixed point because virtuousness represents what all people aspire to be at their best—goodness and nobility—and these aspirations are universal and unchanging in essentially all societies, cultures, religions, and generations (Peterson and Seligman 2004; Kidder 1994). Without virtuousness, it is difficult to identify unchanging fixed points by which to manage change. Thus, virtuousness in organizations can help organizations and societies effectively manage the turbulence and instability typical of the external environment. Virtuousness represents the unchanging standard by which to make decisions and take action.

VIRTUOUSNESS IN ORGANIZATIONS AND WORLD BENEFIT

A great deal of empirical evidence exists showing that organizations characterized by virtuous practices provide benefit to the world. For example, honesty, transcendent meaning, caring and altruistic behavior, gratitude, hope, empathy, love, and forgiveness, among other virtues, have been found to predict desired outcomes such as individuals' commitment, satisfaction, motivation, positive emotions, effort, physical health, and psychological health (Andersson, Giacalone, and Jurkiewicz 2007; Giacalone, Paul, and Jurkiewicz 2005; Fry, Vitucci, and Cedillo 2005; Kellett, Humphrey, and Sleeth 2006; Gittell et al. 2006; Luthans et al. 2007; Dutton et al. 2002; Grant 2007; Cameron, Bright, and Caza 2004; Snyder 1994; Sternberg 1998; Seligman 2002; Peterson and Bossio 1991; Harker and Keltner 2001; McCullough, Pargament, and Thoreson 2000; Emmons 1999). Individuals tend to flourish in the presence of virtuous practices.

For example, demonstrating the virtues of gratitude and humility are associated with enhanced cognitive processing of sensory information (McCraty 2002); highly ordered and coherent patterns in heart rhythms (Tiller, McCraty, and Atkinson 1996); increased efficiency of fluid exchange, filtration, and absorption between the capillaries and tissues (Langhorst, Schultz, and Lambertz 1984); improved health and increased longevity (Danner, Snowden, and Friesen 2001); cognitive flexibility and creativity (Isen 1987; Isen, Daubman, and Nowicki 1987); and heart rate variability, which approaches the highest levels possible when these virtuous states are experienced. In one study of patients with Stage B heart failure, half were asked to keep a daily gratitude journal, and after three months their hearts had healthier resting rates and showed significantly fewer biological signs that their heart disease was getting worse (Redwine, Henry, and Pung 2018).

The virtues of generosity and compassion also produce individual benefits. Older patients with high blood pressure, for example, were given $40 per week for three weeks. Half were instructed to spend the money on themselves, whereas the other half were instructed to spend the money on others (e.g., purchase a gift, donate to charity). Two years later, the blood pressure of giving-patients was significantly lower than the others, and the effects matched the effects of antihypertensive medication or physical exercise as prescribed therapies (Aknin et al. 2015; Whillans et al. 2016). In another study of older adults, those displaying generosity toward others had a 47 percent reduction in mortality risk (Okun, Yeung, and Brown 2013). A study of widows who had recently lost a spouse showed that those who provided instrumental support to others had no depression six months after their loss compared to substantial and lasting depression among those who merely received support but did not provide it. No "receiving-support" factors were positively correlated with an absence of depression, but "giving-support" factors were significantly correlated (Brown et al. 2002).

In addition, organizations are significantly affected when virtuous behavior is demonstrated. For example, Cameron and Caza (2002) and Cameron, Bright, and Caza (2004) conducted a series of studies in which indicators of virtuousness and organizational performance were assessed in businesses across sixteen industries (e.g., retail, automotive, consulting, health care, manufacturing, financial services, not-for-profit). All organizations in these studies had recently downsized so that the well-documented negative effects associated with downsizing were predictable. That is, most organizations engaged in downsizing and retrenchment and that experience turbulent and volatile environments regress in performance. Productivity, quality, morale, trust, and customer satisfaction all deteriorate (Cameron 1994, 1998; Cascio, Young, and Morris 1997).

In these studies, virtuousness scores in organizations were measured by employing a survey instrument assessing compassion, integrity, forgiveness, trust, and optimism. Organizations with higher virtuousness scores had significantly higher productivity, quality, customer retention, and lower employee turnover than other organizations. When controlling for factors such as size, industry, and amount of downsizing, organizations scoring higher in virtuousness were significantly more profitable compared to competitors, industry averages, stated goals, and past performance.

A different kind of study was conducted in the U.S. airline industry after the tragedy of September 11, 2001. This event generated circumstances for a time that mirrored those associated with the recent pandemic. The study investigated the relationships between the virtuousness of the downsizing strategies implemented in the airline companies and their financial performance (Gittell et al. 2006). Virtuousness in this study was defined as preserving human dignity, investing in human capital, and providing an environment in which employees' well-being was the clear priority.

Controlling for unionization, fuel-price hedging, and financial reserves, the study found that the correlation between the virtuousness of the downsizing strategy and financial return (as measured by stock price gains) was $p = .86$ in the first 12 months and $p = .79$ over the next five years, which is a high correlation. The company with the highest levels of virtuousness earned the highest level of financial return in the industry. Virtuousness and financial return were positively and significantly related over the next five years.

An additional study investigated causal relationships—the extent to which virtuousness in an organization produced these performance improvements, rather than the reverse causality (Cameron et al. 2011). The study examined 40 financial service organizations and another examined 30 health care organizations over multiple years to examine what happened to performance when virtuousness scores increased or decreased.

Virtuousness was measured by six dimensions: *caring* (people care for, are interested in, and maintain responsibility for one another as friends), *compassionate support* (people provide support for one another including kindness and compassion when others are struggling), *forgiveness* (people avoid blaming and forgive mistakes), *inspiration* (people inspire one another at work), *meaning* (the meaningfulness of the work is emphasized, and people are elevated and renewed by their work), and *respect, integrity,* and *gratitude* (people treat one another with respect and express appreciation for one another as well as trusting one another and maintaining integrity).

At the beginning of the study period, leaders of the financial services organizations had embarked on systematic efforts to incorporate virtuous practices into their corporate cultures. The performance outcomes of interest were employee turnover, organizational climate, and six financial performance measures, all of which were obtained from company records. Organizations that achieved higher levels of aggregated virtuousness scores also produced significantly higher financial performance, lower employee turnover, and better overall organizational climate one year later than did those organizations with lower virtuousness scores. Organizations that improved their virtuousness scores over two years generated better results in subsequent years than organizations that did not improve in virtuousness scores.

The irony in this research is that virtuousness does not require a visible, instrumental pay-off to be of worth. If observable, bottom-line impacts are not detected, however, attention to virtuousness usually becomes subservient to the very real pressures related to enhancing financial return and organizational value (Jensen 2002; Davis 2008). Few business leaders invest in practices or processes that do not produce higher returns to shareholders, profitability, productivity, and customer satisfaction. Without visible payoff, those with stewardship for organizational resources usually ignore virtuousness and consider it to be of little relevance to important stakeholders. It is often deemed touchy-feely, naïve, or Pollyanna-ish, so its bottom-line impact is not realized.

CONCLUSION

In considering how business can be a better contributor to world benefit, prioritizing virtuousness may be among the very best strategies to pursue. Virtuousness represents the finest of what humankind aspires to achieve, and virtuousness in organizations identifies universally accepted standards for what is best or good.

In addition, the implementation of virtuous practices in organizations produces desirable, excellent outcomes. These outcomes provide advantages for all constituencies rather than benefiting some at the expense of others. Evidence suggests that individuals experience higher levels of positive emotions, engagement (flow), satisfaction in relationships, meaningfulness in their activities, and achievement when exposed to virtuousness at work (Seligman

2002, 2011). Moreover, organizations achieve higher levels of profitability, productivity, quality, innovation, customer loyalty, and employee retention when they implement positive practices broadly, even in turbulent, ambiguous, and challenging times. Virtuousness in organizations pursues the ultimate best for all of humankind—eudaemonism—which in turn broadens and builds the capabilities of constituencies who may never otherwise benefit (Fredrickson 2003).

REFERENCES

Aknin, Lara B., Tanya Broesch, J. Kiley Hamlin, and Julia W. Van de Vondervoort. 2015. "Prosocial Behavior Leads to Happiness in a Small-Scale Rural Society." *Journal of Experimental Psychology: General*, no. 144: 788–95.

Algoe, Sara B., and Jonathan Haight. 2009. "Witnessing Excellence in Action: The Other-Praising Emotions of Elevation, Gratitude, and Admiration." *Journal of Positive Psychology* 4: 105–27.

Andersson, Lynne M., Robert A. Giacalone, and Carole L. Jurkiewicz. 2007. "On the Relationship of Hope and Gratitude to Corporate Social Responsibility." *Journal of Business Ethics* 70: 401–9.

Aristotle. 1999. *Metaphysics*. New York: Penguin Classics.

Asch, Solomon E. 1952. *Social Psychology*. Englewood Cliffs, NJ: Prentice Hall.

Bright, David S., Kim S. Cameron, and Arran Caza. 2006. "The Amplifying and Buffering Effects of Virtuousness in Downsized Organizations." *Journal of Business Ethics* 64: 249–69.

Brown, Stephanie L., Randolph M. Nesse, Amiram D. Vinokur, and Dylan M. Smith. 2002. "Providing Support May Be More Beneficial than Receiving It: Results from a Prospective Study of Mortality." *Psychological Science*, no. 14: 320–27.

Cameron, K. S. 1994. "Strategies for Successful Organizational Downsizing." *Human Resource Management Journal* 33: 89–112.

Cameron, Kim S. 1998. "Strategic Organizational Downsizing: An Extreme Case." *Research in Organizational Behavior* 20: 185–229.

Cameron, Kim S. 2011. "Responsible Leadership as Virtuous Leadership." *Journal of Business Ethics* 98: 25–35.

Cameron, Kim S. 2021. *Positively Energizing Leadership*. San Francisco: Berrett-Koehler.

Cameron, Kim S., David Bright, and Arran Caza. 2004. "Exploring the Relationships between Organizational Virtuousness and Performance." *American Behavioral Scientist* 4: 766–90.

Cameron, Kim S., and Arran Caza. 2002. "Organizational and Leadership Virtues and the Role of Forgiveness." *Journal of Leadership and Organizational Studies* 9: 33–48.

Cameron, Kim S., Carlos Mora, Trevor Leutscher, and Margaret M. Calarco. 2011. "Effects of Positive Practices on Organizational Effectiveness." *Journal of Applied Behavioral Science* 20: 1–43.

Cameron, Kim S., and Gretchen M. Spreitzer. 2012. *Oxford Handbook of Positive Organizational Scholarship*. New York: Oxford University Press.

Cameron, Kim S., and Bradley Winn. 2012. "Virtuousness in Organizations." In Cameron and Spreitzer 2012, 491–512.

Cascio, Wayne F., Clifford E. Young, and James R. Morris. 1997. "Financial Consequences of Employment Change Decisions in Major U.S. Corporations." *Academy of Management Journal* 40: 1175–89.

Cawley, Michael J., James E. Martin, and John A. Johnson. 2000. "A Virtues Approach to Personality." *Personality and Individual Differences* 28: 997–1013.

Caza, Arran, Brianna A. Barker, and Kim S. Cameron. 2004. "Ethics and Ethos: The Buffering and Amplifying Effects of Ethical Behavior and Virtuousness." *Journal of Business Ethics* 52: 169–78.

Chapman, J. W., and William A. Galston. 1992. *Virtue*. New York: New York University Press.

Cialdini, Robert B. 2000. *Influence: The Science of Persuasion*. New York: Allyn Bacon.

Comte-Sponville, André. 2001. *A Small Treatise of the Great Virtues*. Translated by C. Temerson. New York: Metropolitan Books.

Danner, Deborah D., David A. Snowden, and Wallace V. Friesen. 2001. "Positive Emotions in Early Life and Longevity: Findings from the Nun Study." *Journal of Personality and Social Psychology*, no. 80: 804–813.

Davis, Gerald F. 2008. "The Rise and Fall of Finance and the End of the Society of Organizations." *Academy of Management Perspectives* 23: 27–44.

Dent, N. 1984. *The Moral Psychology of the Virtues*. New York: Cambridge University Press.

Dutton, Jane E., Peter J. Frost, Monica C. Worline, Jacoba M. Lilius, and Jason M. Kanov. 2002. "Leading in Times of Trauma." *Harvard Business Review*, January, 54–61.

Dutton, Jane E., and Scott Sonenshein. 2007. "Positive Organizational Scholarship." In *Encyclopedia of Positive Psychology*, edited by S. Lopez and A. Beauchamps. Malden, MA: Blackwell.

Emmons, Robert A. 1999. *The Psychology of Ultimate Concerns: Motivation and Spirituality in Personality*. New York: Guilford Press.

Fredrickson, Barbara L. 2003. "Positive Emotions and Upward Spirals in Organizations." In *Positive Organizational Scholarship: Foundations of a New Discipline,* edited by Kim S. Cameron, Jane E. Dutton, and Robert E. Quinn, 163–75. San Francisco: Berrett-Koehler.

Fredrickson, Barbara L. 2009. *Positivity.* New York: Crown.

Fredrickson, Barbara L., and T. Joiner. 2002. "Positive Emotions Trigger Upward Spirals toward Emotional Well-Being." *American Psychologist* 13: 172–75.

Fry, Louis W., Steve Vitucci, and Marie Cedillo. 2005. "Spiritual Leadership and Army Transformation: Theory, Measurement, and Establishing a Baseline." *Leadership Quarterly* 16: 835–62.

George, Jennifer M. 1995. "Leader Positive Mood and Group Performance: The Case of Customer Service." *Journal of Applied Social Psychology* 25: 778–94.

Giacalone, Robert A., Karen Paul, and Carole L. Jurkiewicz. 2005. "A Preliminary Investigation into the Role of Positive Psychology in Consumer Sensitivity to Corporate Social Performance." *Journal of Business Ethics* 58: 295–305.

Gittell, Jody H., Kim S. Cameron, Sandy Lim, and Victor Rivas. 2006. "Relationships, Layoffs, and Organizational Resilience." *Journal of Applied Behavioral Science* 42: 300–28.

Grant, Adam M. 2007. "Relational Job Design and the Motivation to Make a Prosocial Difference." *Academy of Management Review* 32: 393–417.

Haight, Jonathan. 2006. *The Happiness Hypothesis: Finding Modern Truth in Ancient Wisdom.* New York: Basic Books.

Harker, LeeAnne, and Dacher Keltner. 2001. "Expressions of Positive Emotion in Women's College Yearbook Pictures and Their Relationship to Personality and Life Outcomes across Adulthood." *Journal of Personality and Social Psychology* 80: 112–24.

Hatch, Mary Jo. 1999. "Exploring the Empty Spaces of Organizing: How Improvisational Jazz Helps Redescribe Organizational Structure. *Organizational Studies,* no. 20: 75–100.

Hauser, Marc. 2006. *Moral Minds: How Nature Designed Our Universal Sense of Right and Wrong.* New York: ECCO.

Isen, Alice. M. 1987. "Positive Affect, Cognitive Processes, and Social Behavior." *Advances in Experimental Social Psychology,* no. 20: 203–53.

Isen, Alice M., Kimberly A. Daubman, and Gary P. Nowicki. 1987. "Positive Affect Facilitates Creative Problem Solving." *Journal of Personality and Social Psychology,* no. 52: 1122–31.

Jensen, Michael C. 2002. "Value Maximization, Stakeholder Theory and the Corporate Objective Function." *Business Ethics Quarterly* 12: 235–56.

Kellett, Janet B., Ronald H. Humphrey, and Randall G. Sleeth. 2006. "Empathy and the Emergence of Task and Relations Leaders." *Leadership Quarterly* 17: 146–62.

Kidder, Rushworth M. 1994. *Shared Values for a Troubled World*. San Francisco: Jossey Bass.

Krebs, Dennis. 1987. "The Challenge of Altruism in Biology and Psychology." In *Sociobiology and Psychology*, edited by C. Crawford, M. Smith, and D. Krebs, 81–118. Hillsdale, NJ: Lawrence Erlbaum.

Langhorst, Peter, Gunter Schultz, and Manfred Lambertz. 1984. "Oscillating Neuronal Network of the Common Brainstem System." In *Mechanics of Blood Pressure Waves*, edited by K. Miyakawa, H. P. Koepchen, and C. Polosa, 257–75. Tokyo: Japan Scientific Societies Press.

Luthans, Fred, Bruce Avolio, James. B. Avey, and Steven M. Norman. 2007. "Psychological Capital: Measurement and Relationship with Performance and Satisfaction." *Personnel Psychology* 60: 541–72.

MacIntyre, Alasdair. 1984. *After Virtue: A Study in Moral Theory*. 2nd edition. Notre Dame, IN: University of Notre Dame Press.

March, James G. 1994. *A Primer on Decision Making: How Decisions Happen*. New York: Free Press.

Maslow, Abraham. 1971. *The Farthest Reaches of Human Nature*. New York: Viking.

McCraty, Rollin. 2002. "Influence of Cardiac Afferent Input on Heart-Brain Synchronization and Cognitive Performance." *International Journal of Psychophysiology*, no. 45: 72–73.

McCullough, Michael E., Kenneth I. Pargament, and Carl Thoreson. 2000. *Forgiveness: Theory, Research, and Practice*. New York: Guilford.

Miller, Geoffrey F. 2007. "Sexual Selection for Moral Virtues." *Quarterly Review of Biology* 82: 97–125.

Okun, Morris A., Ellen W. Yeung, and Stephanie Brown. 2013. "Volunteering by Older Adults and Risk of Mortality: A Meta-Analysis." *Psychology and Aging* 28, no. 2: 564–77.

Peterson, Christopher, and Lisa M. Bossio. 1991. *Health and Optimism*. New York: Free Press.

Peterson, Christopher, and Martin E. P. Seligman. 2004. *Character Strengths and Virtues*. New York: Oxford University Press.

Pinker, Steven. 1997. *How the Mind Works*. New York: W. W. Norton.

Redwine, Laura S., Brook L. Henry, Meredith A. Pung et al. 2018. "Pilot Randomized Study of a Gratitude Journaling Intervention on Heart Rate Variability and Inflammatory Biomarkers in Patients with Stage B Heart

Failure." *Psychosomatic Medicine* 78: 667–76. DOI: 10.1097/PSY.000000
0000000316.

Seligman, Martin E. P. 2002. *Authentic Happiness.* New York: Free Press.

Seligman, Martin E. P. 2011. *Flourish: A Visionary New Understanding of Happiness and Well-Being.* New York: Free Press.

Sethi, Rajesh, and Carolyn Y. Nicholson. 2001. "Structural and Contextual Correlates of Charged Behavior in Product Development Teams." *Journal of Product Innovation Management* 18: 154–68.

Snyder C. R. 1994. *The Psychology of Hope.* New York: Free Press.

Sternberg, Robert J. 1998. "A Balanced Theory of Wisdom." *Review of General Psychology* 2: 347–65.

Tangney, June P., Jeff Stuewig, and Debra J. Mashek. 2007. "Moral Emotions and Moral Behavior." *Annual Review of Psychology* 58: 345–72.

Tiller, William A., Rollin McCraty, and Mike Atkinson. 1996. "Cardiac Coherence: A New, Noninvasive Measure of Autonomic Nervous System Order." *Alternative Therapies on Health and Medicine*, no. 2: 56–65.

Weick, Karl E. 1993. "The Collapse of Sensemaking in Organizations: The Mann Gulch Disaster." *Administrative Science Quarterly* 38: 628–52.

Weick, Karl E., and Kathleen M. Sutcliffe. 2001. *Managing the Unexpected: Assuring High Performance in an Age of Complexity.* San Francisco: Jossey-Bass.

Weiner, Neal O. 1993. *The Harmony of the Soul: Mental Health and Moral Virtue Reconsidered.* Albany, NY: State University of New York Press.

Whillans, Ashley, Elizabeth W. Dunn, Gillian Sandstrom, Kenneth Madden, and Sally Dickerson. 2016. "Is Spending Money on Others Good for Your Heart?" *Health Psychology* 35, no. 6: 574–83. doi: 10.1037/hea0000332.

14

—⟋⟍—

Love

The Core Leadership Value and Organizing Principle for Business and Society

MICHELE HUNT

A VISION OF LOVE

I invite you to go on a visioning journey. Imagine it is the year 2030, and we live in a world where *love*, the most powerful, transcendent, energetic force in the universe, is the core value and organizing principle for business and civil society, and leaders value, embrace, and practice *love* as the essential competency for success:

> Envision a world where conscious leaders from businesses, governments, institutions, and communities share a sense of responsibility for the state of the world and are committed to making it better. In collaboration and cooperation with a plethora of diverse stakeholders, leaders are mobilizing the collective genius of people, combined with the innovations and resources of business and governments to solve the seemingly intractable challenges of our time. These conscious leaders are changing the trajectory of humankind. The existential threats of climate crisis; global health; social, racial, and gender injustices; the growing wealth gap; and the pervasive political conflicts that once plagued our world are in a state of renewal.
>
> ALL people, with their rich array of differences, are valued and contributing their unique gifts for the greater good while pursuing their hopes and dreams. Women are leading half of all businesses and organizations, enabling a beautiful dance between the feminine and masculine perspec-

tives and energies, birthing cultures of "realized potential." Young peoples' ideas and experiences are valued, respected, and sought after. They are recognized as the "endpoint of evolution," carrying civilization's collective DNA and most evolved knowledge. Leaders no longer see their positions as an elite status or station in life but, rather, as servant leaders nurturing the health and well-being of people, communities, and the planet.

Conscious leaders are mobilizing people, across all sectors and boundaries, to collectively contribute their energy, creativity, and their gifts to transform our civilization. People, communities, businesses, and nations are cocreating a world where the planet is treasured; the peaceful use of business, science, technology, and governments is the norm; and ALL people and the planet have the opportunity to prosper and flourish.

If you think this is a dream of utopia born out of idealism or Pollyanna-ish sensitivities, think again. A vision of *love* may be the only way for us to change the trajectory of humankind. The tsunami of life-threatening crises engulfing our world has threatened *everyone's* health and well-being and has shaken our sense of reality. COVID came along and placed an all-encompassing mirror in front of us illuminating the threats to our survival, and Mother Nature sent us to our room to get quiet and reflect on the world as we know it. People are now asking crucial questions: *What is important in life? How do I want to live? What kind of world do we want to create for ourselves, our children, and future generations?* As we come out of this experience of isolation and pervasive crisis, most of us cannot help but be deeply impacted emotionally, physically, and spiritually. A vision of *love* may be our only hope to heal and discover the path to a flourishing future.

People are also beginning to understand that the old story where the central plot is that money and power define success is fundamentally flawed. History has repeatedly proven that this story simply does not stand and is never sustainable. We inevitably devolve into two classes, the underserved and the overserved. The underserved exist to maintain the lifestyle of the overserved, and the laws, systems, and structures of this society are designed to maintain that status quo. The overserved claim dominion over people, flora and fauna, and ownership of the planet's natural resources. A form of necropolitics emerges where the elite rich control the lives of the poor and disenfranchised, as well as their access to capital, quality education, wages, housing, and healthcare. This socioeconomic construct causes pain, suffering, fear, and hate, devastating the planet, destroying lives, and dampening the human spirit. In this narrative, those oppressed by the money-power society inevitably rebel, take over, and sadly repeat the same destructive cycle. We have been living and reliving George Orwell's *Animal Farm* scenario since the beginning of civilization. The erroneous belief systems that posit there are only two extreme ways of living, working and being in life (as winners or losers, a belief in supremacy or inferiority, a mentality of abundance or scarcity), creates deep pain, suffering, and devastation. We need a change of heart, a change of mind, and a fundamental shift in consciousness.

THE GOOD NEWS

The good news is that there is a great awakening of consciousness happening around the world. People are waking up to the fact that we can no longer live isolated and insulated from one another or from the planet that sustains us. We are beginning to understand that all life and nature are inextricably interconnected, interdependent, interwoven, and a part of a whole living system and that we fundamentally need each other. This shift in consciousness is catalyzing powerful people movements around the world. Young people are mobilizing, protesting, and challenging world leaders to take urgent action on the climate crisis. People from every sector of life, in cities and communities around the world, are mobilizing to fight social, racial, and gender injustice. They are investing in understanding and respecting each other's differences while discovering the powerful bonds that unite us.

We are also experiencing a rise in conscious consumerism. People are using their individual and collective buying power to support businesses that are making a positive impact on the social, economic, and environmental issues plaguing us. They are choosing to buy from companies that provide safe, healthy products and services. They are realizing the power they have to influence companies to pay equitable wages and treat their employees with dignity and respect. Conscious consumers are taking personal responsibility for their health, as well as the health of the planet. They are becoming more discerning about the ingredients in the products they buy, and they are increasingly moving to plant-based diets. Conscious consumers are banding together forming conscious communities and using their collective power to influence the types of companies they allow into their backyards.

The great news is that decision makers across all sectors and around the world are listening. There is a rapidly growing number of leaders who are creating new economic models and changing the ways they do business. They are moving from profit as a singular aim benefiting elite shareholders to a more inclusive form of capitalism benefiting a broad array of diverse stakeholders.

They are championing socioeconomic, racial, gender, and environmental well-being for all. They are not just talking about or advocating for these changes, they are making tough decisions and taking bold decisive actions. A rising number of conscious leaders and conscious investors are waking up, standing up, and stepping out of the status quo, courageously challenging the old assumptions about the relationship between business and society. They are understanding the deep connection and the interdependence among people, business, society, and the planet, as well as their awesome responsibility to the greater good. These conscious leaders are mobilizing and igniting the rapidly growing *business for good* movement, and it appears to be unstoppable!

Their missions, visions, and values are transforming the relationships among business, society, and the planet. The B-Corps, a global community of over 3,900 rapidly growing conscious businesses from 150 industries and 74 countries, have "one unifying goal . . . using business as a force for good" (Certified B Corporation 2021). Diverse companies like Ben & Jerry's, Eileen Fisher, Patagonia, Cascade Engineering, New Belgium Brewing Co., Danone, Amalgamated Bank, and others belong to this movement.

According to their website, "The B Corp community works toward reduced inequality, lower levels of poverty, a healthier environment, stronger communities, and the creation of more high-quality jobs with dignity and purpose" (Certified B Corporation 2021).

We are also seeing a proliferation of conscious, impact-driven investors. These investors are exploring ways of "marrying profit with purpose." They believe in the potential of a world where peace, prosperity, and humanity are possible for all as the invisible and visible hands of the markets refashion what we all strive toward.

All of these fearless leaders have ventured into uncharted territory. They are cocreating bold new ways of working, living, and being together that transcends fear, hate, superiority, and dominance; they are embracing inclusion, collaboration, cooperation, interdependence, and trust. They are inviting new and different voices to the decision-making table. They understand that women, people of color, and young people bring a rich array of differences and experiences to draw from as we explore and create a new and better world. Halla Tómasdóttir, CEO of the B Team shared in the February 2021 B Team Brief:

> Our biggest barrier to transformative action is the crisis of conformity in leadership. When we change who is given a chance to lead, we can change what issues we tackle and how we tackle them. It's time for all of us to rally around this imperative to build a new inclusive economy. (Tómasdóttir 2021)

THE POWER OF STORY

I am a believer in the power of stories. They help us understand ideas and concepts, and they illuminate lessons learned in powerful ways. One story often attributed to indigenous Americans serves as a fascinating allegory of the origin of our conflicts and wars. It recounts the experience of the survivors of the great flood that came together as a loving community and made a plan to renew civilization. They decided to separate into four groups and set out in four different directions to discover and rebuild the world. The goal was for each group to bring their rich discoveries back for the benefit of the whole world community. One group traveled east, another ventured west, one group went north, and the other south. The group that traveled north learned to become highly efficient, organized, analytical, and conservative—skills and perspectives they needed to navigate through the bitter cold environment and limited resources. Those who ventured east discovered the dramatic topography, from the enormous mountain ranges to the vast deserts. They learned to work in sync with the natural world that overshadowed them. The group that traveled west faced seemingly endless bodies of water. They learned courage, perseverance, and independence, for they had to navigate through unpredictable oceans with no assurance they would find land on the other side. The group that went south learned the art of celebration, dance, and song, for theirs was a world of vast resources, beauty, and warmth.

All of these discoveries, perspectives, and skills were gifts that could have benefited everyone when they reunited, but something went horribly wrong. As time went by, each group forgot that their mission was to explore their part of the world and bring their beautiful discoveries and learnings back for the greater good. Each group began to form their separate culture and norms. Soon their norms became their beliefs, and their beliefs became their truth. They began to judge and fear the other groups, and soon their judgments and fears turned into hate, and hate solidified their separation from one another. Eventually, they began to venture out into the other groups' territories. They fought and killed one another for *their* version of the truth; each group believing *that their truth was the* truth. The love was lost, and the community mission was long forgotten—prejudice, fear, hate, conflict, and war became a way of life.

Love Begins at Home

My unshakable belief in the power of love to transform people, businesses, communities, and complex institutions comes from my journey. My father served in the U.S. Air Force for 27 years, and his family served most of those years with him. He was the noncommissioned officer whose job was to help integrate the de facto segregation on military bases in the 1950s and 1960s. Dad earned that unique assignment because while we were stationed in Arizona, he climbed on top of a segregated table in the chow hall where white airmen were eating, and he gave a lecture on the merits of brotherhood. He was sentenced to 30 days in jail. While serving his time in isolation, the guards urinated and defecated in his food and water; however, my father centered his mind through meditation and held onto love. He had constant traffic of visitors from the chaplain to the base commander and some ordinary soldiers who were curious about the man who refused to hate despite how he was treated. The impact he had on the people who visited him and on the entire base was phenomenal.

People were moved by this Black man who used love to transcend his circumstance. When my dad was released, the commander promoted him over to special services, which encompassed all of the social side of the base, including the chow hall. For the next 25 years, dad was assigned to help bring racial harmony and lift the morale on military bases around the world. He used his gifts in the arts, sports, and his huge heart to transform every place we lived. He created choirs, sports teams, and USO shows; cultures of joy and brotherhood were pervasive. In no uncertain terms, my father was a legend.

After I graduated from college, I worked in the Michigan Department of Corrections. I served two of those years as the first female deputy warden over rehabilitation programs in an adult male prison. I followed my father's path and used love, participation, and collaboration to create inmate-centered treatment programs. The inmates participated in designing the programs that affected them in collaboration with my treatment staff: the teachers, counselors, recreation directors, and even the medical and religious staff and community volunteers. The men felt valued, excited, and proud to contribute their gifts to help develop *their* programs, and their participation engendered shared ownership for the success of those programs. I watched people who came from devastating circumstances and had endured unspeakable violence and abuse, blossom and flourish, despite being in prison.

The next stop on my journey was Herman Miller, then, a *Fortune* 500 office furniture company. In my last interview, while touring one of their manufacturing plants, I saw fresh flowers in the break areas, and people were smiling and waving. Max De Pree, the CEO and chairman, was speaking to a group of employees the day before Thanksgiving break, and he encouraged them to love each other. That did it for me. I chose Herman Miller because the love and joy in that place were palpable. I was blessed to eventually work for Max and serve on the senior leadership team as corporate vice president for people; however,

I joined the executive team when the company fell on hard times. Max initiated a whole company transformation that we called Renewal. We engaged everyone from the housekeepers to the leadership team in cocreating a bold vision and shared values. They were then liberated to work in cross-sector, cross-boundary teams to contribute their ideas to realize the vision and the values. Within 18 months, Herman Miller was thriving. We became *Fortune's* "Most Admired Company," one of *Fortune's* top companies in America to work for, the "Best Company for Women and Working Mothers," the "Most Environmentally Responsible" in the United States, and named the "Best Managed Company in the World" by the Bertelsmann Foundation, by which time we had returned to double-digit growth. Most important, people were beaming with joy and pride for what they had cocreated; this was love in action.

Over the years, I have seen the transformative impact love has on people working in complex, rigid systems, like the U.S. government when I worked for Vice President Al Gore in Reinventing Government, as well as in financial institutions, technology giants, and communities.

ONE COMPANY'S JOURNEY: CONVERSANT

I experienced a beautiful example of the power of love as a core leadership value and organizing principle while partnering with my dear friends at Conversant, a leadership and organizational development company that was founded in 1984 and that has served over 500 global clients in 90 different countries. They have a unique point of view: "We are a diverse, global community of dedicated professionals with a shared conviction: building human connection unleashes collective brilliance and powers sustained evolution" (Conversant Solutions, LLC 2021).

The company recently engaged in a whole-company renewal they call, "Our Collective Re-Enchantment." Deeply moved by the death of George Floyd and pervasive racial, gender, and environmental injustices, they collectively took the time to reflect on what they believe in, what contribution(s) they want to make in the world, and what they need to equip them to realize their highest aspirations.

I was drawn to Conversant because their people exhibited a level of authenticity and courage that I had never experienced in business. They started their re-enchantment journey with a public, bold statement called "It's Time for Change" which was collectively created by the Conversant community in response to the killing of George Floyd. I feel compelled to share this with you in its entirety because this compelling statement is an act of love.

It's Time for Change

At Conversant we are committed to an inclusive, just society without domination and abuse, a world where Black lives more than matter—where Black lives and contributions are recognized as additive to us all. That commitment requires that we face our own shortcomings and participate in building a future that heals and rights the moral wrong of systemic racism.

We are saddened and outraged by the horrific treatment of the Black community that continues every day. Being silently supportive of this movement out of fear of saying the wrong thing or saying it imperfectly is no longer acceptable. We see that we have played a part in allowing systemic racism to be perpetuated through our complacency and insufficient action. It is time for change in the world, for all of us to awaken and take conscious responsibility for our actions. And that requires change in us.

We believe the path forward starts with our own empathy and learning. Over the past few weeks, we have been spending time learning from others. We are continuing that work as we confront these questions: How do we use our privilege now? How will Conversant evolve?

Racial equity has not been paramount in our societal conversations, perpetuating this systemic injustice. We know conversations make a difference—we thank and admire organizers and leaders who have dedicated their lives to reshaping systems designed to oppress. We see the risks you take, and through your actions we are challenged to take risks ourselves.

Over the coming weeks, we will actively seek Black voices and leaders, using our platform to promote other resources that we find helpful. We promise to be transparent about our own learning and public about our commitments. Our first: the next era of our company will look like the world, not like our founders. (Email comm., Mickey Connolly)

Catalyzed by "It's Time for Change," Conversant went on a journey that engaged everyone in the company and their key stakeholders in creating their re-enchanted vision and core values. Indeed, Robin Anselmi, CEO of Conversant, defines love as: "truly seeing another" (Anselmi 2018). They were deeply influenced by Humberto Maturana, a Chilean biologist, philosopher, and co-author of "The Biology of Business," who says:

Most problems in companies are not solved through competition, not through fighting, not through authority. They are solved through the only emotion that expands intelligent behavior. They are solved through the only emotion that expands creativity. . . . This emotion is love. (Maturana and Bunnell 1999, 1)

I felt truly seen while partnering with this extraordinary community of people on their re-enchantment journey; indeed, I fell in love with Conversant.

CONCLUSION

We have all been touched by love in times of crisis. During natural disasters, strangers come together and exhibit extraordinary acts of love, courage, and compassion. It's a powerful natural response that we don't have to teach people because they already know how to make an expression of love. What is that powerful connective tissue that bonds humans during times of crisis, or holds complex ecosystem systems and macro solar systems together? Many scientists and philosophers and ordinary people call it *love*. The new sciences have taught us that everything is energy. We are enveloped and part of this invisible life-giving force, and when we emote loving intentions, we can see each other, our world, and nature in a new light. Love is our greatest hope to heal people's broken trust, mend inequities, and calm the storms. It can transform hearts, change minds, and liberate the human spirit.

We humans have spent thousands of years learning to separate ourselves from one another and from the planet that sustains us. We are only now beginning to understand that we are deeply connected, interdependent, and part of a greater whole. I am beginning to understand that the way out of my problems is the same way out of yours. I was talking with my dear friend Peter Senge recently and he made a statement that rings true: "Start anywhere and you will end up everywhere."

When we truly look at the society we have inherited, accepted, and are desperately clinging to, it makes no sense. We are a collection of people moving in, out, and through the same dysfunctional manmade systems with artificial boundaries—workplaces, communities, educational institutions, healthcare institutions, governments, and nations. The artificial constructs we are living in, for the most part, were not designed to nurture living, breathing human beings or to enable us to live in harmony with nature; rather, they are designed to separate, control, confine, and subordinate people and the planet for the benefit of a few.

Through the shift in consciousness we are experiencing, which I believe is the dawn of a great awakening of human consciousness, we have the opportunity to claim *love* as our core defining value and the energetic organizing principle for business and society. The opportunity to cocreate a far better world born out of love is not just a beautiful utopic dream, it may indeed be necessary for our survival. Love is the most effective, efficient, and powerful force to unleash the creative genius of people to cocreate a world where ALL have the opportunity to not only survive but also to flourish in harmony with the planet. It is our time, our right, and our responsibility to come together to pursue this beautiful vision.

In the "Einstein Papers: A Man of Many Parts," published in the *New York Times*, Albert Einstein eloquently describes our connections:

A human being is a part of a whole, called by us the universe, a part limited in time and space. He experiences himself, his thoughts and feelings as something separated from the rest, a kind of optical delusion of his consciousness. This delusion is a kind of prison for us, restricting us to our personal desires and to affection for a few persons nearest to us. Our task must be to free ourselves from this prison by widening our circle of compassion to embrace all living creatures and the whole of nature in its beauty. (Sullivan 1972)

REFERENCES

Anselmi, Robin. 2018. "Love: The Next Leadership Skill." DisruptHR Talks, DisruptHR Richmond 2.0, April 19. https://vimeo.com/268272871.
Certified B Corporation. 2021. "A Global Community of Leaders." Accessed May 15, 2021. https://bcorporation.net/.
Conversant Solutions, LLC. 2021. https://www.conversant.com/.
Hunt, Michele. 2017. *DreamMakers: Innovating for the Greater Good*. New York: Routledge.
Maturana, Humberto, and Pille Bunnell. 1999. "The Biology of Business: Love Expands Intelligence." *Reflections: The SoL Journal* 1, no. 2: 58–66. https://www.researchgate.net/publication/240275459_The_Biology_of_Business_Love_Expands_Intelligence.
Mbembe, Achille. 2021. *On the Postcolony: Studies on the History of Society and Culture*. Oakland: University of California Press.
Sullivan, Walter. 1972. "The Einstein Papers: A Man of Many Parts." *New York Times*, March 29. https://www.nytimes.com/1972/03/29/archives/the-einstein-papers-a-man-of-many-parts-the-einstein-papers-man-of.html.
Tómasdóttir, Halla. 2021. "The B Team Brief: February 2021." B Team, February 27. https://bteam.org/our-thinking/news/the-b-team-brief-february-2021.

15

The Role of Consciousness in Accelerating Business as an Agent of World Benefit

CHRIS LASZLO AND IGNACIO PAVEZ

THE SEARCH FOR A NEW THEORY of business is driven by a deep misalignment between today's purpose of economic organizing and what society needs to flourish. The reason why businesses exist can no longer be to maximize profits while only reducing their ecological footprint and minimizing social harm. Such an antiquated notion of corporate social responsibility— prevalent in the latter half of the twentieth century—is leading businesses to contribute, at the aggregate level, to a worsening of many of the social and environmental problems addressed by the 17 UN Sustainable Development Goals.[1] The call of our times is no longer for factories that produce goods (the "widgets" of neoclassical economics) to satisfy material consumption, irrespective of the harm done to society. It is for an entirely new form of business—named the positive impact company (PIC)—whose purpose is to create prosperity and flourishing, now and for future generations.[2] PICs are the prototypical instance of business as an agent of world benefit.

When a business purports to "do less harm," for example by cutting its carbon emissions in half, it acknowledges that it is continuing to worsen its negative impacts, only to a lesser degree. Fifth century BCE physician Hippocrates wrote, "In illnesses one should keep two things in mind, to be useful rather than cause no harm,"[3] which led to the modern physician's oath that medical students still take today. Imagine if the medical profession's stated goal had been to hurt a patient less!

The corporate world is slowly coming to terms with this central distinction between doing less harm and making a positive impact, thanks in part to the pioneering work of John Ehrenfeld and many other thought leaders whose work is showcased in this book.[4] Yet in practice, the shift from doing less harm to making a positive impact remains a huge challenge for business leaders and their organizations. The required change is so profound that it implies transforming the very purpose or ethos of business, from a focus on shareholder value to shared value and ultimately to positive-impact value.

We begin by defining terms. *Shareholder value* refers to the *primacy* of shareholder value where the sole purpose of business is to create a profit for its owners. *Shared value* (also called blended value or sustainable value) refers to the more recent "big idea" popularized by Michael Porter in which the purpose of business is to create value for its shareholders and stakeholders without trade-offs. *Positive-impact value* refers to a form of economic organizing predicated on making a positive impact in the economic, social, and environmental domains. Thus, positive-impact value aims to increase economic prosperity, contribute to a regenerative natural environment, and improve human well-being.[5]

Our research on PICs showed that the shift in business purpose from shareholder value to shared value is easier for individuals and organizations than the shift from shared value to positive-impact value. This is because the transition to positive-impact value can only be achieved by crossing a "big divide" in the mindsets of executives. The central feature of the new mindset is a profound sense of the connection and interdependence between individuals, social systems, and the natural environment; a radically different view compared to the fragmented, mechanistic, and utilitarian mindsets characteristic of both the shareholder value and shared value views (i.e., business as usual). A company that exemplifies the shift to positive-impact value is Ørsted, a Danish power company—one of HBR's top 20 business transformations of the last decade and number 1 on the 2020 Global 100 list of most sustainable corporations by Corporate Knights[6]—that radically changed its way of conceiving and running its business. Starting in 2006, Ørsted successfully shifted its business from generating fossil fuel energy in Denmark to "creating a world that runs entirely on green energy."[7] By taking a leading role in creating a better world for all, Ørsted embodies the ultimate manifestation of the executive mindset behind a PIC, which is to attain flourishing as the firm's raison d'être.

In this chapter, we go deeper into the executive mindset that drives PICs by exploring the role of consciousness in enabling the systemwide scaling of business as an agent of world benefit. We begin by discussing the meaning of consciousness.

WHAT IS CONSCIOUSNESS?

A current debate rages about the very nature of consciousness, defined here as the awareness by the mind of itself and the world around it. The physicalist camp, led by the American philosopher Daniel Dennett, argues that consciousness is the product of the neuronal activity of the brain. The opposing camp, led by the Australian scientist David Chalmers, argues that consciousness is a fundamental property of all life and irreducible to physical phenomena. These competing narratives reflect entirely different scientific paradigms—the Newtonian, Cartesian, LaPlacian, Darwinian, and Jevonsian science of the last 300 years, and the emerging new paradigm science of quantum physics, quantum biology, epigenetics, neurobiology, and consciousness research.

The problem of consciousness is not only about competing paradigms in the physics and neurobiology of mental phenomena. It is also the ability to see beyond our egos.[8] It takes the form of deep assumptions we each hold about what it means to be human and the nature of the world. Table 15.1 summarizes today's dominant view of consciousness and the emerging consciousness paradigm based on insights from quantum science and many spiritual traditions.

CONSCIOUSNESS AS THE HIGHEST POINT OF LEVERAGE
FOR BUSINESS TRANSFORMATION

Through the lens of episodic scientific revolutions, we can see transforming consciousness as a disruption in deeply held assumptions about the nature of reality, influenced by successive ontologies in science that exercise a huge, but often hidden, influence on our thinking and acting.[9] In her widely cited practitioner paper, systems scientist Donella Meadows tells us that shifting deeply held assumptions about how the world works is the highest point of leverage for transforming a system.[10] About this highest leverage point, she says the following:

> The shared idea in the minds of society, the great big unstated assumptions—
> unstated because unnecessary to state; everyone already knows them—
> constitute that society's paradigm, or deepest set of beliefs about how the
> world works. . . . [For example] Growth is good. Nature is a stock of

Table 15.1. Dominant versus emerging consciousness

DOMINANT CONSCIOUSNESS	EMERGING CONSCIOUSNESS
• Human beings are essentially separate and selfish. We are bounded individuals who seek to maximize material wealth above all else. • We are driven by competition for scarce resources in a game of survival of the fittest subject to random genetic mutations. • We are born into a cold, mechanical, clock-like universe subject to physical laws like gravity and electromagnetic forces that are predictable but devoid of meaning or spirit. • The only social purpose of business is to maximize profit. • Nature is a resource for human consumption.	• We are spirit-infused beings living in a world that is alive with meaning. • We are connected through vibrational fields of energy. • People, organizations, and the earth are interconnected living systems. • To be human is to be caring and compassionate. • The purpose of human organizing (including business) is to create well-being, prosperity, and flourishing. • Human activity (including business) is an integral part of the ecological realm.

resources to be converted to human purposes. Evolution stopped with the emergence of *Homo sapiens*. One can "own" land. Those are just a few of the paradigmatic assumptions of our current culture, all of which have utterly dumbfounded other cultures, who thought them not the least bit obvious.

To understand why and how consciousness is such a high leverage point, we turn to three pioneering works in the fields of neuroscience, psychology and organizational behavior, and physics. First, we discuss Nobel Prize–winner Roger Sperry's findings that consciousness is not reducible to neural correlates. Second, we build on the work of Martin Seligman and David Cooperrider to embrace prospection—both individually and collectively—as a form of knowledge that can ignite the emergence of new realities. Third, we take the revolutionary ontological and epistemological assumptions of quantum science to situate consciousness as an inherent property of the world we live in. Taken together, these three sets of pioneering contributions provide a powerful conceptual foundation for understanding the role of consciousness in accelerating business as an agent of world benefit.

ROGER SPERRY'S MACRO-DETERMINISTIC "TOP-DOWN" CAUSATION IN MIND-BODY INTERACTIONS

The modern evolution of thinking about consciousness begins with the "bottom-up" causation of positivist science by which the parts micro-deterministically explain the behavior of the whole. In the dynamic model of classical physics, the vector sum of forces operating on or within a particle uniquely determines its trajectory. According to this view, "No physical action waits on anything [sic] but another physical action."[11] Here, mental events such as perception and cognition are governed from below through neuronal physiochemical forces. In neuroscience, this led to the perplexing conclusion that "as neurophysiologists we simply have no use for consciousness."[12] In the social sciences, behaviorism and psychology shared this premise that action is micro-deterministically driven by drives and habits formed in the past. Notable examples are Pavlovian conditioning based on stimulus and response, and Freud's efforts to explain present behavior based on unresolved (and largely unconscious) distal trauma.

Roger Sperry is widely credited with the alternative "top-down" causation view that places mental phenomena (e.g., perception, cognition, and reasoning) at the top of the brain's hierarchy of actions that determine what human systems are and can become. Also called macro-determinism, it gave consciousness and subjective mental phenomena a new legitimacy in science.[13] It places cognition over chemical interactions and physiological neuronal activity. In popularizing top-down causation, Sperry was careful to refute any notion of dualism, for example in his aptly titled paper, "Mentalism, Yes; Dualism, No."[14] Rather he was proposing a new form of monism in which reductionist bottom-up and irreducible top-down processes were distinct but inseparable.

Importantly for our purposes, Sperry concluded that there was no need for the idea of universal consciousness or a consciousness existing outside the brain. It was sufficient to explain consciousness as the irreducible summation of upward and downward causation occurring *within* the brain. Taking this premise, recent studies in neuroscience have shown the existence of specific parts of the brain that can be associated with "consciousness," which is understood as the capacity to integrate information that connects people with the experience itself (e.g., vision, audition, or pain) and enable us to differentiate our internal and external worlds. These studies propose the existence of some neurological conditions (named neuronal correlates of consciousness) that determine to what extent a system has consciousness (or not)—always limited to the boundaries of that system (e.g., a person or an animal)—and suggest that there is a quantity/quality of consciousness available to a specific system. An extension of this perspective is that it might be possible to build conscious artifacts.[15]

SELIGMAN'S PROSPECTIVE PSYCHOLOGY AND COOPERRIDER'S APPRECIATIVE INQUIRY

Martin Seligman built on Sperry's mentalist view of consciousness with his pioneering development of prospective psychology, where prospection refers to the mental representation and evaluation of possible futures.[16] According to Seligman, this ability fundamentally shapes human cognition, emotion, and motivation. While social science typically focused on how the past determines the present and the future, prospective theorizing seeks to move prospection to the center of research on human action.[17] A major function of consciousness becomes to permit better prospection of the future. "Viewing behavior as driven by the past was a powerful framework that helped create scientific psychology," said Seligman, "but accumulating evidence in a wide range of areas of research suggests a shift in framework, in which navigation into the future is seen as a core organizing principle of animal and human behavior."[18]

Seligman's work on prospective psychology was built not only on the power of Sperry's top-down cognition, but it also shifted the historical emphasis on studying problems ("what happens when things go wrong") to studying instances of positive deviance ("how to make things go right"). For much of the twentieth century, psychologists studied the pathologies of the mind and medical doctors studied the diseases of the body. These two fields only recently placed well-being and flourishing at the center of attention. Meanwhile, research into human behavior was offering compelling evidence that people are more willing to change—and that the change is more enduring—when it is built on strengths rather than weaknesses and positive images of the future.[19]

While Seligman was applying prospection to the individual, Cooperrider was developing a similar theory and practice to the behavior of organizations and whole systems. He offers three basic insights. First, organizations are products of the affirmative mind. Second, when beset with repetitive difficulties or problems, organizations need less fixing, less problem solving, and more reaffirmation. Third, the primary executive vocation in a post-bureaucratic era is to nourish the appreciative soil from which new and better guiding images grow on a collective and dynamic basis.[20]

In the context of organizations, Cooperrider observed that reality is conditioned, reconstructed, and often profoundly created through our anticipatory images, values, plans, intentions, and beliefs. Here prospective theory is "generative in the sense that it serves to challenge assumptions of the status quo, opening the world to new possibilities for better living, and propelled by a real sense of intergenerational concern and caring."[21]

In their development of a prospective theory that recognizes "other ways of knowing," both Seligman and Cooperrider prepared the way for the epistemologies of quantum science. "Prospective guidance thus also includes spontaneous cognitive and emotional activity: intuition, undirected recollection, mind wandering, mental intrusions, creative inspiration, uneasiness, surprise, and satisfaction."[22] Cooperrider notes that appreciative inquiry is a "process that tries to **apprehend** the factors that give life to a living system and seeks to articulate those possibilities that can lead to a better future," describing it as "a means of living with, being with, and directly participating" in such systems when they are at their most vibrant.[23]

THE ONTOLOGY OF QUANTUM SCIENCE

The physicalist view of consciousness was challenged by the work of quantum physicist David Bohm, brain scientist Karl Pribram, cognitive scientist David Chalmers, and others who, starting in the 1980s, revived the much older "transmission theory" of consciousness (William James, 1897) that posited consciousness as a field existing outside the brain—a fundamental property of all life that was irreducible to physical phenomena. Based on this premise, this group of scholars started to ask different questions: What if the feeling of being deeply connected to another person reflected an underlying reality in which we were *actually* connected by energy and information? And what if we could experience reality's essential wholeness and connectedness through practices that had a salutary effect on every aspect of our life? Quantum science is revealing answers to these questions that are converging on perennial spiritual traditions and indigenous wisdom held for millennia.

In sharp contrast to the dualist world of classical science, quantum science tells us that we are interconnected not just in the metaphoric sense of feeling emotionally close to someone or in harmony with nature but by vibrational fields of energy. These fields exist only as potentiality. Physical and mental processes interdependently coarise. What this means is that the world does not exist apart from our observation of it. We live in a participatory universe whose manifestation comes into existence through the act of observation. Here consciousness is also viewed as a field.[24] The manifest content of consciousness is the familiar order of space, time, causality, and so on, while its hidden content, which we can only intuit, is the indivisible wholeness and dynamic coherence, or harmony, of the quantum field. When we experience a sense of wholeness and connectedness, through direct-intuitive practices such as mindfulness meditation, we become aware of this underlying nature of reality as whole and interconnected.

THE EPISTEMOLOGIES OF TRANSFORMATION

Even if we understand the role of consciousness in business transformation, the question remains how to cross the big divide from shared value purpose to positive-impact value. How do we durably alter human behavior to be more prosocial and proenvironmental? By rational argument where people try to convince you with empirical evidence? By moral persuasion that appeals to ethics and social norms? Through applying coercive power with sanctions for wrong behavior? None of these have proven particularly effective in getting individuals or organizations to transform their thinking and action in the face of global challenges such as pandemics and climate change.[25]

The quantum paradigm is now converging on perennial spiritual insights to offer epistemologies based on intuiting, presencing, and sensing rather than only on empirical analysis. Direct-intuitive practices ranging from meditation and walking in nature to art and aesthetics, physical exercise, and journaling can give us an experience of wholeness and connectedness, which in turn can change who we are being. Such direct-intuitive practices heighten our awareness of how our actions impact others and the world. They quiet the analytic mind and expand a person's consciousness so that we are more aware of the essential oneness of reality. Adding one or more such practice(s) daily can strengthen a person's learning journey and elevate their consciousness, which in turn changes their way of being at the deepest level of self-concept.[26]

TOWARD A CONSCIOUSNESS OF BUSINESS
AS AN AGENT OF WORLD BENEFIT

In this section, we offer a conceptual elaboration of how consciousness can inform the ethos of business organizations at different stages of their evolution to create positive-impact value. We summarize our theoretical elaboration in figure 15.1, which presents a schematic of the evolution toward a new consciousness for business as an agent of world benefit. Stage ① corresponds to the disavowal of consciousness in positivist science. It embodies the views of the French mathematician Pierre-Simon Laplace who argued, "We may

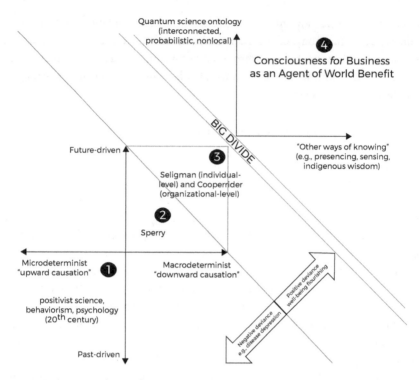

FIGURE 15.1 Foundational stages in conceptualizing consciousness for business in society

regard the present state of the universe as the effect of its past and the cause of its future," according to which the positions and momenta of particles and forces were sufficient to account for the totality of observable behaviors."[27] Stages ② and ③ restore consciousness to scientific legitimacy as an irreducible phenomenon in which prospection plays a central role in determining human thinking and acting. They are neatly divided between research and practice focused on deficit-based approaches ② and those focused on positive deviance ③, with Seligman and Cooperrider respectively applying the latter at the individual and organizational/systems levels. Stage ④ represents an entirely new ontology (Y-axis) and epistemology (X-axis). It corresponds to the quantum paradigm. Figure 15.1 is not intended to represent a comprehensive account of all factors leading to a new understanding of what it means to be human and the nature of the world. It offers one of many possible science-based lenses for conceptualizing successive paradigms of thought affecting business behavior.

Our research shows that a greater sense of wholeness and connectedness—living from a consciousness of the quantum paradigm—has tangible implications for business, as it influences the decision making of organizational leaders. Leaders who embrace this mindset are aware that doing "less harm" is not enough to preserve the balance of the largest social and ecological systems. Thus, they strive to create positive-impact value to preserve the harmony of our planet. This view, however, does not imply viewing business as philanthropic (PICs remain profit-oriented) but as a social institution that plays a fundamental role—interacting with other social and ecological systems—to enable the flourishing of all forms of life. As such, a consciousness of oneness and connectedness can act as a point of leverage to accelerate the transition of business toward becoming agents of world benefit.

CONCLUDING THOUGHTS

The synthesis of science and spirituality, the addition of "other ways of knowing" to empirical analysis, and the new ontology and epistemology of quantum science, offer humanity the best hope today for accelerating individual and organizational behavior in service of business as an agent of world benefit. Through the lens of developmental stages in conceptualizing consciousness, we saw the upward causation "positivist science" view give way to Roger Sperry's macro-determinist downward causation view, effectively restoring consciousness as a legitimate subject for scientific study. Seligman's positive psychology built on Sperry's work to develop consciousness-based *prospection* at the individual level, which Cooperrider did in parallel at the organizational and system level, suggests that consciousness about the future plays a primary role in shaping managerial thinking and action. Here consciousness is holistic and irreducible but remains liminal. Only by crossing the big divide between classical and quantum science do we leap to a universal consciousness—long intuited by indigenous and non-Western spiritual wisdom—that guides the evolution of life in an interconnected and dynamically coherent world. A variety of practices of connectedness gives managers a direct-intuitive experience of such a world, which changes who they are being so that they become agents of world benefit because of who they are.

NOTES

1. "The Sustainable Development Goals Report 2020," United Nations, accessed November 17, 2020, https://unstats.un.org/sdgs/report/2020/. See also

"Time to Revise the Sustainable Development Goals," *Nature*, July 14, 2020, 331–32, https://doi.org/10.1038/d41586-020-02002-3.

2. Ignacio Pavez, Lori Kendall, and Chris Laszlo, "Positive-Impact Companies: Toward a New Paradigm of Value Creation, *Organizational Dynamics* (December 5, 2020): 1–2, https://doi.org/10.1016/j.orgdyn.2020.100806.

3. Hippocrates, "Treatise on Epidemics I," part 2, paragraph 5, in *Hippocrates Collected Works I*, ed. W. H. S. Jones (Cambridge, MA: Harvard University Press, 1868). Original work published around 400 BCE.

4. Rethinking sustainability from a primary focus on doing less harm to one aimed at making a positive impact has enabled the emergence of new business standards and practices such as "full-cost accounting"—that is, accounting methods used to determine the complete end-to-end cost of producing goods or services (see Kathryn J. Bebbington, Judy Brown, and Bob Frame, "Accounting Technologies and Sustainability Assessment Models," *Ecological Economics* 61, nos. 2–3 [2007]: 224–36). New accounting technologies and sustainability assessment models are emerging (see Dominik Jasinski, James Meredith, and Kerry Kirwan, "A Comprehensive Review of Full Cost Accounting Methods and Their Applicability to the Automotive Industry," *Journal of Cleaner Production* 108 [2015]: 1123–39) as well as regenerative business strategies (i.e., businesses strategies that "enhance, and thrive through, the health of social-ecological systems in a co-evolutionary process" (1). See Tobias Hahn and Maja Tampe, "Strategies for Regenerative Business," *Strategic Organization* (2020): 1–22.

5. Pavez, Kendall, and Laszlo, "Positive-Impact Companies."

6. Mike Scott, "Top Company Profile: Denmark's Ørsted Is 2020's Most Sustainable Corporation," Corporate Knights, 2020, https://www.corporate knights.com/reports/2020-global-100/top-company-profile-orsted-sustainability -15795648/; Scott D. Anthony, Alasdair Trotter, and Evan I. Schwarts, "The Top 20 Business Transformations of the Last Decade," *Harvard Business Review* 2, no. 7 (2019), https://hbr.org/2019/09/the-top-20-business-transformations-of -the-last-decade.

7. "Our Vision—And Who We Are," Ørsted, accessed March 31, 2021, https://orsted.com/en/about-us/about-orsted/our-vision-and-values.

8. Judi Neal, "An Overview of the Field of Transformation," in *Handbook of Personal and Organizational Transformation* (New York: Springer, 2018), 2–26, https://doi.org/10.1007/978-3-319-66893-2_26; and Otto Scharmer, *The Essentials of Theory U: Core Principles and Applications* (San Francisco: Berrett-Koehler, 2018).

9. Philip Kitcher, *Science in a Democratic Society* (New York: Prometheus, 2011); and Thomas S. Kuhn, *The Structure of Scientific Revolutions*, 4th ed. (Chicago: University of Chicago Press, 2012).

10. Donella H. Meadows, "Places to Intervene in a System," *Whole Earth*, Winter 1997, quote at 18, https://donforrestermd.com/wp-content/uploads /Meadows-Places-to-Intervene-Whole-Earth-1997.pdf. A second version appeared as *Leverage Points: Places to Intervene in a System* (1999), a publication of the Sustainability Institute.

11. Roger W. Sperry, "A Mentalist View of Consciousness," *Social Neuroscience Bulletin* 6, no. 2 (Spring 1993): 15–19, 16, http://people.uncw.edu/puente/sperry /sperrypapers/80s-90s/274-1993.pdf.

12. J. C. Eccles, cited in Sperry, "A Mentalist View of Consciousness."

13. Sperry, "A Mentalist View of Consciousness," 18.

14. R. W. Sperry, "Mind-Brain Interaction: Mentalism, Yes; Dualism, No," *Neuroscience* 5, no. 2 (1980): 195–206.

15. Giulio Tononi, "An Information Integration Theory of Consciousness," *BMC Neuroscience* 5, no. 42 (2004): 1–22, https://doi.org/10.1186/1471-2202-5-42; and Christof Koch, "What Is Consciousness?" *Nature* 557 (May 9, 2018): S8–S12, https://doi.org/10.1038/d41586-018-05097-x.

16. Prospective Psychology, https://www.prospectivepsych.org/; Authentic Happiness, https://www.authentichappiness.sas.upenn.edu/learn /prospectivepsych.

17. Martin E. P. Seligman, Peter Railton, Roy F. Baumeister, and Chandra Sripada, "Navigating into the Future or Driven by the Past," *Perspectives on Psychological Science* 8, no. 2 (February 27, 2013): 119–41, https://doi.org/10.1177 /1745691612474317.

18. Seligman et al., "Navigating into the Future," 119.

19. Barbara L. Fredrickson, Michael A. Cohn, Kimberly A. Coffey, Jolynn Pek, and Sandra M. Finkel, "Open Hearts Build Lives: Positive Emotions, Induced through Loving-Kindness Meditation, Build Consequential Personal Resources," *Journal of Personality and Social Psychology* 95, no. 5 (2008): 1045–62, https://doi .org/10.1037/a0013262.

20. David Cooperrider, "Positive Image, Positive Action: The Affirmative Basis of Organizing," in *Appreciative Inquiry: An Emerging Direction for Organization Development*, ed. D. L. Cooperrider, P. F. Sorenson, T. Yaeger, and D. Whitney (Champaign, IL: Stipes Publishing, 2001).

21. Fifth Global Forum paper, internal draft, Working Paper, November 8, 2020, 7.

22. Seligman et al., "Navigating into the Future," 127.

23. Cooperrider, "Positive Image, Positive Action."

24. David Chalmers, *The Conscious Mind: In Search of a Fundamental Theory* (New York: Oxford University Press, 1997).

25. Chris Laszlo, David Cooperrider, and Ron Fry, "Global Challenges as Opportunity to Transform Business for Good," *Sustainability* 12, no. 19 (2020): 8053, https://doi.org/10.3390/su12198053.

26. Chris Laszlo, "Quantum Management: The Practices and Science of Flourishing Enterprise," *Journal of Management, Spirituality & Religion* 17, no. 4 (August 2020): 301–15, https://doi.org/10.1080/14766086.2020.1734063.

27. Seligman et al., "Navigating Into the Future," 120.

16

Innovating to Flourish

Toward a Theory of Organizing for Positive Impact

UDAYAN DHAR AND RONALD FRY

SCHOLARS OF CORPORATE RESPONSIBILITY, business ethics, and sustainability have proposed that it is no longer a question of whether a business can "do well by doing good" but of how a business can do so (Glavas and Mish 2015). A review of the six-year history of more than 800 "benefit corporations" or B-Corps (Chen and Kelly 2015) found that these companies had a statistically significant revenue growth rate that outpaced the average revenue growth of similar public companies. Yet, some evidence also suggests that the import of grand challenges into business strategy often gets converted into the mundane and comfortable concerns of "business as usual" (Wright and Nyberg 2017). Therefore, there is a need to explore the synergies between corporate responsibility on the one hand and organizational psychology (Glavas 2016) and organizational design (Mohrman and Lawler 2014) on the other. There has been a recognition (Lynn 2020) that scholars must focus on understanding the provisional and contextual social mechanisms that reward or sanction ethical action. Ultimately, there is a need to continue developing and disseminating knowledge about how to foster and sustain highly functional, humane, ethical, and prosperous organizing (Bright and Fry 2013). The present study responds to such calls and focuses on organizational innovations that aim to create mutual benefit to the business and society, in general.

We began this study with the overarching research question: What are the organizational factors that relate to successful innovations for the mutual benefit (IMB) of business and society? We define IMB as business innovations that advance the United Nations' Sustainable Development Goals (UN SDGs) and create economic value for the investors. We found relevant insights on the dynamics of how an IMB finds inspiration and then gets implemented. In doing so, we were able to identify five key mechanisms of successful IMBs: being socially and ecologically embedded, having a long-term orientation, partnering or collaborating with other organizations, recognizing one's role as a change agent, and implementing circular value chains. Apart from understanding the constituents and correlates of IMBs, the analysis also allowed us to develop a framework on how the innovation journey pans out.

METHODS

Data: Case Studies of IMBs

The case studies for our analysis were collected as part of a global inquiry into business as an agent of world benefit conducted under the aegis of AIM2Flourish, an initiative of the Fowler Center for Business as an Agent of World Benefit (BAWB) at Case Western Reserve University (CWRU). The project is a worldwide initiative using appreciative inquiry (AI; Cooperrider and McQuaid 2012) to inspire face-to-face dialogues about the role of business in society and to discover, amplify, and disseminate stories of innovations in organizations that are creating mutual benefit for business and society (Fry 2017). The world *inquiry* mobilizes students to search for and collect stories of innovations that help a business to prosper while also positively impacting one or more of the UN Sustainable Development Goals. To date, students from 103 schools across the globe have contributed over 3,000 innovation stories. The AIM2Flourish stories are from a variety of businesses similar to (or including) B-Corps, social enterprises, and UN Global Compact members in terms of how they conceptualize the role of business in society.

For our analysis, we selected a randomized subset of 36 cases from among 95 that were based in the United States and were from medium-sized companies, defined as having 50–200 employees. We conducted a content analysis of the cases, allowing categories to emerge from the data. Both authors iteratively grouped similar responses to arrive at a coding scheme based on the extant management literature. We reconciled disagreements through discussion. Based on this initial analysis, we were able to prepare a codebook containing the definitions of the emergent themes. We then systematically coded all of the 36 case studies. Finally, based on the structure of the interviews, which presented information about the innovation from inception or inspiration to implementation, we were able to arrive at a set of propositions around such innovations. The propositions are meant to guide future research and practice in the area of innovations for mutual benefit to the business and society.

FINDINGS

The themes that emerged in the analysis were organized into two categories or phases based on the order of their appearance in the case studies. The first part includes themes that relate to the inspiration behind the innovation, and the second part includes themes that relate to the actions taken to implement the innovation. The case studies suggest that these manifested chronologically, allowing us to integrate the themes into a causal model. We elaborate on each theme and provide a few exemplars below.

Phase 1: Inspiration for the Innovation

The first part of the case studies focused on what inspired or gave impetus to IMBs. The responses in this section showed the presence of the following two themes: social and ecological embeddedness, and long-term orientation.

Social and Ecological Embeddedness

This theme describes cases where the leader or the organization is intimately connected to the local community or the natural environment within which the business operates. In organizational studies, the construct of embeddedness has primarily been linked to social relations, and more recently to a sense of place concerning the natural environment. Social embeddedness has been defined as "the degree to which commercial transactions take place through social relations and networks of relations that use exchange protocols associated with social, non-commercial attachments to govern business dealings" (Uzzi 1999, 482). Ecological embeddedness has been defined as the degree to which a manager or leader is "rooted in the land"—that is, the extent to which they are "on the land and learn from the land in an experiential way" (Whiteman and Cooper 2000).

At Marigold Catering, the first certified Green Restaurant caterer in the state of Ohio, Joan Rosenthal, the founder and president holds a lot of pride and passion for her hometown of Cleveland. She feels she has a responsibility to not only give back to others in the community but also that it is part of her philosophical belief to have business strategies and practices in place that protect the environment. This sense of place that Rosenthal holds shows in the systemic approach to sustainability in the form of the Marigold Outreach Program (MOP). Through it, Marigold partners with local nonprofit organizations to provide donations of either funds or resources, such as volunteer hours, left-over food, or use of Marigold's venues or trucks. MOP allows Marigold to give back to the community and spread their values to a wider audience; it has helped to shape their identity as a "caterer with a heart" (Aim2Flourish 2021).

4ocean, based out of Boca Raton, Florida, offers bracelets made from recy-cled materials and is an illustration of how the ecological rootedness of the founders inspired the business. It began with a postcollege trip by friends Alex and Andrew in which they traveled to Bali in search of a surfer's dream of big waves. When they landed at their destination, they were struck by the enormous pollutants that stifled Bali's shorelines with garbage and waste that had washed up from the ocean. They noticed the battle of Indonesian fishermen as they pushed through hills of plastic. This got Alex and Andrew started on a thriving enterprise that has resulted in 5 million pounds of ocean trash removed and a line of products primarily made up of marine plastic and recycled materials.

Based on this, we can propose the following:

Proposition 1. Social and ecological embeddedness are positively related to inspiration for IMBs.

Long-Term Orientation

This theme describes cases where a leader or organization makes key deci-sions based on a long-term view of the business and society. By building a vi-sion that directs resource allocation and inspires organizational members to achieve sustainable multistakeholder value well into the future, firms with a long-term orientation often engage in activities that do not necessarily gener-ate immediate returns (Wang and Bansal 2012). Examples of such activities are investing in research and development, spotting trends in consumers' preferences that may lead to new markets, and developing strategic resources. In our cases, we found several examples of firms engaging in such activities.

Promess Incorporated is a leader in sensing systems for the manufacturing industry and is based in Brighton, Michigan. Their innovation involved mak-ing a machine that can measure forces directly to test quality. This method can detect if a product is defective, allowing a firm to retool it, thereby reduc-ing defective goods that would become waste. The innovation is a significant improvement over previous devices that relied on hydraulic systems to iden-tify quality defects. This kind of product innovation was expensive for them in the short run, but in the long run saved the company time and money. This also helped with their carbon footprint because the machine time for their operations was cut by about 25 percent due to this innovation.

Another longer-term vision and strategy are that of Impossible Foods, based in Redwood City, California, that develops plant-based substitutes for meat products. "We make meat and dairy products from plants—not because it's particularly easy to do, but because it is one way to mitigate a crisis involving animal agriculture," said Rebekah Moses, the sustainability and agriculture manager of Impossible Foods. Since plant-based protein consumes far fewer resources, Impossible Foods' "meat" would sharply reduce this impact. Articulating a vision for the future Moses said, "This way we can sustainably deliver calories to a population that will be 10 billion people in not too long. We want to see the day when a kid bites into a hamburger and says, 'Wow, to think humans used to make these out of animals'" (Aim2Flourish).

Based on this, we can propose the following:

Proposition 2. Long-term orientation is positively related to inspiration for IMBs.

Phase 2: Actions to Implement the Innovation

This category of themes from the cases focused on the actions that enabled the innovation. The responses here showed the presence of three action domains: circular value chains, collaborative boundary spanning, and enacting the enterprise as a change agent.

Circular Value Chains

This describes cases where the organization focuses on reusing products and byproducts from their production and supply-chain processes. Circular value chains are most frequently depicted in scholarly literature as a combination of reduce, reuse, and recycle activities, whereas it is oftentimes not highlighted that this necessitates a paradigm shift in managing material resources (Kirchherr, Reike, and Hekkert 2017). It is a systemic approach that is radically different from the prevailing economic logic because it replaces a focus on production with sufficiency: reuse what you can, recycle what cannot be reused, repair what is broken, remanufacture what cannot be repaired (Stahel 2016).

CF Global Holdings, based in Bellevue, Washington, makes and distributes coffee flour, a nutritionally dense fruit powder made from the discarded pulp and skin of the coffee cherry. In their innovative business model, coffee farmers collect the coffee cherries that have been picked for coffee and process them into flour. This highly nutritious flour can be used for all types of baking. This reuse of previously discarded waste has resulted in steady revenue streams for the farmers and reduces polluted runoff in nearby ecosystems. Every year, an estimated several billion pounds of coffee cherries around the world are discarded after the bean is harvested. CF is seeking to change the coffee processing industry by eliminating the environmental runoff, attributing more wages directly to coffee farmers, and introducing a healthy food ingredient.

Filtrexx Installation Services, based in Akron, Ohio, is a leader in the research and development of compost-based erosion control and stormwater management systems. Their sustainable technologies are used in diverse applications, such as perimeter control, inlet protection, runoff diversion, sediment trap, green roofs, and filtrations systems. While construction can be a very polluting industry, Filtrexx's Compost Filter Sock innovation can reliably trap sediment and soluble pollutants from being washed away during construction, therefore preventing them from entering waterways. It can also slow, interrupt, and filter stormwater runoff and protect drain inlets. The carbon sequestration benefits come from both plants (the creation of living walls with active growing plants) and compost (when compost is added to soil it increases the microbial activity and promotes plant growth).

Based on this, we can propose the following:

Proposition 3. Incorporating circular value chains is positively related to the successful implementation of IMBs.

Collaborative Boundary Spanning

This theme describes cases where the leader or the organization proactively makes meaningful connections or collaborative alliances with other organizations or external stakeholders to make an IMB successful. Such collaboration has been considered even more essential when organizations aim at ensuring economic, environmental, and social performance at the same time (Gold, Seuring, and Beske 2010). In fact, in the case of social enterprises, which tend by their very nature to be hybrid in structure, this is the norm. They often seek boundary-spanning linkages between the profit and nonprofit sectors. Their exploration of synergies is what has helped foster a new "space between" the public and the private sectors. For example, Mohrman and Lawler (2014) have noted that as companies explore ways to create sustainable value, they have become increasingly engaged in multistakeholder, crossorganizational partnerships and relationships, not only to solicit input from other stakeholders to inform organizational direction but also to collaborate around learning and action.

Union Packaging, a packaging supply store in Yeadon, Pennsylvania, utilizes its partnerships and relationships with different local nonprofits and programs to hire individuals that are often overlooked in the job market. One of their hiring partners in the local community includes the Welcoming Center for New Pennsylvanians, which connects newly arrived immigrants from around the world with economic opportunities to succeed in the region. Another example of a partner is Bridges from School to Work, an organization that offers young people with disabilities opportunities to learn, grow, and succeed in employment.

The founders and team at MPOWERD, based in Brooklyn, New York, have created a solar, lightweight, lamp called Luci light that is "super bright and never needs batteries." More importantly, the company uses its strong retail sales in developed nations to lower their manufacturing costs and, in turn, offers its solar innovation to people in less developed countries living without electricity at a cost each community can afford. MPOWERD reports to have distributed over 200,000 Luci lights in more than 100 countries, impacting more than a million lives. To implement this ambitious initiative, MPOWERD works with its network of over 200 NGO and charity partners to give away one light to a developing country for each one it sells in the United States and other developed countries.

Based on this, we propose the following:

Proposition 4. Collaborative boundary spanning is positively related to the successful implementation of IMBs.

Recognizing the Enterprise as a Change Agent
This theme describes cases where the leader or the organization recognizes their role as an agent for positive change in a larger context, beyond their core business objectives. They see themselves as a catalyst in the transformation of society's values toward mutual benefit in general and within the specific domain of social performance that the business operates in particular.

4ocean, mentioned above, considers outreach and education as an essential part of its business model. According to their website, "People can't be part of the solution until they're aware of the problem. Our job is to help people understand the causes of the ocean plastic crisis and empower them to act. From lesson plans for educators to regional beach cleanups and events, we're committed to sharing our knowledge and inspiring action on behalf of the ocean" (4ocean 2021). Additionally, the public is encouraged to volunteer to work side-by-side with the 4ocean outreach team and this helps ensure that their cleanups are also an educational experience.

TerraCycle is a recycling business headquartered in Trenton, New Jersey. It recycles materials ranging from snack wrappers to action figures. Its programs remind consumers to consider the environmental impacts of their purchasing decisions. Global director Lauren Taylor describes how TerraCycle has helped to raise awareness about recycling in schools. "Parents have said, 'My child was part of a school program, and they've turned the house into a recycling center.' Kids are thinking about what is recyclable and what is not" (Aim-2Flourish). While TerraCycle provides ingenious recycling solutions, the company recognizes that recycling can only mitigate, not fully resolve, the problem of waste. The company, therefore, works to educate consumers to avoid waste in the first place by buying conscientiously, buying more durable or used products, or simply buying less.

Based on this, we propose the following:

Proposition 5. Identifying as a change agent for positive social impact is positively related to the successful implementation of IMBs.

Outcomes of the Innovation

Our analysis of the case studies also showed that the impact of the innovation touched upon both economic outcomes that directly benefit the investors and social and environmental outcomes related to the SDGs. We found evidence that the businesses, through their unique innovations, created value for a variety of internal and external stakeholders, such as owners and shareholders, customers, employees, communities, and the natural environment within which they operated. The impact was evident in all of the 36 case studies.

As discussed above, the product of CF Global Holdings is now being incorporated into food products around the globe, while also transforming coffee-growing communities. The worldwide supply of the cherries has resulted in Coffee Flour operations in Hawaii, Nicaragua, Guatemala, Mexico, and Vietnam, with expansion in Latin America and Asia and new operations in Africa being planned. For the coffee growers, the productive application of formerly discarded cherries creates sustainable jobs and a new revenue source for some of the poorest areas of the world. Environmentally, where billions of pounds of discarded coffee cherries were finding their way to rot near waters that become contaminated with caffeine, ochratoxins, and aflatoxins, Coffee Flour decreases the runoff by using up all parts of the cherry.

Another example is a pioneer in the natural supplements industry, Food-State, based out of Manchester, New Hampshire. They started in 1973 by producing and marketing superior health supplements. Increasing awareness about these products enabled the company to steadily become more financially sustainable. Today, according to their great people finder, Alison Moore, Food-

State is committed to manufacturing the highest-quality product, the promotion of a healthy lifestyle, and care of the environment and its associates by returning to the essence of food consumption intended by nature (Aim2Flourish).

DISCUSSION

To summarize, when leaders and organizations are socially and ecologically embedded, and take a long-term view of their business, it inspires innovations that prioritize and support mutual benefit to the business and society (socially and ecologically). These innovations are successfully implemented through collaborative boundary spanning, circular value chains, and by recognizing the organization's role as a change agent. Ultimately this enables a flourishing enterprise that we define as an organization that makes a positive impact on SDG goals and generates economic gains for investors (figure 16.1).

Based on our findings, we propose that future studies should incorporate the idea of "flourishing" to refer to business practices that aim to do well by doing good. According to Ehrenfeld and Hoffman (2013, 7) flourishing involves shifting from defining ourselves from the materials we possess to defining ourselves by the extent to which we act authentically; at the systemic level, it involves moving away from pure rationalism toward more balance with pragmatic thinking. Tsao and Laszlo (2019) recognize this distinction as well when they

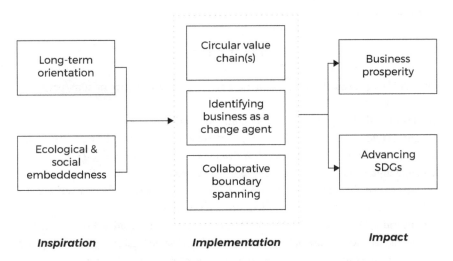

FIGURE 16.1 An empirical model of innovations for mutual benefit (IMBs)

propose that the term *flourishing* is more ambitious than *sustainability* because it is not anchored in mundane notions of continuity; it is instead about a world for which we all yearn. Our study shows that some organizations go beyond the notions of balancing "doing well and doing good" toward "doing well by doing good," specifically through IMBs. Thus traditional terms such as "corporate responsibility" or "mutual benefit" may not adequately capture the range of activities that flourishing necessarily involves. This assertion that "companies do well by doing good" might better reflect the emerging business environment in a post-COVID-19 world (Laszlo, Cooperrider, and Fry 2020).

CONCLUSION

To better understand the movement toward flourishing, we analyzed accounts of innovations for mutual business and social benefit among medium-sized for-profit companies in the United States. We delineated some of the organizational factors related to the inspirations behind and successful implementation of such innovations. In doing so, we contribute to the field of social issues in management by reconceptualizing sustainability in a more holistic manner, notably in the context of flourishing. To this end, we highlight the opportunities for businesses to go beyond the do-less-harm or routine approaches to sustainability management toward a more holistic and aspirational approach. Our findings offer actionable propositions on innovating-for-flourishing that management scholars, educators, and practitioners can experiment with in the years ahead.

REFERENCES

"About Us." 4ocean. Accessed June 14, 2021. https://www.4ocean.com/pages /about.

Aim2Flourish, https://aim2flourish.com/innovations.

Bright, David S., and Ron E. Fry. 2013. "Introduction: Building Ethical, Virtuous Organizations." *Journal of Applied Behavioral Science* 49, no. 1: 5–12.

Chen, Xiujian, and Thomas F. Kelly. 2015. "B-Corps—A Growing Form of Social Enterprise: Tracing Their Progress and Assessing Their Performance." *Journal of Leadership & Organizational Studies* 22, no. 1: 102–14.

Cooperrider, David L., and Michelle McQuaid. 2012. "The Positive Arc of Systemic Strengths: How Appreciative Inquiry and Sustainable Designing Can Bring Out the Best in Human Systems." *Journal of Corporate Citizenship*, no. 46: 71–102.

Ehrenfeld, John R., and Andrew J. Hoffman. 2013. *Flourishing: A Frank Conversation about Sustainability.* Redwood City, CA: Stanford University Press.

Fry, Ron. 2017. "Agents of World Benefit: Business: An Appreciative Inquiry into Business as an Agent of World Benefit." *AI Practitioner* 19, no. 2.

Glavas, Ante. 2016. "Corporate Social Responsibility and Organizational Psychology: An Integrative Review." *Frontiers in Psychology* 7: 144.

Glavas, Ante, and Jenny Mish. 2015. "Resources and Capabilities of Triple Bottom Line Firms: Going over Old or Breaking New Ground?" *Journal of Business Ethics* 127, no. 3: 623–42.

Gold, Stefan, Stefan Seuring, and Philip Beske. 2010. "Sustainable Supply Chain Management and Inter-Organizational Resources: A Literature Review." *Corporate Social Responsibility and Environmental Management* 17, no. 4: 230–45.

Kirchherr, Julian, Denise Reike, and Marko Hekkert. 2017. "Conceptualizing the Circular Economy: An Analysis of 114 Definitions." *Resources, Conservation and Recycling*, no. 127: 221–32.

Laszlo, Chris, David Cooperrider, and Ron Fry. 2020. "Global Challenges as Opportunity to Transform Business for Good." *Sustainability* 12, no. 19: 8053.

Lynn, Andrew P. 2020. "Why 'Doing Well By Doing Good' Goes Wrong: A Critical Review of 'Good Ethics Pays' Claims in Managerial Thinking." *Academy of Management Review.* Online first publication: https://doi.org/10.5465/amr.2018.0250

Mohrman, Susan A., and Edward E. Lawler III. 2014. "Designing Organizations for Sustainable Effectiveness." *Journal of Organizational Effectiveness: People and Performance* 1, no. 1: 14–34.

Stahel, William R. 2016. "The Circular Economy." *Nature* 531, no. 7595: 435–38.

Tsao, Frederick C., and Chris Laszlo. 2019. *Quantum Leadership: New Consciousness in Business.* Redwood City, CA: Stanford University Press.

Uzzi, Brian. 1999. "Embeddedness in the Making of Financial Capital: How Social Relations and Networks Benefit Firms Seeking Financing." *American Sociological Review* 64, no. 4: 481–505.

Wang, Taiyuan, and Tima Bansal. 2012. "Social Responsibility in New Ventures: Profiting from a Long-Term Orientation." *Strategic Management Journal* 33, no. 10: 1135–53.

Whiteman, Gail, and William H. Cooper. 2000. "Ecological Embeddedness." *Academy of Management Journal* 43, no. 6: 1265–82.

Wright, Christopher, and Daniel Nyberg. 2017. "An Inconvenient Truth: How Organizations Translate Climate Change into Business as Usual." *Academy of Management Journal* 60, no. 5: 1633–61.

17

Toward Reinvention of Your Theory of the Business

Five Principles for Thriving in the Disrupted World

NADYA ZHEXEMBAYEVA AND DAVID COOPERRIDER

I find it useful to keep antique ideas around, as a reminder that how we see
things today is not how the world will always see them.
—*Marjorie Kelly*

Forget programming. The best skill to teach . . . is reinvention.
—*Yuval Noah Harari*

SOMETHING DRAMATIC IS HAPPENING in the field of change management, and it has implications for every business that wants to leap to becoming an industry-leading star in the business of betterment and the betterment
of business.

In previous chapters in this volume, authors such as Paul Polman, the former CEO of Unilever and chair of the International Chamber of Commerce,
and Andrew Winston, the coauthor of their recently released book *Net Positive*, have raised the specter of "the elephants in the room." They speak powerfully in their chapter of the need for bold, brave, and principled leadership
combined with a deep enterprise logic reset. We hear them asking: Will our
methods of change truly rise to meet the moment? And why the decades-long
sense of sleepwalking? What is happening is that change management has
failed us—and a plethora of numbers are here to prove it.

For the last few years, we've been conducting a regular change survey with
our clients and partners (Zhexembayeva 2020b). In 2018, out of over 2,000

managers participating, 47 percent reported that to survive, they needed to reinvent their businesses every three years or less. Data from 2020 was telling—the number has jumped to 60 percent.

That should come as no surprise, given the deep interconnections that come with participating in a global economy. The World Economic Forum's 2019 Global Risk Report mapped out 30 critical risks across five categories—economic, environmental, geopolitical, societal, and technological—and showed the interconnections between them. The spread of infectious disease was one of the top 10 (World Economic Forum 2019). COVID-19 (or something like it) was fully anticipated, and many other projected disruptions will likely come to pass, too.

The trouble is that although we recognize and may even anticipate the risks, we are not good at adapting to them. Two decades ago, Nitin Nohria and Michael Beer (2000) observed that "about 70% of all change initiatives fail." Today, according to global consulting firm Boston Consulting Group (2020), we've gotten worse at it: "75% of transformation efforts don't deliver the hoped-for results."

Small wonder then that companies don't seem to stay successful for very long anymore. The 2018 Corporate Longevity Forecast conducted by Innosight showed that in 1964, S&P 500 companies would stay on the list for an average of 33 years; this narrowed to 24 years by 2016; and it is forecast to shrink to just 12 years by 2027 (Anthony et al. 2018). This suggests that there's something profoundly wrong with the way we do change. Our theory and practice suggest that many of our change failures come from our five very basic, ingrained assumptions about what works. It's by flipping these assumptions that we get results—and find readiness to address the elephants and other animals, metaphorically speaking, that are facing business and humanity today.

PRINCIPLE #1
From: Change Happens Rarely. To: Change Is a Constant.

Modern management was born during times of relative stability, as almost every prominent business solution emerged in the West after World War II. This includes the book many treat as the birth of modern business thinking— the 1946 *Concept of the Corporation* by the legendary Peter Drucker.

Of course, some isolated wars and disruptions continued, but in the second part of the twentieth century, the Western world seemed to stabilize: no significant global conflict, relatively stable borders, and few fundamental economic disruptions. Most management functions, such as strategy, human resources, operations research, innovation, and IT (information technology) were professionalized in this postwar era of relative stability. And many of our

most beloved management tools and frameworks, such as just-in-time production, TQM (total quality management), and even fixed budgets were developed for a relatively predictable business environment.

For many years, the data seemed to justify the assumption of stability built
into our business operating systems. Stéphane Garelli, a world authority on
competitiveness, professor emeritus at IMD where he founded the World
Competitiveness Centre, spoke of our no-longer-stable world this way: "You
will probably live longer than most big companies. The large companies of
today are not the same as the ones of yesterday. The process of creative destruction highlighted by Schumpeter is still in action. Indeed, it is accelerating. A recent study by McKinsey found that the average lifespan of companies
listed in Standard & Poor's 500 was 61 years in 1958. Today, it is less than
18 years. McKinsey believes that, in 2027, 75% of the companies currently
quoted on the S&P 500 will have disappeared" (Garelli 2016).

Corporations worldwide enjoyed long and healthy lives, with a slow rise to
the top of financial performance and a gradual decline to annihilation. The
rate of change was so slow and crises were so rare that reinvention was rarely
needed—and when it was, we had all the time in the world to renew our business on our terms, a once-in-a-lifetime project. But that predictable postwar
world, if it ever existed, is long gone.

By the early 2000s, the concept of VUCA—the four world conditions of
volatility, uncertainty, complexity, and ambiguity—turned up in management books, such as *Get There Early: Sensing the Future to Compete in the
Present* by Bob Johansen (2007). And by the 2020s, we have approached a
point where many forces—social, economic, environmental, political, and
technological—are coming together in a whole new way.

Companies are expected to reinvent themselves and their products faster
than ever before. However, to do so, we first must flip the fundamental beliefs
that drive our management systems. The first flip we need to make is to stop
treating change as an exception to a rule and to start seeing it as a normal part
of our daily life.

PRINCIPLE #2
From: If It Ain't Broke, Don't Fix It. To: Break It before Somebody Else Does.

Many axioms drive our personal and organizational life. Along with, "We've
always done it this way," "Don't fix it if it ain't broken" has long been a beacon
of truth to follow.

This approach might be helpful during slow and steady times, but when we enter the era of chaos, turbulence, and constant disruption, it becomes nearly deadly. Consultants Paul Nunes and Tim Breene explain it perfectly: "Sooner or later, all businesses, even the most successful, run out of room to grow. Faced with this unpleasant reality, they are compelled to reinvent themselves periodically. The ability to pull off this difficult feat—to jump from the maturity stage of one business to the growth stage of the next—is what separates high performers from those whose time at the top is all too brief" (Nunes and Breene 2011).

The potential consequences are dire for any organization that fails to reinvent itself in time. As Matthew S. Olson and Derek van Bever (2009) demonstrate in their book *Stall Points*, once a company runs into a major stall in its growth, it has less than a 10 percent chance of fully recovering. Those odds are certainly daunting, and they do much to explain why two-thirds of stalled companies are later acquired, taken private, or forced into bankruptcy. In other words, if we start reinventing on a decline side of our company life cycle, the chances that we'll be able to restore our company to its peak performance are only 10 percent. If we start fixing things when they appear to be broken, it is a 90 percent probability that we are doomed.

To reinvent successfully, we must transcend "If it's not broken, don't fix it." It's time to break our organization, our products, and our processes before somebody else does and to build a new one with our employees fully engaged.

PRINCIPLE #3
From: Run a Sporadic Project in Reaction to Change. To: Build a Deliberate System for Proactive Reinvention.

This particular flip comes logically as a continuation of the previous one: when change comes often, the most efficient and effective way to manage it is to be systematic, deliberate, and proactive. When change was rare, it was OK to treat it as a rare project, an occasional fire to put out, or an opportunity to catch. You also didn't need to develop your capacity for reinvention because it could be outsourced to consultants and specialists.

But once change becomes the norm, it becomes time to build a system, a method, or a process and strengthen one's reinvention muscles to make that system work for you. That way you can prevent most fires and tackle the ones that could not be prevented with greater focus, proficiency, and ease.

PRINCIPLE #4
From: Bet on the New. To: Preserve the Best of the Old
While Fostering the New.

Resistance to change has long been cited as one of the key reasons why companies fail to adapt on time. Research confirms how few employees are ready to take risks needed to reinvent. A team at the University of Toronto surveyed 1,000 American and Canadian knowledge workers (all employed and with college degrees) to assess qualities such as "grit" and "openness to risk" across two countries and three age groups (younger than 35, 35 to 44, and older than 45). While the drive for innovation among participants varied from 14 percent to 28 percent, only two of the six different groups measured broke the 25 percent mark. Willingness to take a risk was even more telling: At best, 19 percent of your company is willing, with some age groups dipping as low as 11 percent (Zhexembayeva 2020a).

Such frustration and resistance are understandable. Often business transformation projects get cooked up behind closed doors by a small group of economists and consultants detached from the reality on the ground. Moving a few numbers in a spreadsheet seems objective and rational until you understand that there are legacies, jobs, and lives involved. To counter this ever-present resistance, it's crucial to find a balance between preserving the old and fostering the new. That way you connect the past, the present, and the future, bringing the resistance down and driving engagement up.

PRINCIPLE #5
From: Fix the Problem We Have Today. To: Succeed Today
While Building Up Tomorrow.

For decades, much of the world developed an unhealthy love affair with quick fixes. Have a headache? Take a pill. Need to lose weight? Go for liposuction. Facing a shortage of cash? Lay off some "headcount." (Yes, we don't even want to call people *people*.)

When it comes to our approach to business investing and decision making, hyperfocus on everything quick and short-term is particularly noticeable. As economic correspondent Alana Semuels (2016) shows, "The average holding time for stocks has fallen from eight years in 1960 to eight months in 2016. Almost 80 percent of chief financial officers at 400 of America's largest public companies say they would sacrifice a firm's economic value to meet the quarter's earnings expectations." That is scary data!

Saving today at the expense of tomorrow has become a norm. Equally dangerous is excessive focus on the future without a grounding in the present. Professionals and companies that manage to navigate the chaos do both: succeeding today while building a foundation for tomorrow. That's the true purpose and measure of successful reinvention.

THE THRILL OF PUTTING THE PRINCIPLES INTO PRACTICE

So, the principles of renewal and flourishing in a volatile world are clear. Now, how can we do it?

Think about CEO Ray Anderson's legacy at Interface, which is now going beyond net-zero to a company that becomes a model for net-positive business. Think about Walmart's Lee Scott years ago announcing, in front of Wall Street, the goal of becoming a company powered by 100 percent renewable energy, with zero waste, and with products that lead in sustainability. Entire industries have moved as a result, including tens of thousands of supply circle partners. Think about how a company, such as Green Mountain Coffee Roasters—at a time when there were whispers of bankruptcy—embedded the conceptual cornerstones of sustainable value creation and the fully human organization everywhere in its culture. They almost single-handedly created the U.S. Fair Trade organization (and went from a small $150 million in company sales, in 10 years, to a company with $24 billion in market value). Think about a Whole Foods, the early growth of the United Nations Global Compact, an Apple corporation being named by Greenpeace as the greatest social and environmentally sustainability leader in the IT industry, as well as others like GOJO (the creators of Purell) and Clarke Industries, both well on the road to becoming net-positive impact companies.

What each of these has in common is that they've pioneered reinvention theory, turned change from an event into a process of decades-long betterment. And each did it by calling all of their stakeholders—employees from every level and function, customers and supplier partners, local communities, industry competitors, and young people into "the inner circle of strategy," to become chief reinvention officers, reconstructing the deep enterprise logic of industrial age business.

How can everyone build on the successes of these companies? Indeed, there is one consistently remarkable practice we wish to single out—one that is especially powerful in the regenerative enterprise work. The practice is called the appreciative inquiry (AI) reinvention summit, and it is a science-backed, game-changing, large-group strategic foresight, design, and implementation meeting that brings a group of 300 to 2,000 people into the room or digitally for a few days of concentrated work, focusing on organizational strengths and opportunities. With both internal and external stakeholders taking an active part (think suppliers, customers, community members, and much more), a whole system is represented where everyone is invited to serve as a reinvention officer and co-designer of the path forward.

After UN Secretary General Kofi Annan brought us (the authors of this chapter) to use the Appreciative Inquiry Reinvention Summit method to facilitate the largest world summit of CEOs from business and society, a UN leaders report singled out the collaborative power of appreciative inquiry and called it "the best large group method in the world today.[1]

Why would you stop everything you are doing to bring together 2,000 people into one room? Three reasons:

1) A shared positive experience builds trust, which in turn creates conditions for greater change results. "Compared with people at low-trust companies, people at high-trust companies report 74% less stress, 106% more energy at work, 50% higher productivity, 13% fewer sick days, 76% more engagement, 29% more satisfaction with their lives, 40% less burnout" (Zak 2017).

2) Engagement. A research group at Gallup released a 2020 meta-analysis of decades' worth of data. The conclusion is striking: high engagement—defined essentially as having a strong connection with one's work and colleagues and feeling like a real contributor—yields a 23% increase in profitability, 41% decline in quality defects, 66% increase in employee well-being (net thriving employees), among many other benefits (Harter et al. 2020).

3) Diversity. Insights from strengths-based management theories (Cooperrider 2012) and theories of complex adaptive coalitions show that in a multistakeholder world it is not about isolated strengths per se, but about configurations, combinations, and interfaces. Having diverse voices in the room means bringing fresh new combinations and configurations of ideas, increasing the likelihood of financial outperformance by 36% or more, according to global consulting giant McKinsey. (Dixon-Fyle et al. 2020)

In a world where learning how to change better is becoming an existential necessity, the Appreciative Inquiry Reinvention Summit allows us to change at the scale of the whole—and thus move with greater trust, engagement, and result. Appreciative inquiry (AI) was introduced into the business world in 1987 by David Cooperrider and Suresh Srivastva, with one of its principles being that a person, organization, or system will excel only by amplifying strengths and never by fixing weaknesses. AI provides the tools and methods for creating new combinations and concentration effects of strengths and ultimately deploying those strengths in the service of a more positive future.

AI is based on the continuity principle of reinvention proposed by the great Peter Drucker, the father of management thought, when he said in an interview shortly before he passed away at 93 that the task of leadership is ageless, in its essence: "The task of leadership," said Peter Drucker, "is to create an alignment of strengths in ways that make a system's weaknesses irrelevant" (Whitney and Trosten-Bloom 2010).

That's what the word *appreciation* means; it means valuing those things of value, as well as increasing in value. This is how reinvention happens, through the elevation, magnification, and cross-multiplication of strengths and solutions and collective discovery of what works, what's better, and what's possible. Appreciative inquiry takes the stakeholder theory of the firm to its logical and more value-creating next stage.

Instead of seeing stakeholders as separate entities forcing companies to choose favorites or to become mired in tradeoff analyses, this method invites radical but exciting shifts, including:

1. The idea that "external stakeholders" is a worldview mistake and that an appreciative system approach specifically refutes the idea of organizations as autonomous, self-sufficient units that have a clear boundary between an inside and an outside. It stresses the fact that all organizations are "wholes of wholes" that interpenetrate one another, thus constituting an intricate, functionally inseparable network of vital relationships, interorganizational relatedness, stakeholder groupings and the ultimate envelope of enterprise, the biosphere.

2. The recognition that the legacy conception of business seriously underestimates the synergy-producing resources available to a business. It underutilizes assets and the vast and available "universe of strengths" in two ways. The first is that the so-called external stakeholders are rarely invited into the inner circle of reinvention and strategy making—for example, how often do companies bring significant numbers of customers or community representatives to the table, with full voice, during the real-time planning of the future? The second is that it's even rarer to bring the whole system of stakeholder groups all

together in real-time and into the inner circle of reinvention for cocreating new designs, dreams, and strategic initiatives. In effect, legacy assumptions of business suppress what the literature calls network effects and "the concentration effect of chemistries of strengths."

3. A third form of leadership is neither top-down nor bottom-up. It helps executives shift their eyes from the parts (a few stakeholders) to the whole (society and world), whereby entirely new options come into view. From the systems perspective, everyone experiences something of an overview effect—not unlike when astronauts zoom out and see the planet for the first time. In the words of the influential organizational behavior scholar and author Bob Quinn (2000), "Appreciative Inquiry is revolutionizing the field of organization development and change."

The next natural question becomes: How do you do it? In actuality, it is very simple. Think of three phases—the pre-summit phase, the summit, and the post-summit.

The pre-summit phase is all about building a strong design team. Together, conveners go through a design session where every element is defined—the right mix of stakeholders to be invited; the articulation of the summit task and agenda; the plans for pre-summit research as well as the post-summit follow-up. The summit takes place typically six to eight months after the key design session—and the post-summit stage includes implementation and follow-through.

Among the benefits of "all-in" reinvention together in one large group is an exceptional speed—whereby hundreds of small committee meetings are bypassed. Leaders—from the CNO of the United States Navy to the secretary general of the United Nations to the CEOs of Apple, Keurig Green Mountain, National Grid, Interface, Whole Foods, and Walmart—are consistently moved by how quickly the best and most positive in their system comes out. They applaud the speed, substantive deliberation, inspiration, unification, trust, and long-term reinvention capacities that are built in the process. And they frequently ask, "We have assembled such great people here—what was all the fuss about, and why didn't we mobilize with this even earlier?"

While the AI summit is new for some, we are predicting that someday—because it so naturally brings out the inherent reinvention capacities and the best in people and groups we think many leaders will feel just as comfortable and at home in these kinds of inclusive, strengths-based, and large-group planning modalities as we do in small groups of 8 to 10 people that, too often, work behind the scenes and "inside the building."

What we are learning is that people do not resist change; they resist being changed. And today we have the methods—whole-system, effective, and fast—to aim higher in ways that build trust, allow everyone to become a chief reinvention officer of one's own life while creating lasting legacies that people are proud of.[2]

Whether it's through running an appreciative inquiry summit or using any other method, one thing is clear: to survive and thrive in a risky, interconnected world of constant flux, you have to make reinvention a part of daily life. And this is not a project you do once. It's time for us to rethink the way we change and make reinvention the cornerstone of the new theory of business for a regenerative and flourishing world.

NOTES

1. *The Global Compact Leaders Summit* (United Nations 2004) documents the impact of appreciative inquiry at the United Nations world summit between Kofi Annan and CEOs from 500 corporations, including Hewlett-Packard, Starbucks, Tata, Royal Dutch Shell, Novartis, Microsoft, IBM, and Coca Cola. In the report CEO Rodrigo Loures concludes, "Appreciative Inquiry is the best large group method in the world today."

2. For more resources on appreciative inquiry—articles, case studies, dissertations, training programs, PowerPoint slide decks, bibliographies, etc.—please see the Appreciative Inquiry Commons at the David L. Cooperrider Center for Appreciative Inquiry at Champlain College: https://appreciativeinquiry .champlain.edu/. Also see Case Western Reserve University: https:// weatherhead.case.edu/faculty/david-cooperrider.

REFERENCES

Anthony, Scott D., S. Patrick Viguerie, Evan I. Schwartz, and John V. Landeghem. 2018. "2018 Corporate Longevity Forecast: Creative Destruction Is Accelerating." Innosight, February. https://www.innosight.com/insight /creative-destruction/.

Boston Consulting Group. 2020. "Apply the Science of Organizational Change." Accessed May 13, 2021. https://www.bcg.com/featured-insights/winning-the -20s/science-of-change.

Cooperrider, David L. 2012. "The Concentration Effect of Strengths." *Organizational Dynamics* 41, 106–17.

Dixon-Fyle, Sundiatu, Kevin Dolan, Vivian Hunt, and Sara Prince. 2020. "Diversity Wins: How Inclusion Matters." McKinsey & Company, May. https://www.mckinsey.com/~/media/McKinsey/Featured%20Insights /Diversity%20and%20Inclusion/Diversity%20wins%20How%20inclusion%20matters/Diversity-wins-How-inclusion-matters-vF.pdf.

Drucker, Peter 1946. *Concept of the Corporation*. New York: John Day.

Garelli, Stéphane 2016. "Why You Will Probably Live Longer Than Most Big Companies." IMD, December. https://www.imd.org/research-knowledge /articles/why-you-will-probably-live-longer-than-most-big-companies/.

Harter, James K., Frank L. Schmidt, Sangeeta Agrawal, Anthony Blue, Stephanie K. Plowman, Patrick Josh, and Jim Asplund. 2020. "The Relationship between Engagement at Work and Organizational Outcomes." Gallup, October. https://www.gallup.com/workplace/321725/gallup-q12-meta -analysis-report.aspx.

Johansen, Bob. 2007. *Get There Early: Sensing the Future to Compete in the Present*. Oakland, CA: Berrett-Koehler Publishers.

Nohria, Nitin, and Michael Beer. 2000. "Cracking the Code of Change." *Harvard Business Review*, May–June. https://hbr.org/2000/05/cracking-the-code-of -change.

Nunes, Paul, and Tim Breene. 2011. "Reinvent Your Business before It's Too Late." *Harvard Business Review*, January–February. https://hbr.org/2011/01 /reinvent-your-business-before-its-too-late.

Olson, Matthew S., and Derek van Bever. 2009. *Stall Points: Most Companies Stop Growing—Yours Doesn't Have To*. New Haven, CT: Yale University Press.

Quinn, Robert E. 2000. *Change the World: How Ordinary People Can Achieve Extraordinary Results*. San Francisco: Jossey-Bass.

Semuels, Alana. 2016. "How to Stop Short-Term Thinking at America's Companies." *Atlantic*, December 30. https://www.theatlantic.com/business/archive /2016/12/short-term-thinking/511874/.

United Nations. 2004. *The Global Compact Leaders Summit*. New York: United Nations. http://www.unglobalcompact.org/docs/news_events/8.1/summit _rep_fin.pdf.

Whitney, Diana, and Trosten-Bloom, Amanda. 2010. *The Power of Appreciative Inquiry: A Practical Guide to Positive Change*. Oakland, CA: Berrett-Koehler Publishers.

World Economic Forum. 2019. *The Global Risks Report 2019*. 14th edition. Geneva: World Economic Forum. http://www3.weforum.org/docs/WEF _Global_Risks_Report_2019.pdf.

Zak, Paul J. 2017. "The Neuroscience of Trust." *Harvard Business Review,* January–February. https://hbr.org/2017/01/the-neuroscience-of-trust.

Zhexembayeva, Nadya. 2020a. "Stop Calling It Innovation." *Harvard Business Review,* February 19. https://hbr.org/2020/02/stop-calling-it-innovation.

Zhexembayeva, Nadya. 2020b. "3 Things You're Getting Wrong about Organizational Change." *Harvard Business Review,* June 9. https://hbr.org/2020/06/3-things-youre-getting-wrong-about-organizational-change.

INDEX

A page number in italics refers to a figure or table.

ABOUT THE EDITORS

David Cooperrider (coeditor), PhD, is a Distinguished University Professor at Case Western Reserve University and holds the David L. Cooperrider Professorship in Appreciative Inquiry and is the faculty director of the Fowler Center for Business as an Agent of World Benefit at the Weatherhead School of Management. David is also the honorary chairman of Champlain College's David L. Cooperrider Center for Appreciative Inquiry. David has authored 25 books and over 100 articles and book chapters. He serves an advisor to many companies and to organizations such as Apple, the U.S. Navy, and the UN Global Compact with its 12,000 companies.

Audrey Selian (coeditor), PhD, serves as director of Artha Impact (Rianta Capital Zurich), an impact investment initiative under the auspices of a dedicated advisory to the Singh Family Trust and has been an advisor and friend of Halloran Philanthropies for many years. Audrey contributed to *The Pursuit of Human Wellbeing: The Untold Global History* (Springer, 2017) and published various reports and white papers on systems change and impact platforms. She holds degrees from the Fletcher School at Tufts University (PhD, MALD), The London School of Economics (MSc), and Wellesley College (BA).

ABOUT THE CONTRIBUTORS

Joey Burton serves as executive director of the Institute for Business in Society at the Darden School of Business, with the mission of helping Darden's faculty change the prevailing narratives about business and capitalism. Burton holds a master's degree in public policy from Brigham Young University and an MBA from the Chicago Booth School of Business.

Kim Cameron is the William Russell Kelly Professor of Management and Organizations at the Ross School of Business and professor of higher education in the School of Education at the University of Michigan. He received BS and MS degrees from Brigham Young University and MA and PhD degrees from Yale University.

Udayan Dhar is a PhD candidate in organizational behavior at Case Western Reserve University. His research focuses on positive identity development in organizations. He also teaches an undergraduate course on human resource management.

John Elkington has three degrees and is an entrepreneur, advisor, writer, and one of the founders of the global sustainability movement. He is founder and chief pollinator at Volans, having cofounded four social businesses since 1978, including SustainAbility in 1987, all of which still exist. He has served on over 70 boards and advisory boards and written 20 books, the most recent of which is *Green Swans: The Coming Boom in Regenerative Capitalism* (Fast Company Press, 2020).

Jed Emerson has been active in the field of impact investing and social enterprise for over 30 years. He has coauthored seven books, including the first book on impact investing entitled *The Purpose of Capital*. He has held faculty appointments at leading institutions, including Harvard, Stanford, and Oxford business schools.

Ben Freeman is a musician, writer, and entrepreneur in Nashville, Tennessee. He has published essays on stakeholder thinking and multiple generations in *Sloan Management Review Online*, the *Economic Times* of India, and a variety of other outlets. He attended the Berklee College of Music and is a cofounder of Red Goat Records.

R. Edward Freeman is university professor, Olsson professor, and academic director of the Institute for Business in Society at the University of Virginia Darden School of Business. He has received six honorary doctorates (Doctor Honoris Causa) for his work on stakeholder theory and business ethics. He is the host of the *Stakeholder Podcast*, sponsored by Stakeholder Media, LLC, and is best known for his award winning book, *Strategic Management: A Stakeholder Approach* (Pitman, 1984; and reprinted by Cambridge University Press in 2010), among others.

Ronald Fry is professor of organizational behavior at Case Western Reserve University, where he has directed the EMBA and MPOD degree programs to national prominence and has served as the Organizational Behavior Department chair. He has published 11 books and over 50 articles and book chapters, and is a cocreator of the appreciative inquiry theory and method.

Marga Hoek is a three-time CEO, non-executive director, and a globally appreciated global thought leader and author on sustainable business. She is a two-time golden awarded bestselling author of the trailblazing books *New Economy Business* and *The Trillion Dollar Shift: Business for Good Is Good Business*. Marga Hoek consistently demonstrates in all of her roles that ESG contribution and financial performance are not mutually exclusive but go hand in hand. She was acknowledged as a member of Thinkers50 as a consequence of her "championing sustainability."

Bart Houlahan (See Andrew Kassoy)

Michele Hunt is a transformation catalyst and strategic advisor on leadership development and organizational transformation. She is the author of *Dream-Makers: Innovating for the Greater Good* and served on President Bill Clinton's transition team, as director of the Federal Quality Institute, working for Vice President Al Gore in the Reinventing Government initiative as well as on the executive leadership team of Herman Miller, a *Fortune* 500 company.

Naveen Jain is the author of the award-winning book *Moonshots: Creating a World of Abundance*. As a serial entrepreneur, he previously founded InfoSpace, Intelius, and TalentWise and is working on current moonshot ventures Viome and Moon Express. He has been named: Entrepreneur of the Year by Ernst & Young, Most Creative Person by Fast Company, Top 20 Entrepreneurs and Lifetime Achievement Award for leadership by Red Herring, among others.

Rosabeth Moss Kanter holds the Ernest L. Arbuckle Professorship at Harvard Business School, specializing in strategy, innovation, and leadership for change. Author or coauthor of 20 books, her latest book, *Think Outside the Building: How Advanced Leaders Can Change the World One Smart Innovation at a Time*, has won a number of accolades. The former chief editor of *Harvard Business Review*, Professor Kanter has been repeatedly named to lists such as the "50 most powerful women in the world" (*Times* of London), and the "50 most influential business thinkers in the world" (Thinkers50, and in November 2019 received their biannual Lifetime Achievement Award). She has received 24 honorary doctoral degrees, as well as numerous leadership awards, lifetime achievement awards, and prizes.

Andrew Kassoy and **Bart Houlahan,** along with their partner, Jay Coen Gilbert, cofounded B Lab in 2006. B Lab is a nonprofit organization with offices in 33 countries, driving economic systems change to build a more inclusive, equitable, and regenerative economic system. Its mission is to serve a movement of people using business as a force for good by shining a light on leaders through a corporate certification (3,800+ certified B Corporations in 70+ countries), thereby providing easy pathways for others to follow.

Mark R. Kramer is a leading researcher, writer, speaker, and consultant on philanthropy, business strategies for social impact, and impact investing. He is best known as the coauthor of seminal articles in *Harvard Business Review* and *Stanford Social Innovation Review* on creating shared value, collective impact, and catalytic philanthropy. Mark cofounded FSG in 1999 with Professor Michael Porter and is a graduate of Brandeis University, the Wharton School, and the University of Pennsylvania Law School.

Chris Laszlo is professor of organizational behavior at Case Western Reserve University's Weatherhead School of Management, where he researches and teaches flourishing enterprise. He is author of *Quantum Leadership* (2019), *Flourishing Enterprise* (2014), *Embedded Sustainability* (2011), and *Sustainable Value* (2008), all from Stanford University Press. In 2012, he was elected a "Top 100 Thought Leader in Trustworthy Business Behavior" by Trust Across America™.

Gillian M. Marcelle, PhD, leads Resilience Capital Ventures LLC, a boutique capital advisory practice specializing in blended finance. She has a proven track record in attracting investment to underserved markets and designing architectures that facilitate partnerships. Her experience includes staff roles with the International Finance Corporation, equity capital markets at J. P. Morgan Chase and M&A with British Telecom. Dr. Marcelle currently serves as a non-executive director with South African fintech Tafari Capital, and she previously was a tenured associate professor at Wits Business School in Johannesburg.

Roger L. Martin was named the world's #1 management thinker in 2017 by Thinkers50, a biannual ranking of the most influential global business thinkers. His newest book is *When More Is Not Better: Overcoming America's Obsession with Economic Efficiency* (Harvard Business Review Press, 2020). His previous 11 books include *Playing to Win* written with A. G. Lafley (HBRP, 2013), which won the award for Best Book of 2012–2013 by the Thinkers50. Roger received his BA from Harvard College, with a concentration in economics, in 1979 and his MBA from the Harvard Business School in 1981.

Ignacio Pavez is currently assistant professor at the School of Business and Economics at Universidad del Desarrollo, where he teaches graduate and undergraduate courses in organization development and change, team development, leadership, appreciative inquiry, and corporate sustainability. He holds a PhD in organizational behavior from Case Western Reserve University.

Paul Polman is chair of social enterprise IMAGINE, which mobilizes business leaders to tackle climate change and global inequality. He is also chair of the B Team, Saïd Business School, and the Valuable 500, as well as honorary chair of the International Chamber of Commerce and World Business Council for Sustainable Development and vice chair of the UN Global Compact. As CEO of Unilever for 10 years, he demonstrated that a long-term, multistakeholder business model goes hand-in-hand with excellent financial performance.

Richard Roberts is inquiry lead at Volans. Over the last decade, he has worked on strategy development and corporate transformation projects with companies in a range of sectors, from finance to heavy industry. Since 2018, he has led Volans' work on Tomorrow's Capitalism—examining the role of business and finance in shaping tomorrow's markets in ways that foster resilience and regeneration.

Louise Kjellerup Roper is the CEO of Volans. A successful entrepreneur, she has spent her career in innovative businesses, pioneering cradle-to-cradle and circular business models. Louise has reshaped Volans, launching thought leadership initiatives such as Tomorrow's Capitalism Inquiry, Regenerative Transformation Architecture, and the Bankers For NetZero Initiative. She also advises leading businesses in their transformation journeys, lectures at a number of universities, and serves on advisory councils across the globe.

John Schroeter is a technology and media entrepreneur. He is the editor of *After Shock*—the landmark book observing the 50-year anniversary of Alvin Toffler's *Future Shock* (in production as a major docuseries). As executive director at Abundant World Institute, he leads a society of the world's foremost technologists, futurists, and entrepreneurs who collectively "imagineer" a better future by connecting the dots looking forward.

Raj Sisodia is FW Olin Distinguished Professor of Global Business and Whole Foods Market Research Scholar in Conscious Capitalism at Babson College, and cofounder and cochairman of Conscious Capitalism Inc. Raj is coauthor of the *New York Times* bestseller *Conscious Capitalism: Liberating the Heroic Spirit of Business* (2013) and *Wall Street Journal* bestseller *Everybody Matters* (2015) and has published 15 other books. He was named one of "Ten Outstanding Trailblazers of 2010" by Good Business International, among other accolades. He has a PhD in business from Columbia University.

Andrew Winston is a globally recognized expert on megatrends and how to build companies that thrive by serving the world. Named to Thinkers50 Radar Class of 2020 as a "thinker to watch," his views on strategy have been sought after by many of the world's leading companies. Andrew's latest book is *Net Positive: How Courageous Companies Thrive by Giving More Than They Take* (coauthored with renowned CEO Paul Polman), and he has published several bestsellers. Andrew has received degrees in economics, business, and environmental management from Princeton, Columbia, and Yale.

Nadya Zhexembayeva is the founder of Reinvention Academy, a U.S.-based research, education, and consulting platform and a former Coca-Cola Chaired

Professor of Sustainable Development at IEDC-Bled School of Management. Nadya's latest book, *The Chief Reinvention Officer Handbook: How to Thrive in Chaos* is a medalist of 2021 Axiom Business Books Awards. She is also author of a number of books, including *Overfished Ocean Strategy: Powering Up Innovation for a Resource-Deprived World* and *Embedded Sustainability: The Next Big Competitive Advantage.*

Berrett–Koehler
BK Publishers

Berrett-Koehler is an independent publisher dedicated to an ambitious mission: *Connecting people and ideas to create a world that works for all.*

Our publications span many formats, including print, digital, audio, and video. We also offer online resources, training, and gatherings. And we will continue expanding our products and services to advance our mission.

We believe that the solutions to the world's problems will come from all of us, working at all levels: in our society, in our organizations, and in our own lives. Our publications and resources offer pathways to creating a more just, equitable, and sustainable society. They help people make their organizations more humane, democratic, diverse, and effective (and we don't think there's any contradiction there). And they guide people in creating positive change in their own lives and aligning their personal practices with their aspirations for a better world.

And we strive to practice what we preach through what we call "The BK Way." At the core of this approach is *stewardship,* a deep sense of responsibility to administer the company for the benefit of all of our stakeholder groups, including authors, customers, employees, investors, service providers, sales partners, and the communities and environment around us. Everything we do is built around stewardship and our other core values of *quality, partnership, inclusion,* and *sustainability.*

This is why Berrett-Koehler is the first book publishing company to be both a B Corporation (a rigorous certification) and a benefit corporation (a for-profit legal status), which together require us to adhere to the highest standards for corporate, social, and environmental performance. And it is why we have instituted many pioneering practices (which you can learn about at www.bkconnection.com), including the Berrett-Koehler Constitution, the Bill of Rights and Responsibilities for BK Authors, and our unique Author Days.

We are grateful to our readers, authors, and other friends who are supporting our mission. We ask you to share with us examples of how BK publications and resources are making a difference in your lives, organizations, and communities at www.bkconnection.com/impact.

Dear reader,

Thank you for picking up this book and welcome to the worldwide BK community! You're joining a special group of people who have come together to create positive change in their lives, organizations, and communities.

What's BK all about?

Our mission is to connect people and ideas to create a world that works for all.

Why? Our communities, organizations, and lives get bogged down by old paradigms of self-interest, exclusion, hierarchy, and privilege. But we believe that can change. That's why we seek the leading experts on these challenges—and share their actionable ideas with you.

A welcome gift

To help you get started, we'd like to offer you a **free copy** of one of our bestselling ebooks:

www.bkconnection.com/welcome

When you claim your **free ebook**, you'll also be subscribed to our blog.

Our freshest insights

Access the best new tools and ideas for leaders at all levels on our blog at ideas.bkconnection.com.

Sincerely,

Your friends at Berrett-Koehler

Certified

Corporation